SITUATING SELVES

SUNY Series, Human Communication Processes
Donald P. Cushman and Ted J. Smith III, Editors

SITUATING SELVES

*The Communication of Social Identities
in American Scenes*

Donal Carbaugh

STATE UNIVERSITY
OF NEW YORK
PRESS

Published by
State University of New York Press, Albany

Production by Susan Geraghty
Marketing by Dana Yanulavich

Printed in the United States of America

For information, address State University of New York Press,
State University Plaza, Albany, N.Y., 12246

Library of Congress Cataloging-in-Publication Data

Carbaugh, Donal A.
    Situating selves : the communication of social identities in
American scenes / by Donal Carbaugh.
        p.   cm. — (SUNY series, human communication processes)
    Includes bibliographical references (p.   ) and index.
    ISBN 0–7914–2827–3 (hc : alk. paper). — ISBN 0–7914–2828–1 (pb :
alk. paper)
    1. Group identity—United States.   2. Communication and culture
—United States.   3. Ethnicity—United States.   I. Title.
II. Series: SUNY series in human communication processes.
HM131.C2525   1996
302.2'0973—dc20   95-16183
                                                                        CIP

10 9 8 7 6 5 4 3 2 1

To the memory of Bernice Carbaugh
For Blair Carbaugh

CONTENTS

PREFACE

The idea that communication could be studied as a personal and cultural accomplishment was introduced to me when I was a graduate student at the University of Washington. At that time, I began thinking of myself as an ethnographer, and began observing some of the scenes of communication in my life, potentially at least, as cultural texts, or cultural games, or cultural battles. I had been intrigued earlier by the idea of becoming an ethnographer through my majors in communication and anthropology/sociology when I was an undergraduate at Manchester College. Since those formative educational moments, I have been trying to make the idea—the identity of an ethnographer who studies communication—a real, active part of my life. The studies of the social scenes collected here reflect some of my efforts, as such.

Upon reflection, I have found that the idea for each of the following studies gained some seminal shape through a kind of crystallizing moment. While pinpointing a precise start to any one would be impossible, I do associate with each a generative seed, with each being sewn in a particular scene. The intellectual planting of each was not highly intentional, and each subsequent cultivation of the field was rather lengthy. Yet, the precipitating moment when the idea for each study solidified was, in retrospect, a particularly intense moment. This kind of moment included puzzlement, anger, or pleasure, sometimes with all of these emotions coming at once. For example, in the first case, I found myself standing with several thousand others, swept into a scene of passionate visceral proportions, screaming at the top of my lungs about a "bad call" made by an "official" during a college basketball game. I remember wondering, at exactly the moment when I, myself, was standing on my feet screaming in a frenzied excitement with thousands of others: "What in the world are we doing here, by screaming this way?" I sat down, right then, and for some reason managed a frame-breaking and shoulder-shaking chuckle. This reaction was somewhat bewildering to me, and bewildered some next to me, yet nonetheless I was delighted at the excuse for reflection my new role as ethnographer had opened to me; even if I awkwardly applied it in this social scene. The moment loosened the grip of the scene on me, opening it for a kind of sustained critical reflection, and culminating eventually in my present, where I continue to be a rabid if somewhat more reflective fan. Created through that moment, in that scene, was the possibility and incentive for some further personal and social reflections, the latter forming chapter 2 in this book.

The last case highlights a complex geographic and cultural (political and economic) scene near to my heart and home, a place where my family and I spend time together. I remember vividly when I discovered, to my considerable dismay, that others, with the support of the state government, were planning the "development" of this place into a major commercial resort. I sat down, then and there, in despair, bewildered and angry. Later, I took the moment as an impetus for further study, trying to figure how others could propose developing such a precious and tranquil place. Eventually I learned much about that proposal for development and the larger scene of which that place was a part. In the process, I learned much about my earlier identification with this land and community. The events surrounding the development became a statewide controversy and are even now of near epic proportions, with the current political battle replaying deep historically based tensions. What I learned about this public space and discourse, and the various identities of people within it, are recorded in chapters 9 and 10.

One's place within communicative scenes like these is of course to some degree a quite personal matter. Yet, when explored ethnographically, communicative scenes become something more than just personally involving. Given enough time and careful reflection, and by traversing scenes through a conceptual system called ethnography, some other insights into these matters can, hopefully, be gained. Listening to fans at basketball games or to environmental disputes, one can begin hearing in communication sociocultural radiants of identity (of being, relating, acting, feeling, and dwelling). By reflecting upon the social and cultural bases of these communicative scenes, and by inscribing what I have found, I have been engaged in, and recorded here, at least one version of an ethnographic life.

The general approach I adopt in the following studies develops an understanding of communication that is based upon social and cultural foundations. A set of guiding assumptions should here be made explicit.[1] As I conceive it in the introduction, cultural pragmatics is a particular variant of cultural communication and a version of the ethnography of communication. It provides a way of doing ethnography that seeks to understand communication systems through the multifaceted lens provided by language use, speech, and nonverbal expression. It proceeds on the assumption that a focal concern of ethnography is discovering the meanings of local communication forms and symbols, that communication everywhere is shaped by local symbols and forms, and that communication implicates distinctive local premises about persons, social relations, activities, feelings, and nature. With such a view, communication comes forth as a potent form for organizing thought, an essential means for engaging in social interaction, and an unmatched resource for knowing one's world and acting within it. The study of communication (of verbal and nonverbal means of expression) joins with the study of culture (of systems of symbols and meanings) in a way that privileges neither, extends the domain of both, and illumines in a sharper way the social scenes in which both operate. While communication and culture can be distinguished analytically, if taken together they can provide two rails to the same station, a way toward exploring social and cultural worlds *in* communication (e.g., Basso, 1990; Bauman, 1986; Carbaugh, 1990b, in press; Fitch, 1991, 1994; Gumperz and Cook-Gumperz, 1982; Hymes, 1972; Katriel, 1991; Philips, 1993; Philipsen, 1987, 1989a, 1992; Sherzer, 1983, 1987; Urban, 1991).

Living as an ethnographic investigator of communication, as I have come to understand it, involves five interrelated dimensions of inquiry. Each contains its own primary attitudes for thinking, with the group together suggesting a holistic guide for traveling the ethnographic path. The trip traverses theoretical, descriptive, cultural, comparative, and critical terrain (Carbaugh, 1990a, 1991, 1993a). Each is, at different times, focal to an inquiry, just as each alone is being informed by the others. Together, the dimensions create a version of ethnography that is attentive to the actual scenes of communication and culture, keeping in view an academic scene (amplifying the theoretical), a local situation or community (the descriptive and cultural), relations among these (the comparative); and, if appropriate, an evaluation or assessment (the critical). Each of these dimensions was figured into the field-work for the following studies; each is thus integrated into the writing of the following chapters. For example, a theoretical framework guides the inquiries, and is foregrounded in part 1, which provides some of the orienting parameters for the studies. Theoretical commentary is also prominent in chapters 6, 8, and 11, showing how theory can be developed through ethnographic inquiry. Descriptive and cultural reports, built with the aid of—and eventually extending—the theoretical frame, form the heart of the book. Here, in chapters 2, 3, 4, 5, 7, 9, and 10, the actual communication practices of specific cultural scenes are explored as they symbolically construct social identities. The comparative dimension appears periodically in ways that emphasize contrasts among social identities within a scene (in chapters 3, 5, 7, 9, and 10), and in a less central way here, cross-cultural analyses between Americans and others (which appear in parts of chapters 1, 2, and 8). The critical dimension foregrounded in these essays is a kind of "natural criticism" (Carbaugh, 1990a), in which participants assess the communication practices through which they live (in chapters 3, 5, 7, 9, and 10). These distinct modes of inquiry bring together into the ethnographic approach theoretical, descriptive, cultural, comparative, and critical dimensions.

The studies presented below follow another in which I explored, not social identities, but American cultural premises for personhood and communication (Carbaugh, 1988b). My efforts in that project were focused mainly upon the common symbols, symbolic forms, and meanings that people—who inhabited various social identities in America today—employed in order to construct a common life together, as "Americans." The communication practices I explored there thus spanned races, genders, social classes, and contexts—in fact, must have done so in order to accomplish the integrative work of culture and communication that was their main task. While adopting the same approach as in that volume, the accent in the present volume shifts from problems of creating a common identity across people, to variability of identities across and within social scenes. Here, then, I focus upon the variety of social identities that operate in various American scenes. In current and forthcoming works, I will explore various practices of communication and cultural identity that are active in some Russian, Native American, Finnish, and popular American scenes, focusing especially upon the ways these are interactively woven into particular intercultural encounters (e.g., Carbaugh, 1990b, 1993c).

PLAN OF THE BOOK

The book is organized into three main parts. Part 1 contains an introduction to an ongoing scholarly conversation about selves, social identities, and communication. The introduction to part 1 reviews literatures that "problematize" the concepts—*individual, self,* and *person,* and previews the general approach adopted in the present volume to address those problems. Chapter 1 begins leisurely with a description of cultural idioms about identity that are prominent in America today, reflecting in a popular way some of the themes discussed in the literature. Chapter 1 continues by building a specific framework for treating social identities as communication performance. As Gumperz and Cook-Gumperz (1982, p. 1) put it: "To understand issues of identity and how they affect and are affected by social, political, and ethnic divisions we need to gain insights into the communicative process by which they arise." The specific thesis that is elaborated there forms the basic theme of this book: Exploring social scenes of living, and the way they are conducted through communication, can show how different versions of self, and different variants of social identities are immanent in the particular communication practices of everyday life (Sapir, 1931).

The heart of the book, its main focus, reflects the commitment to describing and interpreting communication in the actual scenes of sociocultural life. Explored in chapters 2 through 10 are the specific communication practices that help create various social identities in American scenes. These include, in chapter 2, being a fan at college basketball games; in chapters 3 and 4, being a worker at a television station; in chapters 5 and 6, being a married person, through the selection of a style of marital name, and what that style signifies about identity and marriage; in chapters 7 and 8, speaking as a female, a male, or "an individual" on a television talk show and what the play between these suggests about genders and group-based identities; and, in chapters 9 and 10, being a developer or an environmentalist in a particular community's debates and discussions about a parcel of land. This range of scenes was selected for two main reasons: To explore prominent corners of contemporary social life (e.g., leisure, work, marriage and family, television, and community), and to demonstrate the integrative potential of the theoretical approach for studies of public, organizational, interpersonal, group, political, and mass communication.

Chapter 11 summarizes some of the principal findings in the book, proposes a way of integrating social and cultural levels of identification in communication studies, and applies these to popular means of identification in American communities today.

By discussing these scenes as communicative scenes, with an ear toward social identification, I hope to show how we learn to identify important parts of our selves within social scenes like these, and, in turn, to show how we participate in such scenes, partly at least, by enacting our identities. Social identities are not just inside a self but enacted in scenes; communication is not just a revelation of self, but its formative fashioning. In this way, selves are being discussed as situated communication "practices," or performances of practical living, with each self being situated in specific scenes, and with the group of scenes and selves considered here touching some, yet only some, of the prominent features of social identification in America today. Reflecting upon these situated moments, scenes, and selves, with each being accomplished through communication and culture, provides the basic starting points for the book.

Let me conclude this preface with some words about the title. I chose the main title because it distills several of the important points of the book into a short phrase, *Situating Selves*. First, the title draws attention to an intricate link between self and social situations. Without selves, social situations are rather empty, and without situations, selves lack actual contexts for social life. As people engage in and possibly change social situations, so they engage in and can possibly change their selves. This basic idea applies, in various ways, to all human situations and scenes. Second, the word *situating* draws attention to self, not so much as a permanent or core entity—although in some cultural scenes it becomes that—but more as a localized, somewhat contingent process. From this vantage point, self can (but need not necessarily) vary by situation, activity, and time. If the English language permitted it, "selfing" could have been used as a way of emphasizing the occasioned enactment of selves in scenes (as is the "positioning" concept in chapter 8 below). Third, the title implies a generative concept of human action such that self is not necessarily "determined" by a social situation. It can (at least possibly) create and change within (or across) social scenes. Finally, by emphasizing "selves," in the plural, I try to embrace a variety of the versions and variations possible in social identities. I intend to include, then, not only the various cultural landscape(s) that any "self" may possibly inhabit (e.g., as an American, Finn, or Russian), but also the various social identities possible within each of these (e.g., as a fan, female, or forester).

ACKNOWLEDGMENTS

This book and its author are of course situated in their own local-ized scenes. Several people have made it possible for me to con-duct these studies and have provided opportunities for discussing them. Early on, Gerry Philipsen and John Stewart offered courses at the University of Washington that captivated my interests in ethnographic and interpretive studies of communication. In a course offered by Gerry Philipsen, an early version of chapter 2 was drafted. That chapter and those that follow owe an enduring debt to his tutelage, continuing support, and friendship. My initial thinking on communication and culture in organizational settings benefitted from attending the Speech Communication Association and International Communication Association's conference on Interpretive Approaches at Alta, Utah, in August of 1982. I thank Leonard Hawes and Michael Pacanowsky for the opportunity to attend this meeting and thus to discuss the materials in chapters 3 and 4 with the conference attendees; I thank particularly Linda Putnam for comments on an earlier version of these chapters, and William Wilmot and Wes Shellen for the opportunity to discuss these ideas at the University of Montana. A preliminary version of chapters 5 and 6 was presented at the Temple University Discourse Conference in Philadelphia in March of 1989. I thank Robert Craig and Karen Tracy for this opportunity. Also, I thank Lisa Coutu and Kristine Fitch for commenting upon an earlier version of these chapters. Some of the initial thoughts in chapters 7 and 8 were presented at a public forum on Gender and Communication at Nuffield College, Oxford, and at a seminar in discursive psy-chology at Linacre College, Oxford, both in November of 1992. For these opportunities I thank the Reverend Dr. Margaret M. Yee, and Rom Harré. To Rom Harré goes a special thanks for arranging for some rather magical times at Linacre College. While there, discussions with Jens Brockmeier and David Zeitlyn were particularly stimulating and rewarding. The ideas in chapter 8 owe a special debt to these times and discussions. Early versions of chapters 9 and 10 were presented at the Speech Communication Association's Annual meetings in Chicago in November of 1990, and at the First Conference on the Discourses of Environmental Advocacy at Alta, Utah, in August of 1991. I thank James Cantrill and Christine Oravec for organizing this conference, and the many other kindred spirits I met there. To Connie Bullis and Jon Lange goes a special thanks for our continuing conversations. For conversations concerning all of these ideas, and continuous support of these projects, I thank colleagues and students at the University of Massachusetts, far too numerous to mention here. The Office of Research Affairs at the University of Massachusetts, Amherst provided funding for the field research on which chapters 9 and 10 were based, and for help in administering this grant, I thank Bruce McCandless. A Fulbright Fellowship in Finland during 1993 at the Universities of Tampere and Jyväskylä was invaluable for gaining perspective through cross-cultural study. While not frequently integrated into the prose of this volume, the provocative and productive insights gained from living there will be with me for a long time to come. In particular, I thank Michael Berry of the University of Turku, Finland, for reading and commenting on the manuscript. For encouragement throughout this project, I thank SUNY Series Editor Donald Cushman. Finally, my deepest gratitude goes to LuAnne, Andrew, and Jonathan, who continue to provide a familial scene full of life's richness and strong with moral support.

Earlier versions of some of what follows have appeared elsewhere, but all have been revised in order to produce the present volume: Chapters 3 and 4 first appeared as "Cultural terms and tensions in the speech of a television station," *Western Journal of Speech Communication*, 52, 1988, 216–237, with this essay being awarded Honorable Mention in the 1988 B. Aubrey Fisher Article Award competition; an earlier version of chapters 7 and 8 appeared as "Personhood, positioning and cultural pragmatics: American dignity in cross-cultural perspective," in S. Deetz (ed.), *Communication Yearbook 17*, 1994, (pp. 159–186), Newbury Park, CA: Sage; an earlier version of chapters 9 and 10 appeared as "'The mountain" and 'the project': Dueling depictions of a natural environment," in J. Cantrill and C. Oravec (eds.), *Conference on the discourse of environmental advocacy*, 1992, (pp. 360–376),

Salt Lake City: University of Utah Humanities Center, with a differently focused but related version appearing as "Decision-making as social drama," in R. Harré and P. Stearns, *Discursive Psychology*, Newbury Park, CA: Sage.

PART 1

An Academic and Social Scene

Introduction:
A Scene of Scholarly Conversation

Every social scene involves agents in action. Yet within any social scene, what sense is to be made of those agents? How do we think about human beings, as agents? Several important ideas have been proposed for thinking about human beings as such. Some of the more prominent of these treat agents as an "individual," "self," "person," and/or "social identity." Each of these ideas has been created in order to draw attention to an aspect or feature of human experience, with each saying something about agents—as individuals, selves, or persons—as a site of that human experience. Each represents a way in which scholars have responded to a basic question: What basic idea can (or should) be used to make sense of humans? A more specific form of the question is: How does that basic idea shape our views of ourselves, as agents?

My purpose in this introduction is to sketch some of the general conceptual terrain that has been cultivated by investigators who respond to these questions. The sketch I offer is not comprehensive, but it is suggestive, I think, of at least some of the general themes in an ongoing conversation about humans as agents. I will introduce a variety of academic works currently available on the general topic. I will focus my discussion upon three central concepts, "individual," "self," and "person." Beginning this way provides some general sense of the academic scene into which this book enters. Once in it, I briefly discuss the general problems to which this book responds, and then overview the general approach assumed in addressing them. But first, let us survey some of the currents in the ongoing conversations about the individual, self, and person.

The Individual as a Neuropsychological Being

One view of the agent is as an "individual." Such a view foregrounds the human as a separable physical organism and explores,

3

for example, the role of an individual's neurobiological capacities, their development, or impairment. Perhaps the most popular author on this theme is Oliver Sacks (e.g., 1987), who has examined how physiological diseases effect the processes of the brain, and in turn, how the brain controls a patient's conduct. The recent public discussions of Prozac, and the physiological bases of sexual preferences, also point to the important link between biological composition and an individual's behavior. From this view, the agent is deemed an "individual," a complex composition of biological matter and neurological processes, with these generating the agent's abilities to think and act. As explicated in the theory of Allan Schore (1994), human neurological "hardware" plays a key role, along with mental processes, in the development of an agent's ego, psyche, or personality. A long tradition of psychological research examines, similarly, individual traits and preferences, yet here the focal concern is the agent's views of itself, its self-concept and self-esteem, especially as these enter into one's sense of personal identity (e.g., Suls, 1993). Of special concern recently has been the role an individual's affective states and stages play in the developing of the ego, and how these states and stages influence self-awareness and self-knowledge (e.g., Hattie, 1992; Heron, 1992).

Studies such as these, conceived in a language of neurology and psychology, portray the agent as an "individual" that is generated through basic biological and/or mental processes, with the "manifestations" of these processes being evident in human social behavior (see Schore, 1994, for a review and synthesis). Scholars of intrapersonal communication have advanced a cognate view by exploring basic mental processes and their behavioral manifestations (e.g., Fitzgerald, 1993; Vocate, 1994). With these views, the agent is treated, at base, as an "individual" with its own neuropsychological composition.

The Self as Symbolic Interaction

The seeds of a symbolic interactionist perspective were sewn early in this century by Charles Horton Cooley and George Herbert Mead. Reacting to the Cartesian separation of individuals from social orders, Cooley provided a view that integrated self with society. He argued that the self is not something separate from society, but is an agent interpenetrated with the social world. As he put it: "A separate individual is an abstraction unknown to experience, and so likewise is society when regarded as something apart from individuals. . . . 'Society' and 'individuals' do not denote separable phenomena, but are simply collective and distributive aspects of the same thing" (Cooley, 1964, p. 36). For Cooley, society and self are integrated within basic social processes: "Society . . . is a relation among personal ideas" (p. 121).

For Mead, the self begins in childhood as a biological entity, but this "mere organismic existence" succumbs to the child's developing social self. Through this process of socialization, self eventually creates the meanings of its natural physical conditions and social institutions through human interactions (1934, pp. 149–155). Focusing primarily upon face-to-face interactions, Mead's proposal places "the activity or behavior of the individual . . . within the social process" (p. 6). The self then, according to Mead, should be conceptualized from the vantage point of "society, at least from the standpoint of communication as essential to the social order" (p. 1). Mead helped show, early on, how communication and interaction fashion "the social order." He showed also how communication involves the constant fitting together of the potentially diverse conceptions and actions of selves. He emphasized the point: As human agents engage in communication, and interact socially, they generate not only selves, but societal life. The "self," then, for Mead, dwells with "society" in social interaction.

Together, Cooley and Mead set the stage for viewing self not solely as a biopsychological agent, although it is certainly in some sense that, but moreover as an emergent process of social and symbolic interaction.

Within the symbolic interactionist tradition, more contemporary studies of self have investigated self in diverse social scenes. For example, Mark Neumann (1993) has examined how an alternative travel company designs its tours, in part, to meet the desires of "alternative and oppositional identities." He found the tactic of staging an "alternate" social scene at times to be successful, but at other times to lapse into "a familiar social space, one filled with roles that resembled those supposedly left at home" (p. 211). In an exploration of "the postmodern self" using texts from the movie, *Rain Man*, Norman Denzin (1993) implicitly invokes the mythic form of the Odyssey. His objective is to trace how leaving a primary social sphere for self (e.g., home), for elsewhere (e.g., through travel), can provide a means of self-enrichment, but only if self is "willing to listen to that tiny voice that harkens back, always to the world left behind, for that world left behind is the one where the self, if it has any hope for itself, is always anchored" (p. 75). Interesting to compare to Denzin's and Neumann's studies is one by Snow and Anderson (1987), who have examined how displaced others, the homeless, construct and avow identity. Together, these empirical studies explore how self is located in different spheres and scenes of social interaction, and how moving between these different spheres and scenes shapes knowledge of self and social living.

Studies in the symbolic interactionist tradition locate self and society in social interaction, and explore how self varies by societal scene and process. The role of self within and between social processes is apparent in a recent overview of the symbolic interactionist approach (see Denzin, in press). A highly synthetic, refined, and ambitious overview is Turner's post-Parsonian theory of social interaction that explicitly integrates Mead's theories of the self, act, and interaction with the later theories of Goffman, Schutz, Giddens, and Habermas (Turner, 1988).

Self as Social Construction

While the symbolic interactionists have been exploring self in various spheres and scenes of social interaction, social constructionists have been busy formulating philosophical arguments about the social and discursive bases of self. Similar to the symbolic interactionists, the social constructionists often rally behind this general claim: Self, and its social significance, is not a given in nature, but is a consequent of discursive and interactive life. While symbolic interactionists tend to be working within and extending a complex intellectual heritage (couched mainly within a sociological tradition), social constructionists are revisionists, exploring the rather weighty implications of their general claim in various academic literatures. For example, several social constructionists have formulated specific and highly influential arguments that are designed to revamp the nature of scientific explanations (e.g., Harré and Secord, 1972), to rethink individual psychology (e.g., Harré, 1984; Harré and Stearns, 1995; and Smith, Harré, and VanLangenhove, 1995), to introduce discursive theory to social psychology (e.g., Potter and Wetherell, 1987), to advance textually based theories of selfhood and identity (e.g., Shotter and Gergen, 1989) and, more recently, to present a discursive theory of the mind, self and agency (Harré and Gillett, 1994).

In an interesting piece of social commentary, Kenneth Gergen (1991) has argued that contemporary postmodern society has so saturated the self that any essential core of self has eroded. A consequence of this erosion, he claims, is a fundamental challenge to the very sacred notion of self that has been so prominent in many western societies, from the romantic to the modern era. The social constructionist school has proceeded rather ardently by advancing the idea that self is socially constructed through various relational and linguistic processes. By tracing the implications of this claim, these scholars have argued for radical transformations in various disciplines of thought, especially in philosophy, literary theory, and psychology.

The Person as Culturally Configured

A long tradition of studies in anthropology has responded to the above questions about self and person with a dual allegiance. Based upon basic fieldwork, one accent has been placed upon the universal importance of the concept of individual or self or person to people everywhere. As Hallowell (1955, p. 77) wrote: "A concept of self not only facilitates self-orientation but enables the individual to comprehend the nature of his own being and, by inference, the nature of other selves with whom he interacts. Since concepts of this category define the most typical and permanent attributes of a phenomenal class of objects among which the personal self is included, their importance in any culture is obvious." The cross-cultural utility of the concept has been affirmed and discussed more recently by several others (e.g., Fortes, 1973, p. 288; Geertz, 1976, p. 225; Hymes, 1961, p. 335; Singer, 1980). Earlier, the concept of self had been stipulated as a kind of culmination of a developmental, evolutionary process (Mauss, 1938). In each school of thought, the concept of self or person, and perhaps its development, has been demonstrated as useful in cultural and cross-cultural studies (Carbaugh, 1988b, pp. 15–19, 109–120).

The concept of person, or self, within this tradition, even if of "obvious" utility for cultural studies around the world, as Hallowell claims, also has been used to emphasize the voice of cultural distinctiveness and difference. As Marcus and Fischer (1986, p. 45) put it: "Perhaps the most effective focus for descriptions that would deal with the ways in which cultures most radically differ from one another is a consideration of conceptions of personhood—the grounds of human capabilities and actions, ideas about the self." This second accent, then, comprises perhaps the most celebrated feature of ethnography. This is the commitment to analyzing models of the person as these are differently configured in cultural scenes of contemporary societies. The general objective is to demonstrate how "person" is conceived and lived variously in communities around the globe.

Several recent anthologies on this subject demonstrate this view of the person through intriguing ethnographic analyses (e.g., Shweder and LeVine, 1984). Some of these include explorations of Pacific models of the person (e.g., White and Kirkpatrick, 1985), Eastern and Western versions of self (e.g., Marsella, Devos, and Hsu, 1985), and ways the current concept of person relates to Mauss's earlier evolutionary formulation (e.g., Carrithers, Collins, and Lukes, 1985). Extensive ethnographic analyses have analyzed concepts of the person and emotions in Micronesia (Lutz, 1988), in the Philippines (M. Rosaldo, 1980), among the Balinese, Moroccan, and Javanese people (Geertz, 1976), among a Hindi speaking people (Shweder, 1991), and among Japanese workers, with special attention being given to the influences of power and gender (Kondo, 1990).

While maintaining a vigilant watch upon the cultural shaping of selves in the practices of many peoples, and taking the time to understand the diversity involved, these scholars amply demonstrate not only the cross-cultural utility of the concepts of self and person, but also the unique configurations of each of these in societies and cultures around the world.

Self in Communication and Rhetoric

In 1976 and later in 1985, Donald Cushman and his colleagues built upon the views of George Herbert Mead and others in order to argue that the self-concept was central to the conduct and interpretation of interpersonal communication (Cushman and Craig, 1976; Cushman and Cahn, 1985). Similarly, Barnett Pearce and Vernon Cronen (1980) developed a theory of communication in which the self, or the particular biographical qualities of participants, were used as resources for conducting, understanding, and explaining communicative interactions. Some recent developments in communication theory have detailed social interactive processes that are sites of cultural identities (e.g., Carbaugh, 1990b; Collier and Thomas, 1988; Philipsen, 1987), while others have discussed how communication activates dialectical tensions within self and social relationships (e.g., Baxter, 1994; Carbaugh, 1988b, 1988/ 1989, 1990c; Hecht, 1993; Rawlins, 1992). Clearly, these studies have begun to show how communication involves self in social interactions, and further how social interaction can mediate the personal and social dimensions of selves in human relationships.

These communication studies, as do many of those cited above, bring to fruition the prescient insights of rhetorical theorist Kenneth Burke (1937). As he saw it, identity and self derive from a kind of socially infused dialectical dance among various levels of "identi- fication." As he put it: "'Identification' is hardly other than a name for the function of sociality" (pp. 266–267). And further: "Identity involves 'change of identity' insofar as any given structure of society calls forth conflicts among our 'corporate we's.' . . . For since the twice born begins as one man and becomes another, he is at once a continuum and a duality. Such changes of identity occur in every- one" (pp. 268–269). As readers of Burke already know, his view of rhetoric is built largely around this concept of identification. He uses the concept as a way of entitling basic dialectics in symbolic action between the separation of people (e.g., "conflicts") and their union (e.g., "continuum"), between changes in identificational ori- entations and their permanence (Burke, 1965).

Building upon this Burkean view, George Cheney has explored "the nature of organizational rhetoric (or organized persuasion) as the management of multiple identities" (1991, p. 2). His rhetor- ical approach is turned to the Catholic bishops' development of a pastoral letter on nuclear arms. His findings detail how complex organizations require the rhetorical management of multiple iden- tities, with some of these being in concert, while others are in con- flict (see esp. 164ff.). And so the self, person, and identities are fig- ured into contemporary communication processes, as a kind of grand dialectical process of identification, alternating between divisions among persons and their union.

THE PROBLEMS OF STUDY

The basic claim that is a condition for the above studies, and upon which I want to build, is this: Each approach to the human agent derives from a common way of communicating in a scene. The communication in the above scenes involves communities of people (i.e., academic communities) using a particular language—and other means of expression—and in so doing identifies human people as kinds of agents (as an individual, self, person), and thus relates to them accordingly. In any community or social scene presumably, whether academic or not, this process of identification is conducted in particular ways. The main problem I want to raise and address, then, with the benefit of these colleagues' insights, is the question of how the agent is both conceived and lived in particular American scenes. How is communication shaping agents there? This is the *basic problem* of this study.

Several recent studies help suggest a second problem: the difficulty of hearing "macro-notions"—such as society, class, ethnicity, institutions, culture—within "micro-processes." The studies that follow explore situated communication practices as "radiants" of cultural meaning—including history or society or class or politics or economics. From this view, it is not, then, that culture, or society, or class, is merely a larger "environment" or "context" for a social scene. I argue instead that these features, to the extent they are socially active, are immanent in the actual patterning of actual social interactions, themselves (Sapir, 1931). As much has been demonstrated in studies of racial discrimination in South Africa (Chick, 1990), gender (West and Zimmerman, 1991), and cultural identity generally (Wieder and Pratt, 1990). For example, in the following studies, one can hear in chapters 3 and 4 the communication of social class among workers, in chapters 5 and 7 the communication of gender and politics, and in chapters 9 and 10 political and economic dynamics. Race, gender, culture, politics, economics, and so on are not just abstractions or infrastructures, or deep forces to be posited a priori in order to account for surface actions. Such things are figured in a social communicative way into the actual patterning of actual interactive processes themselves. How these "macro" features get woven into American social scenes raises a second problem for this study.

Another line of work helps raise a third, related problem: Can one hear, in interaction, notions previously deemed "psychological" or "mental"? Several authors have proposed relocating mental notions, moving them from inside the brain or head, or somehow underlying human action, into concrete communicative practices. Rather than moving notions (e.g., culture) from the outside into discourse, as above, the problem here is moving notions from the inside (e.g., personality) out. Of special concern here has been shifting the bases of concepts like "self," "person," "identity," "personality," and "attitude" from mental to discursive matters. Social constructionist (e.g., Billig, 1987, 1991; Edwards and Potter, 1992; Gergen, 1985; Harré, 1991a; Potter and Wetherell, 1987) and some anthropological works (Kondo, 1990; Sherzer, 1987) have advanced discourse based theories of these various concerns. Studies such as these can enrich communication theory as they suggest, similar to ethnomethodology, how concepts about "mentation" refer not just to mindful matters, but are immanent in historically transmitted, socially structured communication practices. How notions of "self," especially those related to play, work, marriage, and gender, enter actively into routine communicative life, is the third, main problem of this study.

CULTURAL PRAGMATICS

To address these problems and examine the processes outlined above, I have adopted a particular communication perspective. As applied here, it seeks to "see"—speak, listen, sense, or feel—the "micro" and "macro" concerns of identity, from the vantage point of situated communication practices. The general substantive objective is to bring into view particular ways social identities are practiced in situated social scenes. The general theoretical objective is to provide an account of these practices by explicating the basic communicative forms, symbols, and meanings of those practices. After a brief introduction to this approach, I will mention a set of key terms that figure prominently in the following analyses: *cultural dimensions, communicative practice, cultural scene, social identity,* and *identification.*

Background

The general approach I adopt is indebted to the insights of several authors, including Kenneth Burke (1937), Erving Goffman (1967), and Clifford Geertz (1973; see also Richard Shweder, 1991). In an effort to bring micro and macro features into view, it seeks to integrate the interactionist focus, for example, of Goffman with the more heavily cultural focus, for example, of Geertz. Generally, the approach seeks to describe communication practices, to interpret those practices with reference—partly at least—to the participants' point(s)-of-view, and thus to explore how participants' meaning systems get woven into the means of actual communication practices (see the Appendix to this volume; Carbaugh, 1993b; Moerman, 1988). Grounded first and foremost in actual scenes of routine communication, and turned to the problems at hand, it explores ways of hearing in culturally situated practices, social identities at work (e.g., Basso, 1990; Hymes, 1961, 1972; Katriel, 1991; Philipsen, 1992; Varenne, 1977).

As discussed above, some scholars and lines of research have been searching for ways to hear communal processes of identification in concrete social interactions. One of the earliest modern writings on the topic is Bakhtin's demonstration of ways, for example, speech genres are caught up in forms of joint action. As Bakhtin shows, forms of communication enable some identities while constraining others. Bakhtin regularly refers to this general process as "speech communication," "speech communion," and "cultural communication" (Bakhtin, 1986). Although not drawing explicitly on Bakhtin, Philipsen (1987) has noted similar dynamics, and made a plea for explorations of "cultural communication" especially through the "cultural communication forms" of ritual, myth, and social drama. Exploring the relationship between specific interactions and cultural contexts, Eriksen (1991) has shown how ethnic identities are contextually managed through cultural forms of interaction. Fitch (1991) has interpreted how the symbol of "mother" gets culturally coded into everyday communicative forms in Colombia, a coding that sharpens knowledge about both the cultural shaping of that identity and patterns of identification that are much more general. A closely related and well-established body of work in the "coordinated management of meaning" seeks to integrate cultural dimensions, interactive episodes, and identity (Cronen and Pearce, 1991/1992).

The studies included here attempt to keep communication and culture in view. Effort is thus given to integrating the pragmatics of everyday communication with the cultural meanings that are presupposed for and implicated by those very practices. The approach is thus pragmatic and cultural: It draws attention *both* to the situated and momentary character of meaning-making in any society (the pragmatic), *and* to the conceptual and actional forms of identification that are both immanent in and a necessary condition for that very interaction to be, indeed, richly meaningful (the cultural).

A Cultural Dimension

The cultural dimension draws attention to the twin interactional accomplishments of *coherence* and *community*: What indigenous meanings are being (re)created with this pragmatic action (i.e., the focus on coherence); and, for what people are these meanings intelligible (i.e., the focus on community)? Responding to these questions, one attempts to explicate, at least partly, how participants' meanings are associated with their situated symbolic practices (Carbaugh, 1991). For purposes of this study, we ask a specific question about coherence in the scenes of a complex community: What situated communication practices are being used in specific American scenes, and how do they meaningfully constitute participants' identities, as such? Attending to the cultural features of communication in these scenes enables one to understand the symbolic resources of identification that participants use in their routine communicative practices, as well as the meaning system associated with those situated communication practices.

Note that the questions about coherence and community are *mute on the criterion of approval or agreeableness*. Agreement of opinion or value is not a necessary condition for coherence. Communities differently identify agents (e.g., as Democrats or Republicans), as do families (e.g., as father, son). This is often done quite coherently, if disagreeably. Also, in some scenes, identities are played rather coherently within relations that are sometimes laden with disapproval and conflict (as in chapters 3, 5, 9, and 10 below). Questions of (de)legitimacy thus are sometimes—but not always—central, as are the processes in which such questions are raised and addressed.

Accomplishments of coherence and community are done in particular ways. Specific social identities are creatively configured around the dimensions of *particular* cultures. For example, for some communities and scenes, it is coherent to communicate in a scene to disembodied spirits (such as "fairies"), just as in others one can speak to dispirited bodies (the "possessed"). For others, in other scenes, this is incoherent. Cultures thus set stages, or discursive parameters, for what is coherent as identity, with different versions of those identities being differently practiced in the social scenes of life. The communication of social identities is cultural, then, to the extent that the practice of those identities coheres (is deeply sensible, or intelligible) within the particular scenes of that community (Carbaugh, 1988a).

Within any particular community, a social scene can be set for the practice of identity in very particular ways. In some scenes, meanings of separation and hierarchy between identities might be amplified, just as in other scenes meanings of unity may preside (see chapters 3 and 4). The social organization(s) that coheres with prominence within any one scene of a community—whether harmonious or contested—derives therefore, at least in part, from the creative uses of communication practices. And so the communication of social identities plays upon culturally coherent axes of identification, with various social identities, relations among them, and institutional arrangements being immanent in that very process. As communication coheres social identities, and plays them variously into various social scenes, so it structures the various relations of a community's life (further discussion of the point appears in chapters 1, 3, 4, 8, and 11 below; also see Carbaugh, 1988a, 1988b, 1990a, 1991; Carbaugh and Hastings, 1992; Goodwin, 1990).

Communication Practice

I use the concept of "communication practice" to refer to a patterned means of expression (a recurrent symbol, image, or form) and its meanings; as practice, it refers to the actual use of that means by, and its meanings to some people in a particular social scene. A communication practice—or a discursive practice—is, then, an actual means of expression in a community, given that community's specific scenes and historical circumstances (in the broadest sense).

The concepts "symbol" and "form" help elaborate the particular means and meanings of communicative practices. Any practice can be composed, presumably, of symbols (i.e., potent words, phrases, tropes, or images), forms (i.e., sequences of acts and events), and their meanings (e.g., premises of belief and value that are associated with each symbol and form of expression). The primary objective of an ethnographic pragmatics is to describe particular communicative practices-in-use and to interpret the symbols, forms, and meanings that comprise them.

Cultural knowledge of pragmatic communication, built this way, suggests that one know something of the larger "expressive system"—as Goffman (1967) put it—of which each single practice is a part. This larger *system*, this expressive system of symbols, symbolic forms, and meanings, contains features that are typically presumed across scenes, in order to create a large, "super-sense" of the cultural community. This sense of the "landscape" becomes, in turn, a resource for the ethnographer when analyzing any one particular communicative practice. In the process, one can learn how the various features of communicative practice—the particular symbols, forms, and their meanings—operate generally and particularly, and interpret how each might possibly be substituted, associated, contrasted, hierarchically arranged, causally organized, vis-à-vis the others. In this way, one can build senses both of a general "cultural landscape" and of the particular communicative practices that invigorate its social life.

Cultural Scene

As indicated in the book's title, and above, the concept of "scene" is central to these studies. Following Hymes (1972), this concept provides the anchoring of the studies in social settings that are inhabited by actual people, people who conduct their own version of communicative life. Further it gives a central place to participants' senses of what they are doing, and being, while acting there (Geertz, 1976). No specific feature is ruled into a scene or out of a scene in an a priori way. If participants "say" (implicitly and/or explicitly) that their identities rely on political and economic features, then cultural analyses should take up that lead. While any one account, provided by any one participant, may or may not ably represent the actual communication in a scene, the ethnographer wants to know nonetheless what the participants have to say (Briggs, 1986). If participants repeatedly say that identities revolve around certain axes, then the ethnographer should pursue that lead, at least for some of the time. The concept of scene, then, draws attention to actual social settings, the communicative practices being used in those settings (an order of enactment), and the participants' senses of the communicative practices that are being used there (an order of reports about enactment). Ethnographic interpretations are creatively formulated then, by describing communicative practices in social settings, and by being cognizant of (but not necessarily constrained by) the participants' reports about those practices and scenes.

A second sense of cultural scene—a kind of over-text—is also being used. This involves the analyst's investigation of the larger system of communication, the "culturescape," of which any one particular situated practice is a part. Whether participants say it is relevant or not, one would want to know the history of the community, its social demography, economic composition, political structures, occupations, educational system, legal processes, objects of art, and so on. Additionally, and ideally, one would want to know all possible scenes in the community, and the communicative practices and social identities that make them what they are. This "cultural knowledge" then becomes a general resource with which to describe and interpret, to account for, the communication in any one particular scene.

With these two senses, the concept of scene suggests a practical knowledge that is attentive both to a particular situation of communication practice, and to the cultural landscape in which that practice plays a creative part.

Identity, Identification

Following Burke (1937, pp. 263–273), and based upon the dialectics discussed above, I use the terms *social identity* and *identification* as ways of drawing attention to two aspects of communicative practices. One is the use in communicative practices of particular *symbols of identity*, those that identify human agents. Reflecting some of the concerns in the following chapters, examples of these include: "fans," "shakers and movers," "Mrs. Nobleton," "men," and "women." The other aspect of practice of concern to us here are the communicative *forms* being used to enact social identities. Examples of these are, at one level, culturally specific actions, such as "cheers," "chants," "using my husband's name"; or, more generically, rituals and social dramas. The use of any such symbol or form implicates meanings about social identity. Through exploring these symbols and forms of communicative practice, and interpreting their meanings, we are able to hear identities being constituted through participants' practices.

From a cultural pragmatic view, then, communication activates culture, and does so through situated communication practices, with social identity being immanent in those actual practices. As this view of self and social identity integrates self and societal processes, it is indebted to the symbolic interactionists; as it integrates social and discursive processes, it is indebted to the social constructionists; as it is based upon culture theory and concepts, it is indebted to interpretive anthropologists; as it derives from interpersonal and rhetorical concerns, it is indebted to communication theorists. With the focus upon communication practices, and the cultural features being used to identify agents in specific social scenes, it hopes to contribute to this ongoing scholarly conversation of agents-in-action.

By joining this important conversation among scholars, we have engaged largely in the language of academic books and journals and educational classrooms. What if we explore these concerns elsewhere, in the popular discourses and discussions of an American public? What communicative practices and idioms are available there for discussing social identity?

CHAPTER 1

Social Identities as Communication

POPULAR DISCOURSES OF IDENTITY

One of the central questions of social and communication theory, indeed of philosophy and psychology, has been Who am I? Popular responses to this question have been given in at least three different idioms. As with the literature reviewed above, one has taken as its basic starting point the biological composition of human organisms. On this basis, the question Who am I? is responded to by reference to basic human biology, and presumable types of biology. For example, a person might claim to be a kind of person such as a male or female, based upon his or her biological sex. Similarly, one might claim to be a kind of person such as a caucasian, Black, Asian, Irish, Italian, Native American, and so on, based upon his or her genetic composition. For each such claim, one can trace at least some of its force to the basic factors of human biology.

This first set of responses constitutes a sometimes potent *idiom of biological identity* and is the basis, for example, for some of the government policies concerning Native American tribal membership, for deciding who indeed is a "real" Indian (according to the government). Some of these policies are based upon "blood quantum." In some cases, to qualify for tribal membership, one's body must contain a minimal proportion of Indian blood or a certain biological composition. For example, at least one of one's grandparents must be or have been a full-blooded Indian. An equivalent biological composition would also suffice, so that a parent of one-half blood, or all grandparents of one-quarter blood each, and so on would be sufficient to qualify for tribal membership. Without having this biological make-up, regardless of how one acts, or thinks one is acting, one cannot, according to this policy, become a member of a Native tribe.

An analogous argument could also be developed about one's sexual composition, or racial composition, or ethnic composition, basing such claims upon one's permanent, or ascribed, biological make-up. From the vantage point of this response, "who I am" is contingent upon an individual's basic physiology. This is, of course, an assessment that is made independently from an individual's actions, or thoughts. For example, one can lay claim to being a biological Native American, without doing any action as a Native American. That biology forms powerful sources of claims about identities, at least in some scenes, cannot be disputed, as the examples above, and events in parts of the world under the rubric of "ethnicity," or even "ethnic cleansing," make all too apparent.

A second popular idiom has taken as its starting point the psychological composition of human individuals. On this basis, the question Who am I? is responded to by reference to an individual's human psychological traits. For example, a person might claim to be, like Woody Allen, a bit neurotic, depressed, or obsessive. Similarly, one might attribute psychological qualities to others, some perhaps even identifiable as paranoid or psychotic. On a larger scale, whole groups of people might be identified as narcissistic. For each such claim, one can trace some of its force to the internal domain of human psychology.

This second response is couched in a popular *idiom of psychology* and is the basis for claims being made about the enduring dispositions of individuals. Some such qualities are said to be rather stable, with others being more transient, but all such claims rely upon a particular kind of internal cognitive reality for this claim of identity to make sense. From this vantage point, the question Who am I? is contingent upon the individual's (in psychotherapy) or group's (in social therapy?) internal traits, or psychological make-up.

Some popular claims of identity are also forged with hybrid versions of both of these idioms. For example, as a female, it is sometimes presumed that whatever one "is," one is that kind of person not only because of biological factors, but also because the individual is psychologically composed in that particular female way. Similarly, as an African, presumably for some, one is not only a particular kind of biological entity, but also psychologically composed (or programmed or endowed) in a particular African way.

The biological and psychological claims of identity are mostly operationalized at the level of individuals. That is, through these idioms, we lay claims to identities, or attribute identities to others, largely on the basis of biological and psychological factors and dimensions that apply to that particular individual or organism. This is the case, for example, when white parents adopt black children with the stated objective of creating a multicultural world. Their belief is that the biological and psychological composition of their child is "black" just as theirs is "white" and their family will demonstrate how these different identities, so conceived, can live together. As a result, each of us can be led to thinking that "who I am" is, at least to some degree, predetermined by basic biological or psychological factors and dimensions. Whether male or female, Italian or Indian, black or white, presumably one is who one is by being so—biologically and psychologically—designed.

Up to this point, in this admittedly sketchy story about popular forms of identification, we have neglected "environmental" factors, or the contexts in which people live. In other words, up to this point our discussion has neglected this form of our basic question: is "who I am" dependent partly, at least in some ways, upon where I am? A third set of responses has taken as its starting point the largely cultural and social structural factors of human living. On this basis, the question Who am I? is responded to by diagnosing one's cultural orientation and one's position in the social structural arrangement of society. For example, a person might claim a particular identity because of one's nation of origin or a group's presumed features. One might claim to be "American," or "British," or "Finnish," based upon one's place of birth or residence, or use these identifiers as a way of saying, respectively, that one is talkative, refined, or silent. Similarly, one might claim to be "poor" or "wealthy," "professional" or "laborer," based upon one's position in the social structures of society. The opening of the "Chunnel" (the tunnel under the English Channel between Britain and France), for example, if one believes some news reports, has been oriented to very differently by the British and the French. The former have shown a rather haughty indifference, as the latter have excitedly charged into the event rather opportunistically. That owners and shareholders of the Chunnel orient to it differently than do the laborers who built it reveals the social structuring of identities in this process.

This third set of responses creates a popular *idiom of cultural and social identity* and is the basis for claims being made about *people* as members of groups. As such, *people* are assigned particular qualities or features because they are group members, or because they hold a particular social position. Each is being identified as a bearer of that group's habits or customs or position of living. As we of course know, any one individual within the group may or may not conform to the particular quality or feature being attributed to it, but nonetheless, it is presumed, being a member of that group exposes (or socializes) or predisposes one into that particular being. From the vantage point of this third response, the question Who am I? is contingent upon particular cultural orientations or social structural positions within the life of a society.

Each of these three idioms for claiming an identity is only sketched here, yet each can be distinguished analytically, one from the other. Whether one is laying claim to a biological, a psychological, or a sociocultural identity, each can be distinguished from the other, at least in the abstract. In real scenes of social living, however, these claims to identity, and the resulting processes through which they are made and remade—which I call cultural discourses—can easily overlap and ambiguously affirm, or deny, one another. For example, saying in a scene that "I am a woman" is, perhaps at once, to say something—or at least to be heard possibly as saying something—about one's biology, psychology, culture, and social position. Making this claim in another scene, perhaps, can be heard to say something that is explicitly, or intentionally, biological, psychological, and social-structural, yet also as something that is beyond any culture, or underlying every culture. Some claims within the women's movement are being so stated.

One commonality runs across these claims as they are typically made. Each presumes the primary site of identity is "in the individual." If we ask where, fundamentally, identity is located, I think this question is largely responded to, at least in prominent American scenes, on the basis of a primary psychobiological idiom, with culture and social structure heard as laminations onto, or social developments of these. When formulating an alternate response to the question (e.g., identities are in social patterns), one might be challenged by Americans: Where is identity, if not fundamentally in people? If no other location can be found (that is, if and when the primary site of identity is presumably biological and psychological), then identities become, at base, like material resources, properties or possessions of individual persons. As such, they become something that derives from, or if not deriving from then a basic part of, the biological and psychological conditions of living. This is a prominent American conception of identity (Carbaugh, 1988b, 1994).

With this cultural view and these popular idioms, social identities are conceived or conversed as something inside the agent, something an individual "has" or "has become"; they are a part of one's internal "self." This sense of internalizing an identity, of having it inside as a deep part of one's being is important, especially to Americans today. Yet, identities are also, perhaps, something more than this. They can be (thought of as) something people "do" on occasions. They are, in this sense, something invoked, used, interpreted with, displayed, performed, and so on in particular social scenes (e.g., Wieder and Pratt, 1990). What if we conceive of them in this way?

With the following studies, I want to draw attention to the communication of identity. This suggests shifting attention to an alternate site of identity. The basic site of identity, in this view, could be formulated in this way: What exactly one is being, or saying, or doing, by being such a person as a worker, or a woman, or a man, or an environmentalist, or a German, is largely contingent upon the scene in which one is acting, and the way that scene is set, cast, and communicationally improvised. Focusing on this performative mode of identity, or selves, as in social interactions in actual scenes, in a particular social somewhere and not just an abstract anywhere, leads me, following others, to add a fourth "cultural pragmatic idiom" to the above.

While each of the above claims to identity is analytically distinct, the discourses being used to state and interpret them, the situated communication of them, needs to be understood, especially as these are used in particular scenes. I propose the cultural pragmatic approach as a way of doing this, as a way of embracing and extending these by exploring actual scenes where people are living together. This suggests shifting attention from psychobiological factors to conversational scenes. I enter the academic and popular discussions about selves and identities, then, not fundamentally on the basis of biology, psychology, culture (in the abstract, encompassing sense), or social structures (in the predetermined sense), although each of these can and does hold considerable importance in some conversational scenes. I do enter on the basis of actual scenes of social interaction in which selves are fashioned and conducted. From this vantage point, we examine social life as scenes of practical living, and identities as something created and subjected to particular conversational dynamics. For example, this perspective opens the possibility, if not the likelihood, of hearing in some scenes males and females who act not as "men" or "women" but as "colleagues," muting for now their gendered compositions. With this approach, gender becomes less a condition for all conversation, and more a quality of communication in some conversational scenes. As a result, we can add an alternative basis to our thinking about the ways biology, psychology, culture, and social structure get played into social scenes. From this vantage point, the question Who am I? depends partly on "where" I am, with whom I am, and what I can ably do there, in that scene, with those people, given the (material and symbolic) resources that are available to the people there. The primary ontological site of identity is, then, not solely psychobiological, although these might turn out to be active features in some scenes. Who I am, from this vantage point, depends upon both actual scenes and sequences of living, and what I become as I interact through these situated, communication practices. To be able to develop this, however, we must enrich our sense of the communicational bases of identity.

IDENTITY AS COMMUNICATIVE PERFORMANCE: SOCIAL AND CULTURAL FOUNDATIONS

How does one begin conceiving of identities as communicative accomplishments? Building on these introductory comments, I develop here three specific working assumptions from which to start examining social identities as communication. I propose first, as stated above, that we think of identities as dimensions and outcomes of communication practices; second, that we think of each identity as a system of communicative practices that is salient in some but not (necessarily) all social scenes; third, that we think of communication, and the everyday practice of social identities, as a cultural accomplishment.[1] Let us examine each.

The first working assumption suggests that we think of selves as both dimensions and outcomes of particular communication practices. If a message about identity is a dimension of communication, this suggests that communicative actions carry weight, in part, because they show who the people are who are engaged in that very action. For example, to praise one's child for her high grades is, in part, to be one who is a parent. The same communicative scene—of having one's school performance appraised—is also creating part of what it is to be a child. Such scenes creatively invoke identities of parent and child, and create social relationships between them (e.g., one who can evaluate, and one who is subjected to evaluation). Presumably, a dimension of all communicative actions and events is presenting who one is, and who another is, by the way that very event is being conducted. This insight was established forcefully by Goffman (1967), as he demonstrated how selves are fundamentally subjects in social presentations, with each sense of self hinging upon the ongoing lines of face-to-face interaction. Goffman's insights about self-presentations is thus partly the basis for the present proposal.

The first working assumption also suggests thinking of selves as an outcome of communication. This implies that one's sense of who one is derives from the particular arrangement of social scenes in which one participates. Boldly, it asserts that whatever identity is deemed important derives from the social scenes in which one lives. Without a social scene in which to enact an identity, and without having some degree of validation of that identity in those scenes, as many immigrants know, the force of that identity is communally empty, or without social life. This emphasizes the importance of actively and efficaciously practicing an identity within and/or across social scenes. To assume an identity is, then, something more than a simple declaration or avowal of that identity in a particular scene. It is to know ways to express that identity efficaciously, that is, to express it and have it validated, through a variety of actions, in a variety of scenes (see chapter 8 for further discussion).

Thinking about identity as communication is, then, to think of it as both a general dimension of all communicative action, and as a particular outcome (e.g., a particular identity) of specific communicative actions in the scenes of social life.

The second working assumption suggests some fine-tuning of the above, that is, to think of any particular identity as a set of communicative practices that is more salient in some social scenes than in others. Just as an individual is more adept at some identities (e.g., being a teacher, or an American) than others (e.g., being a business executive, or a Russian), so too are social scenes designed for some identities more than others. This is a way of elaborating our shift of focus, and moving the site of identity from the individual into actual scenes of communicative actions (see

Bakhtin, 1986, p. 87). From this view, who you are does not rely solely upon your body or mind, although your body and mind are played forcefully into certain scenes (at least in some cultural landscapes). The alternate basis suggests thinking that who you are hinges upon your actual conceptions and conduct of identity in real social scenes. Any social scene supports some communicative performances more than others, some identities more than others. The scene, how it is being scripted, cast, and acted; or the game, how its rules work and who can play; or the text, how it is being written and read; or the social fabric, who is spinning it, into what design—all of these suggest metaphors about scenes and the ways each designs particular versions of selves. Any scene, through the nature of its communication, then, involves individuals in playing some arrangement of selves over all possible others.

The third working assumption draws attention to the social and cultural, less as prefigured templates and structures, and more as features of actual communication practices. Through a social emphasis, and following the above, attention is drawn to communication as actional and eventful, as performance in the actual scenes and sequences of interactive living (Goodwin, 1990, pp. 8–10). For example, if speaking is necessary, who speaks first, who next, and who gets to speak at all, can matter. Ways it can matter can say something about social identities, who each person is, the ways they are being related, and even what role institutions play by way of organizing these identities and relations. How social interaction like this is being managed, moment by moment, and how that management displays and relates social identities perhaps through institutions, keeping these concerns in mind is to hear the social life of communication.

As mentioned in the introduction, the cultural axes of action draw particular attention to participants' meaning systems. What is it that these people, in this scene, think they are doing by communicating in these ways? One tries to interpret the participants' meanings of their communicative practices, how they cohere through their communicative actions, their ideas about who they are and the activities they are doing. One seeks to know how present concerns are significant and important to them, keeping the symbolic landscape of their community in mind. This is to hear cultural life in communication (Basso and Selby, 1976, pp. 3–6; Geertz, 1976). Knowing what coheres conversational scenes from the view of participants, in a way that resonates with their terms and meanings, this is to hear in community scenes, cultural communicative action (Carbaugh, 1991; Hymes, 1972; Philipsen, 1987).

Together, then, and in summary, one might think of social identities as a dimension and outcome of communication performances, as more salient in some scenes than others, and as socially negotiated and culturally distinct. To address the problem this way means that responses to the question Who am I? may be developed at least in part by explicating the shape of particular communication practices in particular scenes, and by exploring how those practices activate, for the people in those scenes, means of social identification and meanings of cultural lives (Carbaugh, in press).

One important implication of relocating identity into scenes of practice is the opening it creates for possibilities in conversation (rather than a reliance upon preconditions of necessity). For example, whether one is a Native American or White is, from this view, contingent upon whether one is being subjected to—or making a bid for—a conversational scene in which one is deemed a Native American or White. This might suggest something radical for some readers: There are, possibly, some scenes where one's identity can be conversed in a way that is mute on its ethnic composition. Some e-mail connections, and interactions among young children, provide evidence of this fact, as do, more subtly, some face-to-face encounters in which people identify and orient to each other through their communication, not on the basis of ethnicity, but through practices that identify participants in other ways. Whether this identification is beneficial or detrimental of course depends upon the particular dynamics of that scene and the cultural landscape of which it is a part (see the introduction and chapters 5–8 for discussions on this general theme).

If this can be so, if we imagine social identity as communication in these ways, as a dimension and outcome of communicative practice, as salient in some but not all social scenes, and as activating participants' frames of coherence and community, how might we formulate a general framework for this kind of understanding?

A SIMPLE RECIPE FOR SOCIAL IDENTITIES AS COMMUNICATION

Following the foundations laid above, I want to continue by distinguishing social and cultural levels of identification. I will take up this difference in more detail in chapters 4, 7, 8, and 11. Here, I want simply to introduce a basic distinction between what I call "cultural agents" and "social identities," then propose a form of statement for thinking about the communication of social identities. As we shall see, the basic difference between "cultural agents" and "social identities" is a matter of emphasis, with each influencing the other.

The Cultural Agent

The communication of identity, as a "cultural person," is built through certain unquestioned premises, or taken-for-granted features of conversation (Fitch, 1994; Hopper, 1981). Premises can be thought of as basic beliefs and values about what constitutes person, about what person is (and should be), what person can (and should) do, can (and should) feel, and ways "it" can (and should) dwell in nature. These premises create a scene of coherence about what has often been called "personhood." For example, in many American scenes, it is widely assumed that people are, in the first and last analysis, "individuals." This belief is elaborated as people talk about individual "rights," "needs," and "equality." A further belief is that the "individual" has a "self" or something inside of himself or herself that is special, unique, yet rather stable across scenes and times (e.g., their "personality"). These ideas about the person, as an "individual" with a "self," are valued, and are often elevated above "social roles" or "society" as a source of identity (Carbaugh, 1988b, 1994). These themes are taken up in chapters 7 and 8. From the vantage point of this American model of identity, then, in some prominent American scenes, people are conversed as "individuals," and because of this, "relationships" and "communities" are not given, but must be made, constructed, or built (Varenne, 1977).

As different premises for the cultural person hold sway in some other scene and culturescape, then the American model of the agent, of course, does not hold. For some Hindi-speaking people, in other scenes, the person is conversed not as "an individual" but as a "dividual" (Marriott, 1976, p. 111). The basic ingredient in this Hindu "cultural agent" is not the human body, but various more fundamental particles and substances. Any organism might be changed materially, as these particles are shifted, or are recombined, and reshaped. This quality is expressed through the Hindi concept *rasa* (juice) and is used in scenes of marriage: "A woman merges and loses her entire personality into her husband's *substance* at the wedding . . . she actually changes her natal essence for that of her husband's, she merges it with his quite literally— not through sex and childbirth as romantic western readers might be inclined to think, but in a truly material sense" (Bharati, 1985, pp. 220–221). An actual person, here, is conversed not as contained in a single biological or organismic membrane, but as deriving from more basic particles and substances that can be differently arranged, at different periods in one's life, making one a different material being, for example, by going through a marriage ceremony.

The examples given here mark a shift, at the cultural level, between scenes of identification. From the vantage point of the American premises, the Hindu person is nearly unintelligible. As such, an American, with typical American premises, would find it hard to believe, even incredible, that a social ceremony *literally* changes the biological or "natal essence" of a person. Similarly, from the vantage point of this Hindu model, the American "cultural agent" seems less intelligible and incredible. This is the way shifts in the scenes of identification, at the cultural level, can seem incoherent, one to the other (Carbaugh, 1993b, 1993c).

An Emphasis on Social Identification

In the following essays, however, I want to focus primarily not at this cultural level of personhood, but at the social level of identification. Again, the two levels are distinctive, but interrelated. The basic move is this: Within any cultural communication system, erected upon cultural premises of the person and action and nature, there will be available a variety of social identities. For example, on the basis of American premises, there will be a variety of discourses available for communicating specific social identities such as an American man, woman, husband, wife, teacher, student, worker, owner, environmentalist, developer. Each discourse of identity will play upon certain presumed (i.e., cultural) premises about what a person is (and should be), can (and should) do, feel (and should feel), and how that person dwells within nature (Carbaugh, 1994). Other people, with other cultural premises, will make available their own discourses of social identities, erected upon their cultural premises of the person. At both levels, even if the identities are called the same thing, for example, "a marital partner," the cultural premises—and larger cultural landscape—of the social identities will probably vary (e.g., an American "marital partner," a Hindu "marital partner"). In short, any set of premises for a cultural agent will support a variety of social identities. And, as intercultural marriages make readily apparent, any one social identity (e.g., "spouse") will vary by different cultural premises (e.g., American and East Indian).

The focus of the following studies is upon social identities that are situated in American scenes. How can we understand social identification as a conversational and cultural accomplishment?

Recall that my basic proposal is built upon cultural axes and scenes, and upon Burkean processes of identification (discussed in the introduction). As further developed in this chapter, this suggests treating identity as a dimension and outcome of communicative practice. The proposal suggests shifting attention to cultural scenes of conversation in order to understand the particular social identities enacted there. Focus is drawn later to psychological, biological, cultural, or social structural conditions, and earlier to situated, conversational practices. A statement of the following basic form should help us operationalize that conceptual shift, and focus upon the communication of social identities:

> I know who I am, in part, by the way I symbolize in situated social scenes.

First, note the "in part." With this phrase, I want to show that I think this way of conceiving social identities is only part of whatever a whole picture of identity might be. "Being" and "social identity" can and do reside, also, outside of communicative scenes, sometimes in very lively ways. For example, parts of who one is might be revealed in moments of personal reflection, or in transcendental experiences with natural environments, or in physiological mechanisms that are beyond participants' range of expressions. While these experiences can be productively treated as communication, they are also, as any such experience would be, more than that. I do not want to preclude this "more" from the general picture or sound of identity. In other words, a communication theory of social identity can, I think, tell us a lot for example about being a fan, a worker, a husband or wife, a man or woman, a developer or an environmentalist, but I do not think it can account for everything that is relevant to any one social identity (Carbaugh, forthcoming).

With that caveat made, note how the statement can be played with. A shift in pronouns and predicates can help shift the focus from one person to interactions among the present participants. For example,

> I know who you are, in part, by the way you symbolize in situated social scenes.

Or,

> You know who I am, in part, by the way I symbolize in situated social scenes.

A collective orientation can of course also be formulated:

> We know who we are, in part, by the way we symbolize in situated social scenes.

Playing with the forms of pronouns thus helps one shift the focus to various participant identities, or roles, or "selves–2" in Harré's sense (Harré, 1991a). It also can help identify the nature of social relationships and how these are being created between persons. For example, one might reformulate the statement by saying:

> I know how we are related, in part, by the way we symbolize in situated social scenes.

One can also explore how social relationships are differently symbolized within or between social scenes (e.g., Baxter, 1993; Rawlins, 1983, 1992). In this sense, analyses using the form can help capture not only the communication of social identities, but dialectical dynamics as well, including social relations of intimacy, solidarity, and power (e.g., Brown and Gilman, 1960; Brown and Levinson, 1987; and chapter 8 below).

Playing with the basic verb *know* should also prove instructive. Perhaps *know* suggests something too mindful, or too guided by perception and cognition, and one wants to emphasize social activity. This could be formulated:

> I show who I am . . . , *or*, You show who you are . . .

While this captures active, perhaps even strategic features of identities (e.g., I pretend who I am . . .) , some might be bold enough to claim that such action is indeed formative of that very identity. This point can be made:

I constitute who I am . . . , *or,* You constitute who you are . . . , *or,* You constitute who I am . . . , *or,* We constitute who they are, in part, by symbolizing in situated social scenes.

The last preposition, "in situated social scenes," gives the statement its crucial toe-hold in the actual practice of social living. This condition again emphasizes the situating of identities and selves into cultural scenes, with scenes here, intended broadly, implying particular physical settings, cultural senses of those settings, and the larger cultural landscape of which each is a part. This includes (1) the material conditions (2) among particular participants (3) who are engaged in specific activities and events (4) in particular ways (5) about specific topics (6) through their own norms (6a) for acting (6b) and for interpreting that action (Hymes, 1972). Attention is thus drawn to actual communicative practices, the social identities activated through them, and the larger scenes of which they are a part.

This poses a challenge to those who make general claims about any one identity (e.g., "the feminists" or "white men") or any one social arrangement (e.g., "the patriarchy"). In what social scenes are people operating, as such? In what particular ways, about what topics, and so on? It is time our knowledge of social identities, their affordances and limitations, as well as the institutions and societies they help create, were built upon the subtleties and requirements of social interaction itself (Moerman, 1988, pp. 1ff).

I have left perhaps the most important term for last: *symbolize.* Other terms could be substituted for this term, such as *practice, communicate, perform,* or *participate.* The point is to draw attention to the various means of communication (including silence and absence) through which action gets done, and the various meanings these means can have for participants.

Some particular ways communication gets done and the meanings it holds in some scenes are elaborated in the following studies. At a general level, though, the ways of symbolizing that are available to a people are historically rooted, occur in verbal and nonverbal channels, and guide the conduct and interpretation of activities.

Before concluding these remarks, let us summarize the full version of the basic form of statement with which we have been working. A full-blown version with a variety of options would look something like this:

$$\left[\begin{array}{l} \text{I} \\ \text{We} \\ \text{You} \\ \text{They} \end{array}\right] \left[\begin{array}{l} \text{know} \\ \text{show} \\ \text{constitute} \end{array}\right] \text{who} \left[\begin{array}{l} \text{I} \\ \text{we} \\ \text{you} \\ \text{they} \end{array}\right] \left[\begin{array}{l} \text{am,} \\ \text{are} \end{array}\right] \text{in part, by the way}$$

$$\left[\begin{array}{l} \text{I} \\ \text{we} \\ \text{you} \\ \text{they} \end{array}\right] \left[\begin{array}{l} \text{symbolize} \\ \text{perform} \\ \text{participate} \end{array}\right] \text{in situated social scenes.}$$

This framework for thinking about social identities as symbolized in scenes underlies the studies that follow, and is used to explore just how various social identities, various versions of the "I," the "you," and the "we," and social relationships among them, are being practiced in particular social scenes.[2]

Symbolizing: Forms, Symbols, and Meanings

Before sketching the "symbolic" component, one must identify and describe a communication practice, a pattern of communication that recurs with cultural significance. Then, one can interpret the particular forms, symbols, and meanings of identification that comprise it. When each—a symbol and its meanings, or a form and its meanings—is present in communication practices, a social identity is being symbolized in distinctive ways.

Following Burke (1968) and others (e.g., Frentz and Farrell, 1976), a *communication form* can be understood as a recurring interactional sequence that has a cultural and symbolic integrity. Some examples of generic communication forms are rituals, myths, social dramas, and agonistic discourses (Philipsen, 1987; Carbaugh, 1988/1989). Some examples of American communication forms are "being honest," "sharing feelings," and "communication" (Carbaugh, 1988b; Katriel and Philipsen, 1981). Let me reiterate: Even if "identity" is not being discussed explicitly as part of the form of a communicative practice, it is being implicated at some level in the cultural meanings of that practice.

Symbols of identity are particular words, phrases, or images that are used to identify a person as an example of a kind of person. Examples would be "a real Indian" (Wieder and Pratt, 1990), "a man" (Philipsen, 1992), or a "self" (Carbaugh, 1988b). Each communication form, and each symbol of identity, when used in a social scene, implicates some meanings rather than others. In other words, the effective meaning of a particular symbol, or form, is contingent upon its use by someone, and the particular social scene in which it is used (Hymes, 1962). The *meanings* of communication forms and symbols are interpreted below through such various concepts as "premises," "semantic dimensions," "dialectics," "norms," "rules," and "codes." Together, then, the symbolizing component of identity consists, minimally, in a communication form and its meanings, and/or in symbols of identity and their meanings, as these are being used in situated communication scenes.

Any communication practice can be understood, then, as part of a cultural landscape, a landscape in which particular socially situated, symbolic identities—so formed, symbolized, and meant—are being actively played (Carbaugh, 1991, in press). A more detailed discussion of particular communication symbols and forms appears in the appendix. In the meantime, each part of the book will demonstrate, in various ways, how symbolizing in particular social scenes helps constitute the practice of social identities. By explicating the communication of social selves, we can develop a way of thinking about identity that is not grounded solely in human biology or psychology, but also in particular social scenes of symbolic activity: This is the proposal. Now, let us see what it produces when applied to particular social scenes.

PART 2

Five American Scenes

SCENE ONE:
PUBLIC LEISURE

CHAPTER 2

The Playful Self:
Being a Fan
at College Basketball Games

Sport is the very fiber of all we stand for. It keeps our spirits alive
—Franklin Roosevelt

Every society or group or organization of people somehow manages to arrange social selves into private and public versions, so that one acts privately here, and publicly there. Critics have claimed that a predominant focus for any group on one to the neglect of the other can carry attendant problems. For example, contemporary Western, and more specifically American society has been criticized for losing a "proper respect for the public as something meaningful in its own terms" (Halloran, 1981, p. 523). Other students of American social life have argued that the public sphere has become threatening as an "ominous source of tension" (Berger, Berger, and Kellner, 1973, pp. 185–186). It has been persuasively argued that Western societies lack the stable social contexts, or arenas of sociality, in which to engage in meaningful public activity. This critical theme attributes "a built-in identity crisis" and "a deep uncertainty about contemporary identity" to a withering of a robust Western public life (p. 92).

This critical theme is developed most ably in Richard Sennett's *The Fall of Public Man* (1978). A summary of four of Sennett's central points will illustrate this criticism while providing several claims to which this chapter responds.

A central point which pervades much of Sennett's critique is that "all social phenomena, no matter how impersonal in structure, are converted into matters of personality in order to have a meaning" (p. 219). When a people regard all interaction as a reflection of one's deeper "personality," Sennett claims, the social structuring of public relationships is obscured. In fact, Sennett argues, what one "really feels" or is "genuinely like," becomes the sole measure of public sociability. Standards of personal authenticity have so much dominated social life, Sennett claims, that an egological standard has tyrannized public discursive acts and judgments. In his words, "In modern social life adults must act narcissistically to act in accordance with society's norms" (p. 326). Meaning is judged only as far as the individual self extends, with social scenes falling prey to the dictates of personal identities.[1]

Second, Sennett correlates this decline in public culture with a decline in civility. By civility he means "the activity which protects people from each other and yet allows them to enjoy each other's company" (p. 264). Sennett sees contemporary Western interaction as a repertoire of intimate skills that render civil relations problematic. Through Sennett's lens, one sees Western public interaction as ill-fitting residuals of private scenes. The consequences are a lack of coordinated public activity, a loss of protection for the cultural participants, and a cultivated inability to perform civilly with people on a nonpersonal level. Authenticity reigns over civility.

Third, Sennett argues that Westerners participate and experience community life as isolates (pp. 299–300). Rather than communally validating people through the impersonal webs of public interaction, he claims that people seek the comfort of small interactive hubs, as a way of orienting to and maintaining (one's and all others') privacy and personal identities. Sennett sees this kind of public life as inducing a type of psychotic frenzy due to the demands of coordinating action around endlessly diverse private and personal matters. While "small-scale" situations involving private scenes may be managed most comfortably, the arena of public and impersonal interaction results in participatory isolation and at times even chaos. While finding a personal tree or two, one is lost in the public forest.

Finally, as a result of this mass psychological articulation, declining civility, and participatory isolation, Sennett believes adult actors have been deprived of an art of publicly expressive "play": "In modern society, people have become actors without an art. Society and social relations continue to be abstractly imagined in dramatic terms, but men have ceased themselves to perform" (p. 314). The passage from childhood to adulthood becomes a rite in which there is a loss of play. Consequently, the child is weaned of fun and inducted into the serious business of adult culture.[2]

While Sennett's perspective is both provocative and persuasive, "he offers no solution to the problem he so ably describes," nor does he highlight public scenes of activity which counter his arguments (Halloran, 1981, p. 328).

Sennett's critique invites this question: Are there scenes in contemporary American life where adults ably participate in expressive play, in a relatively civilized way? To explore a response to that question, we will examine crowd behavior at American college basketball games. We enter the communication of this scene, and puzzle over one kind of self that is acting there. How can one describe and interpret public interaction in which these statements are boisterously made: "You stink"; "In your face"; "Hey, do you shave your knees?"; and "Give him another tranquilizer!" How can one account for these statements as parts of a scene of public discourse? What does this say about "being a person" there? Eventually, we will see how the responses to these questions are responsive to Sennett's critique of contemporary discursive life. As a result, we will find that Sennett's potent critique of contemporary public life, while particularly apt for many social scenes, elides at least one scene for public communication. To cut to the chaff, there is at least one public scene in America where people exercise a public and playful self, and they do so in a largely civilized, if somewhat peculiar, way. In this scene, they know who they are, in part, because they can symbolize in their rather impersonal and playful ways. The inability to describe and understand public, participatory, and playful patterns such as these in contemporary public life, then, reflects not just a simple oversight, but also a gap in perspective. Such a gap provides an invitation, or a challenge to students of communication to explore how playful selves are conducted in some scenes of public life.[3]

Some caveats are in order up front. One might ask: How typical or general is the pattern of conduct described here? I have observed it from coast to coast, with little variation, and trust, therefore, that most American readers—at least those who are basketball fans—will find it somehow familiar. However, I do not claim that the patterns analyzed here are typical of all basketball games; only that the analysis presented here demonstrates that some actions at some basketball games are culturally patterned, and that these actions provide practical resources from which people draw to "do" one kind of social identity. Second, I do not claim that all people, even as they are being "fans," engage in the patterns described here; only that the patterns described here provide one such discernable form. Finally, I do not claim that the sequence or meanings of communication discussed here are generalizable to other sporting events. Certainly other people in other locales have developed uniquely patterned ways of acting; humans tend to do such things.

METHOD

There are perhaps two very interrelated ways to attend a basketball game: one as an observer of the game, as one who comes to see the teams play; the other as a participant in a particular kind of talk, as a part of the communication practices of the event. Over a period of three years, I attended about forty college basketball games and two professional basketball games as an observer of the game and as a participant in the talk. The scenes in which I experienced these events spanned three medium to large university coliseums, each seating between six to twelve thousand people. Attendance at the events I attended averaged about five thousand people per game. Of these games, six were selected for intensive analysis. During these games, my exclusive role was as an ethnographer. My purpose was to observe and record the way people talked when experiencing this public event. All available data including field records, participants' comments (both spontaneous and elicited), and players' accounts of the event were used to construct the cultural account. Data were analyzed using the cultural pragmatic framework discussed in part 1 of the book.

A CULTURAL SCENE OF PUBLIC CONDUCT

Any cultural event is situated in a context which is acted in by some group of people. The setting for the basketball game is much like a "giant bowl." The center arena or court is often decorated in the home team's colors, with the team's emblem or symbol near the center. Frequently the home team or host school's name is written across either end of the court (as they often are in the end zones of a football playing field). A basket, ten feet high, is situated at each end of the playing surface or court. The people, fans, or crowd sit in an ascending arrangement above the court. All seats point toward the court in which the teams play.

Several symbols in the setting are salient as aspects of the basketball event. Often an arena includes a series of banners on its walls. The banners are generally of two types. First there are those which place the home team within a larger collective, or conference, such as the Southeast, Big 10, ACC, PAC 10, Big Sky, Atlantic 10, and so on. This affiliates the team with a larger community or institution. Second, there are those banners which commemorate the home team's past achievements, such as conference titles, tournament victories, or, in the case of professional basketball arenas, divisional or world titles. Other symbolic features in the setting include trophy cases placed in central locations which are visible upon entering and leaving the arena. These also signify past achievements of teams and players. Often the hallways entering the arena reserve a place for pictures of past "great players." The banners, pictures, and trophies add an explicit sense of the school's sporting history, and set the current scene as a possible extension of the successes of the past. The setting, then, is more than merely a physical place; it is a scene, a historically rich cultural arena, where players, and fans, come to play.

There are six general kinds of participants in the basketball scene. First, and of foremost concern in this study, is the crowd, or "fans." The fans of course are those participants who come to the basketball event to "see the teams play," and to cheer for their favorite team. The fans, though the largest in quantity, have the least restricted of the participants' roles. Most basketball events also include in the crowd "a mascot." The traditional mascot dresses as the team's nickname, such as a minuteman, a husky, a grizzly, a spartan, a bobcat, and so on. Recently, however, there has been a variation on the mascot role that, to my knowledge, has no generic term. These neomascots are often large animal-like "things" dressed in outfits apparently modeled after those used on the American television program *Sesame Street*. Some that I have observed are a chicken, a duck-like thing, and a bear-like body with an ostrich-looking head. It is very significant, I think, that these "things" are not visually related to either team's name or traditional mascot. Yet, during the game, there they are, visible at court side, or during the "breaks" in the game, playing around in the center of the court. I will return to the neomascot later; for now, make note of this—apparently odd—participant in the basketball event.

Another kind of participant in the event is the band. The band frequently includes twenty-five to fifty musicians who function to entertain, energize, and direct the fans in song and cheer. The band is normally seated close to the court, and is therefore visible to the crowd. Complementing the band's role are "the cheerleaders." As the name implies, their primary function is to lead the fans in cheers. Yet, they often entertain the crowd by dancing to the band's tunes or by performing gymnastic mounts. Like the band, the cheerleaders are centrally located along court side in front of the "main cheering section" or are visible to the most expressive part of the crowd. The cheerleaders are easily noticeable because of their uniform (and frequently scanty) dress.

Other participants in this cultural scene are "the players." The players, of course, represent two teams of about twelve members each, which wear the same style, yet different colored uniforms. The colors are easily distinguishable, with the home team usually being dressed in a light color and the visiting (or "away") team dressed in a dark color. In other words, the "good guys" or home team most always wear white or light. The person who coordinates the team's activities is "the coach." The players, then, compose two teams which are directed by coaches.

The final kind of participant is the referees. The two or three referees are noticeably clad in black-and-white striped shirts and black pants. The function of the "refs" is to mediate the competition between the two teams and assure that the basketball game proceeds according to preestablished rules. The referees are the final and official arbiters of all disputes in the game.

These six kinds of participants—the fans, the mascot(s), the band, the cheerleaders, the teams (players and coaches), and the referees—constitute the main identities in the cultural scene of the basketball game. From the vantage point of the fans, the communication in this scene can be understood as a coordinated and playful performance.

FOR THE FAN: A RITUALIZED DISCURSIVE GAME

There are five main phases of communication that combine to form a rather integral sequence of conduct. To act within this sequence is, largely, to be a fan at this sporting event. The talk of the sequence, and of each phase within it, may be understood as a playful game in itself.

1. *The Warm-up*

Most of the fans arrive at the basketball game between a half-hour and five minutes prior to the start of the game or "game time." During this time they, like the players, are warming-up. This stage of the event is characterized largely by talk about two topics. First, some talk centers on the arena, the crowd, and the event at hand. For instance, about the arena ("Those seats sure look comfortable"); to the crowd ("Hey, there's Bob", "Here comes the guy selling mixer" ["mixer" referring to soft drinks to be "mixed"—illegally—with alcoholic beverages], or "Do you believe how many people are here?"); to unique aspects of the event ("Hey, we're going to be on TV", "We got to get on TV"); to the cheerleaders ("That was a nice routine", or "Boy she's good-looking," or "wow, what a hunk"); to the teams ("They've (the other team) got a seven-footer," or "Camby has been on a hot streak lately"). The second dominant topic is rather generally sociable and refers to current events (the weather, political issues), to common friends, or to previous basketball games. The function of the talk at this stage is to acquaint individuals in the crowd to those seated around them (even if indirectly) and to orient the crowd to the event at hand.

During the above conversations, and at about twenty minutes prior to game time, the arena clock begins a countdown. While the beginning of the countdown has no apparent impact, the clock helps orchestrate an intricately designed sequence of events. With about twelve minutes left until game time, several things begin occurring at once. By this time both teams are on the floor warming up. The band has begun playing several lively songs, loudly. The cheerleaders are performing dances to the band's music and doing gymnastic mounts. The referees and coaches are often gathered toward center court and talking. Public announcements are being made of upcoming events. There is an incredible amount of visual and aural and verbal stimulation! The conversations become more lively. A crescendo of talk appears, as if someone were gradually turning up the arena's volume. Then, suddenly, with about eight minutes left on the clock, the teams leave the floor.

2. *The Salutation*

As the teams leave the floor, the volume in the arena quickly lowers. A military or service group marches onto the floor prominently displaying the American flag (among others). The announcer states, "Now ladies and gentlemen, please rise for the playing and singing of our national anthem." Those within sight of the flag rise to attention, with some "crossing their heart" and (some) singing the national anthem.

For most Americans this is not an unusual sight, yet it is interesting to the cultural analyst. Contrast the tone of reverence introduced during this salutation—if not maintained for its entirety—with the frenzy of stimuli occurring only seconds earlier. By playing a controlled reverence against a frenzied excitement, each symbolic stage serves dramatically to heighten the impact of the other. As the "warm-up" sets the stage for play and wild excitement, the salutation provides Americans with a kind of reverent political gesture, a cooperative activity paying homage to a national heritage. The salutation ritual provides a practice in which all participants rise, attend to, and/or orient to a common symbol, the nation's flag, thereby uniting through this common gesture. This is a compellingly integrative sight in a predominantly competitive sporting arena.[4] Some of the members of the crowd (or readers) may not agree about the full meaning or sense of the salutation (for example, who is being united toward what ends?). Additionally, those from elsewhere can find the salutation stage to be quite puzzling in the context of a sporting event. Nonetheless, the salutation is always an integral part of the American basketball event. In the salutary performance, the fans typically cooperatively stand, in a common and shared way, and thus co-orient to the American flag. In this sense, this phase provides a form whereby a symbol, the flag-nation, is cooperatively celebrated, within the larger competitive ritual of the game itself.

The second (or seconds before) the anthem is over, a frenzied excitement begins.

3. The Introductions

Soon after the salutation, the teams reenter the arena. As the home team comes into view, the band breaks into song, the crowd claps, and the cheerleaders lead yells. With between forty and fifty seconds left on the clock, the band begins the home team's fight song, which ends as close to "zero time" as possible. With the clock running down, a strongly expressive style pervades the arena (dramatically extended from the tone set at the end on the warm-up). Yelling and "blurting out" characterize the introductions as the crowd discursively divides into two groups of fans, the home-team fans and the "away-team" fans.

The announcer begins by introducing the away team. As the announcer says, "we would like to welcome the visiting (team name) to (the home team's arena)," a moan or at times even a loud "boo" is often heard. If the home team fans orient to the away players at all, their attention seems to follow the rule: one should playfully disconfirm and/or ridicule the other team. For example, when a smaller player was introduced he was met by "Hey runt!" or "Squirt!" Another player whose name rhymed with lemon was called "Lemon" from the introduction to the end of the game. One player with very hairy legs but peculiarly unhairy knees was greeted by "Hey, do you shave your knees?" These exemplify individuals' comments that orient to an unspoken consensus: that fans playfully disconfirm and/or ridicule the other team.

Groups often coordinate communicative acts to orient to the rule that fans disconfirm the opposing team. For example, the band often leads a particular cheer after each opposing player is introduced. The announcer may say "starting at guard, wearing number 44, six-foot-four-inch, John Smith!" He is greeted by the band and some of the fans yelling "So what?" After being introduced, the next player is greeted by "Who cares?" the third by "Big deal!" the fourth by "Go home!" and so on.

Several other coordinated acts orient to this rule. When a university team from Idaho was being introduced, it was met by several dozen potatoes which were rolled across the floor. (Idaho is the state known for its "famous potatoes," as written on its automobile license plates.) When the U.S. Air Force team was introduced, it was met by a barrage of paper airplanes. When another school, which had a canine nickname, was introduced, the fans rolled several dog biscuits across the floor. Another tactic, used while the opposing team was being introduced, involved almost everyone in the main cheering section opening and casually perusing newspapers, negating any concern about or contact with the away team.

Although the above acts may seem nasty or even tactless, they are almost always done in a spirit of fun, in a playful (rather than serious) tone, and are usually understood (even expected) as part of the basketball event. During the away team introductions, the talk is very expressive and competitively based as it emphasizes and embraces lack of support for the other team, and relentless support of one's favored team.

If the away team consists of disconfirmed players, there is no doubt about who is familiar and supported at home. Home team introductions usually follow a sequence of acts, a kind of mini-ritual, which itself functions to celebrate the team. The sequence is initiated by the announcer, who says, "And now, ladies and gentlemen, your University of Massachusetts Minutemen!" Upon this announcement, the band bursts into a rhythm, the crowd stands up, claps, whistles, and yells. The cheerleaders form a dancing tunnel through which the celebrated players enter, one by one, into the arena. There is an explosion of sensorial and even sensual energy after each player is announced (although each time it becomes harder to hear the announcement). As the players join each other at center court they slap each others' hands, smile, and take apparent delight in the highly energized scene. After the final player is announced, the band turns the pounding rhythm into an electric song, the cheerleaders dance, the players "psyche up," and the fans continue to applaud, clap, yell, and celebrate. The band plays one last rendition of the fight song, ending right at the moment the game begins.

Through participating in the introductions the fans celebrate the home team while attempting to intimidate and disconfirm the away team. Sometimes it is stated that the fans are the "sixth man" on the team, playing a key role in the game itself. As the differences and competition between the teams, and between the fans of each, is emphasized, the introductory talk is highly coordinated in its performance and competitive style. As the players have, so the fans have come to play.

To this point, the playing of the game itself has no effect on the cultural event. In other words, the sequencing of events to this point is, to a degree, not dependent on the playing of the game. At times, especially if the home team loses, much of the fans' cheering and excitement ends here. The final two phases in the basketball event, however, are dependent on the playing of the game itself.

4. *Game Talk*

Once the game begins there are several kinds of talk practiced by the fan. I will discuss these in the following order: individual comments, group chants and cheers, and halftime talk.

Individual comments normally are spoken, during the basketball game, as fans express their approval or disapproval of the events in the game. During these times it is appropriate, perhaps even preferred, for individuals to express—sometimes by standing up and yelling through cupped hands—his or her opinions about various plays and players in the game. Continuing the theme of the introduction, these "fan solos" often criticize or disconfirm the opposing players, but also turn similarly to the opposing coach, or the referees. For instance, after an opposing player had made a defensive error a fan yelled, sarcastically, "Nice defense!" Another opposing player had played intense defense on a favorite home player, but the home player eventually scored. A fan responded to this play by yelling "In your face!" Fans also seem to have an affinity for telling the opposing coach what to do. As the coach stands up to advise or admonish his players or the referees, he is told to "Sit down!" or to "Take another tranquilizer!" The opposing players and coach are the recipients of such verbal criticism and disconfirmation.

While the opposing players and coach may also have some supportive fans in the stands, the referees are less fortunate. No one yells in favor of the refs, only *at* them. The referees, as the official authorities in the rules of the game, bear the brunt of many fan solos. When a fan is dissatisfied with the game, he or she does not verbally fault the home team, cannot fault the visiting team for playing well, so he or she "lashes out" at the referees. During these times the fans might describe their opinion of a call ("Horrible call, ref!" "Terrible call, ref!"); explain to the referee what, in their opinion, the proper call was ("That was a foul, ref!" or "Goal tending ref!"); or they simply tell the referee what they think of him ("You smell!") or what to do ("Take a shower, ref!" "Hey, put your glasses on!" or "You might as well put on a [the opposing team's color] shirt!"). These verbalizations function as an emphatic support of the desired team. An example on this theme makes the point rather clearly. In this case the referee had made an obviously good call—against the home team—and a hometown fan seated high in the stadium on the opposite end of the arena from the call yelled, in the commercially televised style of Bob Uecker, "No way, ref!" The crowd chuckled and "took delight" in such an unquestioned and loyal support of the home team.

One anomalous act deserves mentioning. During the first few minutes of one game, the home team had fallen badly behind. At this moment a person seated near me in the home team rooting section yelled rather cynically, "And you think they (the home team) are going to win?" After this snide comment he was showered with popcorn, hit with a couple paper wads, several scornful glances, and a thumb extended toward the exit. This act, and the reactions to it, illustrate how fans orient to, defend, and are expected to be loyal to their favored (in this case the home) team. Perhaps this person did not understand that an individual's criticisms and disconfirmations must function to support not only one's own favorite team, but also, if civil (in Sennett's sense), must be appropriately cognizant of those seated nearby. What counts as the desired team, and desirable actions of a fan, is, then, negotiated by the particular social context of proximate fans.

While individual comments or fan solos support one's favorite team by criticizing and disconfirming the opposing team, group chants and cheers coordinate means of explicitly supporting the fan's favorite team. Many verbal chants during time-outs or "breaks in the game" are led by cheerleaders. One example illustrates a call-response interplay between the cheerleaders and the fans as they "spellout" the team name. Other verbal chants occur during specific points in the game. When the opposing team has possession of the ball the crowd may chant "defense (clap, clap) defense" and so on. At other times when the desired team needs support, the crowd may chant "here we go (team name) here we go (clap, clap)". Certain fans have designed a chant used to criticize the referee during an alleged "bad" call. These fans chant "zebra, zebra" (playfully referring to the referees who are dressed in black and white striped shirts).

The fans' nonverbal cheers occur regularly and perhaps most intensely when the opposing players are shooting fouls (or most needing to concentrate), or similarly when they call time out, or when they miss shots at the basket. Silence performs the communicative counter-function as it occurs during the home team's foul shots.[5] Vociferous cheers of support obviously occur when the desired team scores.

Every basketball game has an intermission or halftime, which seems to serve a conspicuously phatic function. The expressiveness of the event seems to carry over into halftime as fans yell to friends, "Yip-yippee, it's Shannon Lee!" or simply "Hey, (friends name)!" with a smile and wave. Loud and expressive talk seems to be a visible aspect of halftime—perhaps a residual of the fan solo style above—yet with a cordial rather than a critical and competitive objective.

5. *The Dissipation*

At the conclusion of the game the band plays an appropriate song. Upon winning, the popular songs "Celebrate" or "Another one Bites the Dust" have been played. When losing, the fight song or some other song is played. The announcer sometimes summarizes the performance of both teams while fans dissipate, chatting about a players performance, a key play, team effort, and other aspects of the event. During this phase, the manner of talk is usually quite cooperative and conversational, although competitive flare-ups may occur. I will elaborate on the potential problem of the flare-up in a moment.

DIMENSIONS OF THE RITUAL FORM

The communicative phases described above can be summarized through the manner and style of communicative practice involved in each. By manner, I simply point to the kind of relational tone being targeted in the practice of that phase, ranging from cooperative to competitive. For instance, the talk that occurs during the warm-up would appear to be highly cooperative as the participants discuss the arena, the game, or other everyday affairs. Contrast this with the communicative acts of the game talk when fans choose a desired side and thus verbally "play" on the competition in the arena. By style, I point to the intensity of discursive expression in the phase, ranging from rather low, subdued, and conversational to rather high, frenzied, and excited. For example the "warm-up talk" involves conversations in a style that contrasts to the later parts of the introduction phase when the fans fanatically express support of their desired team. Using the two dimensions of manner and style of communication practice, we may parsimoniously summarize the nature and sequence of fan actions in the basketball scene.

Using figure 2.1, one may get a shorthand sense of how talk progresses during this cultural event. During stage 1, the warm-up, talk is normally cooperative and held at a rather low level of intensity. The crowd filters in and chats about the arena, the event, other public events, and so on. During stage 2, the salutation ritual, the

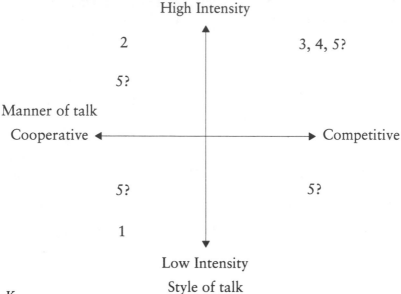

Figure 2.1
Communicative Dimensions in Some Basketball Events

crowd is highly cooperative and at least mildly expressive in their singing of the national anthem. Stage 3, the introductions, includes the division of the crowd into fans who support their chosen team during the introduction of the players. As described above, a high level of competition and expressiveness enters fans' utterances as they support one team against the other. Stage 4, game talk, continues the competitive manner and highly expressive style established during the introductions with fans' solos, verbal chants, and nonverbal cheers (e.g., claps and yells). Stage 5, the dissipation, is somewhat more difficult to place. Normally, the fans return to a cooperative and relatively lower level of expressiveness in order to facilitate leaving the event. However, this is not always the case. Scuffles, abusive statements (perhaps residuals of game talk), even nonverbal attacks have happened during the dissipation stage. This exhibits a degree of ambiguity, at least for some fans, when they leave the basketball event, for they continue a highly competitive and expressive style, especially when the event includes little by way of a concluding phase of conciliation. Perhaps some type of ritualized activity is needed at game's end to create a coordinated transition from a competitive to a cooperative communication climate. Some effort has been taken in this direction when the "public address" announcer, in some scenes, gives a balanced presentation of the game's statistics. He (or she) is presenting information about the game, but moreover, that "giving of information" marks an important transition in the style and manner of conduct. Similarly, the final games of basketball tournaments are often followed by the presentation of trophies to both teams. Perhaps understanding the quality of the interaction at the end of the game—as both highly expressive and competitive—provides a needed insight for designing a conciliatory kind of transitional cultural activity for the final, dissipation stage.

The dimensions also show how the social identity of a fan largely involves, in this scene, participating, if vicariously, in a kind of public discourse that is at once highly competitive and highly expressive. "Doing" this social identity cultivates both a competitiveness and a way of being competitive that is, at least for many, intensely expressive and passionately involved. That one should win, that one should express one's interests verbally, that the opposing team is playfully denigrated, all of this is part of the practice of being a "fan." Notice, in turn, that lower, more subdued levels of expressive competitiveness are not evident in figure 2.1 nor in many scenes of sport. Perhaps this is yet one more example of the work-hard, play-hard theme so prevalent in contemporary American culture. Perhaps the metamessage of the scene for the fan, as for the player, is already abundantly clear: Come to play, and compete, and do so together, with intensity.

ENLARGING THE SCENE
THROUGH SYMBOLS AND MEANINGS:
LOCAL LORE, MASCOTS, AND THE BOUNDARY
BETWEEN PLAY AND DANGER

While the focus in the above is upon phases of a ritual form, and the meanings of each phase, perhaps a slightly richer understand-

ing may be gained if we examine symbols of what is being celebrated, starting with the "home team."

One pertinent question about basketball events would be
What constitutes "the home team"? What is it that fans cheer and
celebrate in these events? Let us recall, for a moment, the arrangement of objects in the cultural arena. Upon entering the halls of
the arena we see team trophies and pictures of past "great players." Inside the arena we see banners of past team championships.
A player has commented on the banners, saying, "Y'know, every
time I walk into this gym I can look up and see those banners. Boy
does it feel good." The banners and trophies convey a sense of the
history and tradition of the team. In this larger scene, when the
fans expressively cheer for their team, it is not just the current
team, but a history of the sport in the town or institution that is
cheered. The meaning of being a husky, a minuteman, a spartan,
and so on is not confined to one particular game or team, but
builds upon a particular tradition of teams, which helps set the
stage for each subsequent performance. When one fan said, "I am
a Nittany Lion fan and proud of it," he said these words thinking
perhaps of one football team. However, he also invokes the history of meaning in being a Nittany Lion fan that is built upon past
Nittany Lion teams, and which provides a larger context for this
year's team, this game, and this social performance.[6] Of course,
this can work in a different direction as a history of losing teams
attests. In any event, as a fan, one is cheering not only a particular
game, or team, but *in* a particular place, with its own history and
lore (about players, teams, coaches, officials, and fans).

If banners and trophies can symbolize the content and history
of the fans' discursive celebrations, where does one learn how to
"be a fan"? Most certainly fans learn from each other how to be
fans. And one peculiarly visible and significant other out there on
the floor as head instructor is the neomascot, that irrelevantly
attired, and often irreverently acting *Sesame Street*–looking
"thing." What purpose does this goofy "thing" serve in this cultural scene? During a game this "thing" is usually quite active,
often in an exaggerated way, responding to the action on the
court. When a great and favorable play is made, the "thing"
jumps all around, and waves frantically in support. But when a
referee makes a bad or unfavorable call, the thing may fall over,
play dead, or throw a tantrum. I have seen one point its rear-end
right at the referee while waving its hands over its back. Yet, this

same creature is cuddling children during time outs, putting its arms around the elderly, dancing with an elderly woman at center court, sitting on a lap throwing kisses, and so on.

There is an analogic message here, a model of, and for, how to be a fan. Even if in an exaggerated way, the neomascot shows everyone how to act playfully when stepping into the social identity of a fan. For such a performance, questions of authenticity or sincerity of course are muted. One need not wonder so much about the individual ego or self at work, for the message is a portrayal of a how-to-be-playful-here. For example, if there is a great play, then cheer, clap, yell, be intensely expressive, or, as it is so often put, "go crazy!" If there is a "bad" call, then throw a fit, yell, criticize. What is relevant to this performance is less who you are as an individual, and more how you act as a playful player in this scene's discursive game. For the enactment of this social identity, there is a foregrounding of a playful agency and scene over the psychological qualities of the particular agent. And the neomascot "thing" provides cultural actors with analogic messages of that agency and agent, of how to be a fan. If the banners and trophies signify the historical content of a fan's celebration, the neomascot models a particular manner and style of how to be a fan, of how to intensely, playfully, and passionately celebrate the desired team, together.

That these performances foreground a kind of public silliness in crowd behavior, and do not hold serious repercussions for one's personal identity, has been noted by the humorist Dave Barry: "Sports cheers tend to be demeaning to everybody. I have watched students at prestigious Yale University shout: 'Bulldogs! Bulldogs! Bow wow!' I don't care what your SAT scores are, you can't shout something like this without appearing to have the intelligence of luncheon meat. That's what being in a sporting event crowd is all about: a mass lowering of IQs. That's why, after all of these years, we are still vastly amused by our own cleverness when we manage to execute 'The Wave.'"[7]

To be a fan, then, is to play with the generally accepted model of a person. In the basketball scene, one largely "plays" with the more serious side of life—such as one's personal dignity, economic competition, and hard work—yet does so in ways that counter that serious side—through a public persona, symbolic cooperation, and play. The neomascot offers everyone a model for doing just this, in a way the traditional mascot (e.g., a husky, lion, trojan, etc.) cannot. Why? Because the neomascot models a nonpartisan, intensely active, spontaneous, and unquestionably playful actor. Symbolic actions of some fans mirror those of the neomascot. Some enter the arena intentionally dressed in unusual costumes—as Elvis, as sheiks in robes, wearing sunglasses, colorful shorts, headbands, masks, sheets, with a basketball on the head, a surfboard in hand (in January snow). What appears at first to be an effort for personal attention turns into a playful model for acting that others in the crowd can follow. The function and appearance of these actors is similar to the "thing's," as each provides models for how to be a passionately expressive, socially involved, and playfully public fan. The emphasis in the performance is drawn away from the selves or personalities of these people, away from the normal routines of economic competition and hard work, and toward the group's symbolic identification through their common play.

There is of course a dangerous side to any play (Basso, 1979), as the rare end-of-game fights attest. One might summarize a metacommunicative moral of this scene: When faced with a contest, play the good game properly through the proper form, and words, not improperly with fists and physical aggression. This moral is steeped in an American ethic, the freedom to play and participate, to compete with rivals, and to deliberate with reference to the rules of the game. For players, of course, the rules are officially set. For fans, however, they are governed not by officially codified procedures, but by normative and community constraints, and are thus somewhat more negotiable.

One such normative rule is this: That fans can and should be competitive and passionate in conduct. Another rule that is not entirely acceptable to everyone (in fact I found myself prohibiting my children from acting on its basis, even if I slipped into it occasionally) is this: Disconfirm others in this scene. Danger can arise, of course, when this scene of competition, passion, and intense physical activity, combines with the rule of disconfirmation, to create verbal and physical confrontations. For fans, the scene suggests a way of dealing with foes not through a refined ability to deliberate verbally (as through some appeals of the coaches), nor by mediating contesting positions by reference to the rules (as with the officials), but by asserting a more visceral emotional reaction. While this undoubtedly helps ventilate and thus integrate fans through an unabashed display of loyalty, it can also bring community members with different allegiances dangerously close to the edge of physical battle. Because the activity in the scene is so competitive and intense, and because, in this scene, one fan's amusement can become another's denigration, the line from play to hostility is ever close for the crossing. But also because of this, the scene tests one's limits in passionate battle, and requires one to monitor that ever-present line between proper play and improper battle.

Fans gather, then, as fans, not only to *celebrate* their favored team, and not only for some degree of *release* through competition and intense social activity, but moreover for some degree of communal *integration* through the celebration. Within the particular bounds of a cultural scene and identity, they target public play. Because of the element of danger in the playing, this is not flawlessly executed by all fans. Whatever the outcome, there are always overriding messages for both players and fans: Play the game properly and stay within the rules, with these moral dictates, as with all similar dictates for social living, being shaped and designed in the cultural scenes of social life.

The above analyses suggest one way to think of identity as moving into and eventually out of a playful scene, as moving in and out of "fandom." Perhaps we are "fully" fans in these events as we move, or are moved, through a rather ritualized public performance: from being rather cordial and sociable in warm-up; to being a somewhat reverent citizen during a salutation (thus paying homage to a political union); to being a passionate, expressive, and competitive ally with vested interests during introductions; and similarly, to being a more impulsive and intensely involved reactor to the immediate action during the game (thus paying homage to union through competition). Clearly there are other qualities to "being a fan" that are not necessarily involved here, such as reading the literature of the sport, and perhaps supporting the team financially, but performing as a "fan," in this scene—unlike the more passive viewing of the sport on television—constitutes perhaps the most prominent performance of the identity in America today. To be identified through this human web of public, ritualized activity is to be a fan, to be one happily caught up in a frenzied crescendo of unmatched, playfully passionate, communal proportions. In the process, the practice provides for people a shared means of identification, a release from routine affairs, and a means of identifying with the common life of a community. This is the ritual communication of a public identity in an American cultural scene.

RITUALS OF PLAY, PUBLIC LIFE, AND CULTURES

A question I have been asked frequently is this: Why do you go to the game when you can stay home and see it better on television? My response to that question should be clearer now. Basketball is not just a game to see; it is (or can be) a potent cultural event, a highly involving, playfully expressive ritual of communicative practices, in which one participates. To be a fan is at least in part to be one who goes to, witnesses, and sometimes participates in these communicative practices, in the discursive life of the game. Without these discursive practices, the sport itself would become a less lively, if not lifeless public event.

By understanding the scene this way, and by conceiving a collective social identity as being performed through it, the chapter suggests several responses to Sennett's potent critique. First, Sennett claims that contemporary social interaction is translated into psychological terms in order for it to be meaningful. While some interaction, perhaps most public interaction is translated this way, the data here warrant a different conclusion. Some American utterances belong to a community of discourse that is being articulated at the community level. These utterances—the fan solos, verbal chants, and nonverbal cheers—are not primarily meaningful as reflections of personality, but are meaningful as a collective performance of a shared identity in a cultural event. In other words, the communal function of communication is highly active here (Philipsen, 1989b). Second, Sennett fears the end of public culture or civility. This study provides at least one example of a kind of communicative event that demonstrates a public alignment within a cultural conversation. Essentially it points, using Sennett's definition of civility, to an "activity which protects people from each other and yet allows them to enjoy each other's company" (p. 264). Civility in this sense is hardly gone, nor is public culture, for both are symbolically nurtured and socially identified in crowd activities at basketball and other public games. Third, is participation in community life a form of isolation? This cultural event can be seen as a highly communal and integrative performance, constituting ways people can identify with each other by being a part of the scene, as a fan. The common meanings in being such a person provide a means of collective identification, rather than a scene or scenario for secluded isolates. Finally, have adults lost the art of public play? The basketball event seems to invoke a particular set of practices that constitute a type of play. Even Sennett, in passing, acknowledges that sport offers adults a moment of "passion" (p. 323). But is this event or other sporting events atypical instances of American public life? Consider a variety of public conduct in markets, on planes, in restaurants, in schools, at the "gigs" of Arkansas highlanders, and so on. Any gathering where people are together may be interpreted or translated into a variety of perspectives. Perhaps when all events are seen in psychological terms, or in strictly personal terms, as Sennett claims, play is lost. Yet, this chapter demonstrates a cultural scene of a general kind, where cultural actors can and do coordinate their play. To claim that these phenomena are exclusive to basketball scenes or sporting events seems untenable.

In addition to responding to Sennett's critique, I hope to have illustrated a type of cultural perspective on the communication of social identity. With a cultural lens, (1) we have seen a way of conducting a social identity, as a fan, through a ritual form; (2) we have summarized the discursive phases of this form with two dimensions; and (3) we have sketched some symbolic aspects of the event with reference to the particular histories and communal functions of the fan identity. Perhaps such a reading of this social identity and its communicative performances in America offers but one instance for understanding how the communication of this social identity gets done. For example, while attending some hockey matches and a basketball game in Finland, I could not help but compare and contrast the way a "fan" acts there, compared to here (in the United States). Some similarities were evident during the warm-up, introductions, and game phases. But largely absent in Finland, however, were the constant outbursts of fan solos one encounters in American sporting scenes. Further, the ease of synchrony in mass group cheering that is evident during Finnish fanfare is noticeably different from that found in the United States. The uniform enactment of the Finnish fan contrasts with the more uneven, somewhat asynchronous conduct seen during many American group cheers. As Finnish scenes are enacted in ways that take rules quite seriously, Americans seem everpoised to play with and negotiate them.

By exploring social identities through the communication of particular cultural scenes, such as at basketball games, we may gain an insight into the role of communicative practices in everyday social life. By examining the public actions we perform daily, we may better come to grips with our social identities and the various notions of public life related to these, a quality many critics fear has died. Cultural conversations and social identities are alive in the scenes of contemporary life, but their contexts and practices, manners and styles, themes and contents, like all cultural phenomena, must be noticed and described to be understood. By doing so, it is hoped that we can gain a better insight into the communication of identities and thereby understand our cultural scenes as practices that are not entirely dead, nor only serious, nor overly personal, just misunderstood.

SCENE TWO: WORK

CHAPTER 3

The Working Self: Making Television and Tension between Workers

The concept of "organizational culture" burst onto the intellectual scene in the early 1980s as a new tool for organization analysis. On the corporate level, the concept was used to plan and implement organizational decisions, to analyze and change corporate norms, to assess public managers' roles, and to understand the particular orientations of various corporate offices.[1] As a conceptual perspective on institutional life, it was used to study commitment and loyalty in organizations, to examine workers' mutual beliefs, and to explore powerful discursive themes such as "the mighty machine" and "the computer" in organizational life.[2] These various uses demonstrate the utility of the concept and led to various approaches to its study.[3]

This chapter uses a particular approach to organizational culture.[4] The organization is viewed, from this perspective, as the expressive system of symbols, symbolic forms, and meanings that, when used, constitutes a common sense of the working self and work-life. The assumption is that a particular sense, a situated system of symbols, symbolic forms, and meanings, is used systematically by workers to make sense of themselves as workers, and to make sense of their work-life. This expressive system is always, to a degree, organization specific, and through its use, workers show who they are, by symbolizing in their scenes of work. Thus the immediate task is to discover and interpret the expressive system that is being used by particular workers when in, and when discussing, their scenes of work.

Several additional assumptions ground this task. First, following Hymes (1962), the study explores ways speech is used in a social group "in terms of its own patterns." Of primary concern is the language and meanings workers use to organize their social contexts. Clearly there are systems of signification operating other than the oral, such as codes of dress, furniture arrangements, and so on. But it is assumed that the oral life of the organization has patterns of its own, ones worthy of investigation. Put in terms of Giddens' (1984) structuration theory, the essay explores the "discursive consciousness" of this group more than its practical or unconscious life (see also Bilmes, 1986). A further assumption is that the verbal resources both enact and reconstruct work life. In Giddens' terms, discursive practices are both a "production and reproduction of social systems," thus serving as "both [a] medium and [an] outcome of the [social] practices they recursively organize" (p. 25). Finally, the essay follows a specific suggestion grounded in the cultural approaches of Hymes and Geertz, that is, if one wants to understand the action persons do, from their point of view, one should listen for the terms they use to discuss it. Thus, the interpretive framework adopted here organizes discursive action and interpretation from the standpoint of participants' terms and forms of action (Hymes, 1962; Geertz, 1976).

This chapter explores the workers' terminological system, and uses it as the primary framework for interpretation. This approach is unlike others where analysts' frameworks are focal. For example, Goodall, Wilson, and Waagon (1986) interpreted "performance appraisal" interviews by applying a Burkean framework of "The Order, The Secret, and The Kill." Their "meaning-centered approach" enabled them to interpret from an outsider's standpoint the form of stories told *about* those interviews. The two essays however have some common concerns: Both explore symbolic action, its motives, and meanings. Both also explore different social identities or classes of people. The approaches are thus distinct from, yet complementary to, each other. The concern in this chapter, however, is to explore discursive action from the standpoint of the cultural actors, through the terms, forms, and meanings they use to characterize and conduct that very action. Rather than foreground the analysts' framework and meanings through *reports about* action, the focus here is to foreground a cultural framework and participants' *meanings in* action. Rather than offering an outsider's appraisal of workers' symbolic forms, then, this essay asks: What local discursive resources are being used by workers? How do these order, interpret, and motivate their working selves and lives?

The immediate purpose of this study, then, is to discover and interpret the communication in an organization—a television station—in order to understand how cultural communication and organizing get done there. While the substantive claims apply to this particular social group, the general approach could be used in any organizing environment.[5]

Three questions, which reflect station employees' discursive concerns, organize the central themes in this study:[6] (1) What is meant when station employees describe coworkers by saying, "There are completely different types of people that work here" and "The building situation exacerbates and reinforces the differences"? (2) What is meant as coworkers talk about "the communication problem," or as one "production crew" member said, "Without a doubt, and I've been through the United States Army, this station is the most inefficient organization from a communications standpoint that I have ever witnessed or participated in"? (3) What is the symbolic meaning of "the product," for example, a manager called it, "the thing everyone can rally behind"?[7]

My responses to these questions provide an interpretation of the station's communicative life. The particularities of this case demonstrate *how a cultural analysis of an organization's communication embraces social and symbolic tensions, especially by creating social classes among workers.* What is discovered in this organization's speech is an intricate system designed around what workers call "tensions." The various kinds of workers' identities and their relations with one another create a deep tension, for example, as "the movers" are placed over and above "the secure." Another symbol, "the building situation," exudes "tensions" among those who work in different locations. Yet, while these symbols radiate tension and divide workers into social classes, there is another symbol, "the product," that expresses a grand, regnant unity. Thus, the communication system used by this group of workers creates and reproduces tensions between different classes of people, between different work sites, and between this theme of division and another, the integrative product. Note, then, to begin, that this communication system, as a social and cultural system, creates a system of stratified social identities and relations between them of tension, but does so through the discursive practices common to their work lives (cf. Schneider and Smith, 1987).

In a review essay about organizations and interpretive research, Eric Eisenberg (1986, p. 91) applauded studies that explore "the sharing of modes of expression" rather than, simply, "systems of shared interpretation." One goal of this chapter is to display "modes of expression" that are so shared, the range of meanings commonly evoked through such expressions, and the tensions issuing from such patterns. Thus, the picture drawn here, as in this organization, is not one of "like-mindedness" nor of uniformity or blind conformity, but of common resources that are essentially contestable, with each playing a prominent role in a routine communication system, and all constituting tension among social identities and "buildings" through local symbolic actions. That work can occur in such conditions is remarkable.

THE SCENE AND METHOD

The cultural communication I describe occurs in a television station in a metropolitan area of the western United States. The station employs approximately one hundred and fifty people in five major departments (programming, marketing, finance, development, and promotion). A unique characteristic of the organization is its physical division into three separate buildings, one five blocks from the other two.[8]

I spent nine months in extensive contact with station workers between February and October of 1982. During that time I interviewed station employees at all levels and in each of the three buildings of the organization. I observed the production of several television shows and volunteered during a ten-day fund-raising telethon. All available data, including field records, participants' comments (both spontaneous and elicited), tape recordings of interviews, station memos, and public accounts ("on air," in the newspaper, and in the station) provided the evidence from which the cultural patterns were derived.

All data were scanned in search of potential commonalties or themes. Idiosyncratic cases were tested against the themes which were then reconceptualized to include the case, or judged to be outside their domain. Deviant episodes were also subjected to tests in workers' speech. All analyses examined the patterns of everyday communication actually used in the workers' daily lives.[9]

"COMPLETELY DIFFERENT TYPES OF PEOPLE": IDENTITY SYMBOLS ABOUT PERSONS AS WORKERS

One prominent feature of the routine communicative life of any social group is its creation of a sense of the types of people who comprise it. This television station is no different. Employees here, in particular, describe their colleagues as "completely different types of people," "specific types of personalities," and as "oriented so differently." They also express a "tension" between the "completely different types." For example, one employee said, "You've got the different tasks they all do and the different kinds of people who are willing to do those tasks—and each brings totally different expectations in what they bring and get from the work experience. It is why in this station these people don't relate at all."

Station employees identify three types of coworkers through three clusters of terms: (1) "the movers," "the shakers," and those "on the fast track," (2) "the secure," "the stable," and "the satisfied," and (3) "the paper movers" or "administration." While workers' speech does not always describe *particular individuals* as exclusively in one of these types, it clearly uses this system of terms as apt descriptions of coworkers, and as sources of "tension."

"The Movers"

The "fast-track movers" are described as "on the move in the community, making television," as "highly motivated," and as "young bright professionals who are better than what they are doing." These persons are "movers" in two senses, as they travel "in the community making television" and as they are "motivated" professionally to advance to a better job.

To be "on the move," however, is not just to be "making television" and upwardly mobile, but also to be immersed in one's job. Employees claim that the movers are "very 'into' what they do. It's their hobby and their job. They're very egoistic and throw themselves at their job." They are discussed as "in the limelight" and as "visible personalities."

Movers are also discussed through terms of high interpersonal status, specifically as "domineering," "powerful," and a part of "the idea-generating aspect of the station." A coworker's use of terms such as "a mover," "a shaker," or "on the fast track" therefore invokes associated terms such as "mobile," "motivated," "egoistic," "visible," and "powerful."

"The Secure"

A second group of workers is described as "those who are secure in their jobs." As one manager put it, "There are lots of people within this organization who are happy doing what they are doing and where they are doing it because they like the environment." Later, I asked him what he meant by "the environment" and he replied, "It's a state agency with a lot of stability [difficulty in firing] and retirement benefits." This statement reflects the stability which is associated with "the secure," "the satisfied," or "the stable." Another informant (referred to by another worker as "one of the secure") contrasted his "secure" identity with the movers as a way of introducing some of the expressed "tension" between the two. He said, "I have another life away from my job, whereas others live, breathe, and eat their job. I think they're crazy." Other workers, perhaps "movers," nurture the expressed "tension" as they accuse those (secure) who "know that it's difficult to fire here and say 'I have to do X and no more.'" Still others criticize the secure for having a "union mentality," being "loyal, minor-task oriented," and for "leaving their job at five o'clock." Some even claim the secure lack a "professional competitiveness."

"The Paper Movers"

This group is described in terms that emphasize organizational task and lack of visibility. As one worker said, "You've got the administration in the classic sense of the word. They're there to move paper." In addition to their task, the "paper movers" or "administration" are seen as "low profile," "preferring an anonymous element of their job," and thus as those "not seeking [or getting] recognition."

SEMANTIC DIMENSION OF THE "TYPES OF PEOPLE"

The meanings of "the movers," "the secure," and the "paper movers" may be differentiated along five semantic dimensions.[10] The dimensions were derived from workers' speech in which "types of people" were the topic of discussion. I tried to make sense of these terms by asking, "What do speakers need to know in order to portray these different identities intelligibly? What sense do I invoke by using such terms as I work here?" The following dimensions will help explicate the meanings that are distinct to each cluster of terms and identify points of contrast between the clusters. The analysis of dimensions thus will help refine what workers mean when they speak of "tension," both through the cluster of "types of people" and, as will be shown below, when discussing "the building situation."

Station employees use five dimensions of meaning when using these symbols—the movers, the secure, and the paper movers. These are: mobile/stable, work as life-style/work as job, egoistic/complacent, visible/unseen, and influential/yielding. The essential element in the *mobility/stability* dimension is the relative degree of activity in workers' styles, both in specific daily tasks and in professional advancement. Those identified as movers are typically described as highly "mobile" in both their work routine and their assumed desires for professional advancement. The secure workers are discussed as relatively stable or "loyal" to this organization. The use of this dimension creates a degree of "tension" between those who are highly mobile and those who are relatively stable.

The second dimension, *work as life-style/work as job*, refers to the workers' degree of day-to-day time spent in their occupation. As workers discuss others, they contrast those who "live, breathe, and eat their job" with those who "like to work from nine to five." Some workers treat their work as, as one person said, "a hobby," a place to stay "until midnight and no one thinks a thing of it." Others enjoy the nine-to-five job, implying interest in "another life away from my job." The work-as-life-style sense is aligned with the "mover" and mobile style, while the work-as-job sense is aligned with the "secure" and stable style.

A third semantic dimension, *egoistic/content*, reflects judgments concerning the degree of psychological, or ego involvement in one's work. The "egoistic" or self-serving worker is said to translate work-related activities into self-elevating tasks. The other pole, however, is not altruism but a type of contentedness or complacency, a style of work that reveals satisfaction in a current routine. The dimension thus contrasts egoism (doing the job with maximum concern for self) to contentedness (filling a social role in a rather contented and satisfying way). The workers discussed as "movers" and "on the fast track" are talked about as more ego-involved in their working style, pitting them against the "secure" or "paper movers."

The fourth dimension, *visible/unseen*, suggests workers' levels of prominence in the organization. One is visible to coworkers not only because one is mobile, calls attention to oneself, or frequents the workplace at "all hours," but also because one "hangs [one's] work" (which sometimes includes themselves) "out for critical judgment." Some workers are, therefore, "visible personalities" who place self or product "on the air" for critical judgment by others. In contrast are those workers described as unseen, "behind the scenes," or as those who "don't seek recognition." While the movers are said to be visible, the paper movers are predictably described as unseen and, generally, unsung participants in the stations' activities. The level of prominence reflected in the visible/unseen dimension also accounts for an element in the expressed "tension," as one type of worker—the mover—receives more visibility than the others.

The fifth dimension (*influential/unyielding*) refers to the degree of interpersonal power exercised in the station's interactive life. To be influential is to be able to solicit certain activities or duties from fellow workers. This ability may or may not be sanctioned by structure or formal status. Influence is primarily created in employees' routine talk; it is an index of the oral competencies of workers and their ability to use the available means of persuasion. Being *yielding* is contrasted with being influential—not as powerless, but as in a position where one defers to those with assumed power or influence. Generally, the worker style discussed as being a mover and "on the fast track" is more influential than the secure or paper movers, who are discussed, relatively speaking, as yielding.

The five dimensions formalized here help make explicit the semantic domain station employees use to discuss the "completely different types of people" with whom they work, and the "tensions" between workers. The workers referred to as "movers," "shakers," and "on the fast track" are spoken of as *mobile, visible, influential*, and as treating *work as a style of life*. That type of worker discussed as "secure," "loyal," and "minor-task-oriented," is described as *stable, yielding*, oriented to *work as a job*, and as being somewhat *contented in that role*. Finally, the "administrative" "paper mover" is said to be, for the most part, *unseen*.

The point here is not that there are three types of people in this organization. In fact, few fit any "pure" definition. But station employees do talk *as if* there are three distinct types of workers. This talk renders the identities of workers as distinctive, coherent, and marked by explicit tension. Thus, to speak in an informed way in this organization is to command, in part, this symbolic system of identification, and its meanings.

"THE BUILDING SITUATION": SYMBOLS OF PLACE AND WORKERS' IDENTITIES

If this description of "types of people" is accurate, then the dimensions should be instructive in understanding how, as station employees say, "the building situation exacerbates" the differences among workers.[11] As was noted, the station is divided among three different buildings, one five blocks from the other two. Employees' extreme dissatisfaction with this physical "situation" is illustrated by comments like, "Having three buildings is one of the worst things you can do to an organization that needs to work together." And, "the building situation is a pain in the ass. We all hate it. It's uncomfortable."

Apparently, the primary point of discomfort is the fact that, as one person said, "The building situation is so polarized. It helps accentuate and perpetuate the polarization in types of people. Because of the very wide split, it is a very wide chasm." Others articulate the same theme, claiming, "the polarity of the buildings is ridiculous," "the building situation exacerbates and reinforces the differences [in the types of people]," and "peoples' worlds revolve around their own little buildings." One person went so far as to say, "I cannot imagine this organization being in one building."

In order to pursue this dimension of the organization's life, I asked: If "the building situation" is used to emphasize and reinforce the differences in types of people, then what discursive sense is assigned to those in each building?

The Rockefeller Building is located five blocks from both of the other two. It houses the offices of the upper-level management, some production staff, and a few others. During my involvement with the organization, two of the upper-level managers from this building accepted positions at other stations. Given these circumstances, I posited the following: workers will discuss Rockefeller employees along dimensions of "the movers."[12] When I asked what type of person works there, employees responded by discussing qualities of *mobility* (e.g., "moving," "hustlers," "shakers and movers") and *influence* (e.g., "domineering" and "powerful"). Additionally, and consistently, employees added a general description of the task which those in Rockefeller do. For example, they "generate ideas" or are the "dreamers." This does not mean that there are only movers in the Rockefeller building; it does mean that employees' speech concerning those that work there activates two mover dimensions, *mobile* and *influential*, and includes a task of creative thinking.

The Bundy Building houses many technical staff. Initially I expected Bundy workers to be described along a variety of dimensions including mover, secure, and paper movers, and was surprised when that did not occur. Bundy personnel were described as relatively *stable* and *content*, as "state-of-the-art people who are content," "the twenty-year family man," and "those who have never been replaced, just not fired, hangs on." Bundy personnel were also discussed regarding their tasks as "the doers," and "the arms and legs of the station."[13]

The basement of the Administration Building was located about one-half block from Bundy, and houses, among other things, most of the "administrative" staff for the station. Much of the accounting and fund-raising activities are located there. Those in Rockefeller and Bundy described the administrative personnel as "not flashy" and "not wanting to be on television," and the building as "where the old producers go out to pasture." Those in the Administration Building described themselves as "bypassed" and "isolated." One employee there complained about the sense of isolation: "I don't think the others realize that we are the foundation of the station. Without the money, we wouldn't get paid." The sense of isolation and lack of importance constituted and enacted in these utterances indicates the nonvisible or *unseen* role relegated to those in the Administration Building. Their task was mainly "dealing with money."

"The building situation" is said to "exacerbate," "perpetuate," "reinforce," and "accentuate" the "chasm" between the "types of people." Specifically, Rockefeller personnel are discussed as *mobile* and *influential*, creative thinkers; Bundy personnel as the stable and content doers; while the Administration personnel are spoken of as the *unseen* financiers. The personnel in each building is thus rendered sensible through particular symbols and meanings, associating a place of work with a worker's identity.

"THE COMMUNICATION PROBLEM": SYMBOLS ABOUT SPEAKING

Given a social group whose speech thematizes tensions among persons and buildings, it is of little surprise that workers would discuss "the communication problem." The intensity of this problem would be hard to overemphasize. At the beginning of one interview, one informant—before I had a chance to introduce myself, my purpose, or my first question—said, "there is a tremendous communication problem because of the three buildings." This was not an unusual statement. Other workers described the station's communicative life: "There is such a separation of personnel that communication problems are tremendous"; and "I will say, for an organization devoted to communications, this place, internally, communicates terribly bad. It communicates just awful." The currency and intensity of "the communication problem" led me to ask: What cultural features elaborate "the communication problem" here? Three emerged: the "non-trickle-down" of information, the difficulty in coordinating routine speech concerning daily tasks, and a problem in maintaining a minimal degree of "casual communication."

When workers speak of "the communication problem" they often mention that "information does not trickle down" from upper-level managers. As one person said, "the dynamics in upper management do not trickle down for everyone else to see. " The "non-trickle-down" of information is manifest in a policy for department head meetings (held in Rockefeller). The policy is stated by a department head: "Everything is not to leave the room. It's not for general information because a lot of it could be conjecture which may or may not happen. We need not get people excited for no reason." Those who are not department heads seem somewhat mystified by the meetings. As they say, "I've never seen any minutes generated from those meetings. There aren't reports sent to the staff"; "I spend a lot of time gathering information that doesn't come out in all of those meetings." The sense of mystery regarding some information is also complicated by "the building situation." As one person from the Administration Building said,

"There is plenty of mystique on the part of the staff about the way some of the information winds up in another building. A lot of it is word of mouth and spread through the ranks about what is happening. People [in Bundy], I don't think, have any idea about upcoming productions other than word of mouth. They're not involved in planning meetings so they hear things second, third, fourth, and fifth hand. There are situations with my job where I don't know what the hell is going on over there [in Rockefeller]." Others emphasize the same sense of uncertainty about how information gets exchanged between upper-level management (in Rockefeller) and others (in the Bundy and Administration Buildings). Some express disgust ("My boss is in [Rockefeller] and s/he doesn't know what goes on here [in Bundy]"); others simply dismay ("This whole situation is silly").

This failure of information to trickle down is clearly illustrated in a speech event in the station, "the staff meeting." The meeting occurs in Bundy with all employees present, and unfolds as follows: A "boss" begins by talking about current station affairs such as upcoming documentaries, fund-raising activities, and other general topics. The current status of the station is represented and summarized in a monologue of anywhere from thirty minutes to "great length." Next, the boss asks the others at the meeting what they are doing with their projects, and each person responds. This dialogue is rather informal, as workers can question each other if they have any concerns. Finally, the boss asks if anyone has anything else to say. Sometimes during this phase, workers may ask the boss a question but, as one person said, "the questions tend to be evasively answered since (the boss) doesn't want to disseminate the nitty-gritty until the decision has been made, it's been cast in cement, the cement has dried, and it's been checked by the cement analyzer."

This speech event is clearly a ritualized communication form, consisting as it does of a structured sequence of symbolic acts that provides a cooperative way to celebrate a sacred feature.[14] The topic of the ritual is current station affairs. The participants in the ritualized event are those staff members who could come to the meeting (attendance is voluntary, with about twenty out of fifty attending) and the boss. The tone of the event is rather detached, routine, and boring. The structured sequence of acts may be interpreted as unfolding within three stages: the monologue, the reports, and the evasion and/or conclusion. This speech event, controlled by the boss, appears to be structured to celebrate the boss's sacred status and privileged closeness to generally inaccessible information. As the boss engages in monologue, evasively answers questions, yet invites discussion among staff members, the sacredness or inviolate nature of his/her status and influence is clearly affirmed. At the same time, the speech event illustrates the "non-trickle-down of information" in its ritualized structure *and* particular managerial style.[15]

A second shared sense conveyed in the "communication problem" involves a difficulty workers have in coordinating routine speech. For example, one informant said, "It's not like you can walk down the hall to see certain people. You have to set up an appointment to see them because you just can't catch them when they are between certain things. The problem we have is when we need to get together." Given the "building situation," there are continuous problems in coordinating daily schedules and unending frustrations in attempts to accomplish everyday tasks.

Not only do most workers often find it difficult to meet with fellow employees to talk about their work-related tasks, but they also find it difficult to coordinate efforts using the telephone. As one person said, "Everyone has different phone extensions and the information is in offices where the phones aren't conveniently linked. We *must* run around."

A third common theme of "the communication problem" involves difficulties in maintaining a minimal degree of "casual communication." In this organization the well-known "grapevine" is virtually nonexistent. A worker expressed this common theme by noting, "There is a lack in the causal communication which communicates a lot about what is going on. I'm a great believer in conversational flow of information rather than memos and written things like that." Another person expressed the same theme, saying, "A lot of the most valuable information is exchanged in casual conversation. It hurts us not having that here." A manager explained an indirect, but important, consequence of the lack of an informal network by describing a situation involving him: "If someone is upset, often it doesn't get expressed until three to four days or a week later. Then it's too late, a decision has been made and you're in the middle because that person has been trying to get in touch with you." Often, workers expressed amazement at what other workers did not know. Information they had taken for granted was simply unknown to a fellow worker.[16]

In summary, when station employees' speaking includes references to "the communication problem," they evoke a frustration with information not "trickling down" (from department head meetings, between buildings, and in ritualized staff meetings), a common difficulty in coordinating routine conversations, and a problem in maintaining a minimal degree of "casual communication."

The three previous themes—"types of people," "the building situation,' and "the communication problem"—consist of a system of cultural terms which station employees use in making their common work-life mutually intelligible. The use of each of these phrases creates a particular order, and constitutes a specific sense, in employees' work-life. If the cultural analysis of their speech was completed here, one would interpret an organizational culture which consists only of social tension and division. This is not the case for station employees, however, for there is one compelling regnant symbol which all employees articulate, accept, and respect. It is "the product," or what gets broadcast "over the air."

CHAPTER 4

Unifying Workers through "the Product": An Epitomizing Symbol

"The product" is a cultural symbol used by station workers to create a unifying identity in their routine work life. It is a key symbol that co-occurs with terms of collective identification like "everyone," "group," "we all," and "we." As several said: "The thing everyone can rally behind is the product on the air." Or: "As a group, as a whole entity—maintenance, production, programming, operations, crew—everyone has something to do with what the final product looks like. Everyone is able to relate their work to that product. That's the primary purpose in being here." Or: "The fact that we have a very visible product that we all, in one way or the other, are working towards, makes a common bond." Or: "We have a common product. It's what comes out on the screen." (Almost every office has a prominently displayed color television set that is continually playing "the product.")

"The product," as a regnant, integrative cultural symbol, is the means by which "everyone's" shared identity is expressed. It is a way to talk about the goals and sentiments of "everyone" in the organizational "group." It provides workers with a discursive resource through which the different identities can be transcended, for a while, in the station. As one influential manager put it:

> There is one great equalizer in television. There is a piece of product that is easily measured that all agree on. For all the normlessness that exists, there is a standard for the product. It must be good. . . . We only communicate as much as it takes to get that product—which occurs on television—to be good. The product is the thing at the end which must pass, not fail, the test on the air. That's the great equalizer.

Since creating "the product" is the central and public focus of the station's life, the workers' collective image and sense of pride is dependent upon its quality. As a visible and tangible entity, it must meet employees' standards for first-class production. As an informant said, "that product is probably a direct reflection on how well everyone in the organization works." Others articulate the connection between a quality product and worker pride, saying, "We're all motivated by the same thing. We want the end product to be first class." "We all have a pride in what we do, [which is] making good, quality television."

When "the product" fails to meet workers' standards, that failure damages station pride, and workers are motivated to co-orient to the failure. The activity that orients to product problems is called "putting out fires," and is done in two general ways. First, and frequently, the problem is entered into the organization's discourse as a way of publicizing the violation and upholding the workers' standards for the product. In one informant's words, "If we look bad, anybody in the station can call and say 'Did you see such and such last night?' They feel they could do that because we all have a vision of the standard we are achieving. When we fall below that [standard], people respond, because everyone knows what that standard is. The deviations are what you notice more than anything else." Another employee states: "I feel very comfortable about coming to work, calling someone up and saying, 'Y'know that [program] is really bad stuff. We shouldn't air that. Have you seen it?' Surprisingly enough, I don't know of anyone in the building [Bundy] that doesn't feel that way. Most people feel comfortable enough to say 'that's terrible' or 'that's bad.'"

In this way, product problems or "fires" are publicized, co-oriented to, and frequently rectified, as station workers negotiate and reaffirm their shared standards for a high quality product. It is, as one person said, "up to all of us to monitor what's on the air." One of the ways the product is monitored is by entering the problem, the violation in quality, into the station's informal discursive paths.[1]

A second way that product problems are managed is a more formal or institutionalized version of the first. This procedure involves the filing of "the discrepancy report." The report involves a written communication in two parts. First, a violation is specified, such as "dead air," "faulty placement of credits," "audio problems," and so on; and second, the corrective action, which solved the problem, is outlined. Discrepancy reports are examined once a week in the "D.R. meeting." This procedure, as one worker said, "is the institutionalized way to deal with the standards and quality of the product"; it is a recording of past "fires" and the specific ways they were "put out." As this procedure is followed, workers co-orient to their common problems, and reaffirm their shared standards for a high-quality product.

The above communicative processes demonstrate a *social dramatic* form of communication, a process in which participants negotiate, transform, and/or reaffirm their shared cultural standards.[2] The *participants* in this particular drama are, potentially, "everyone," "all" station employees, for all employees are responsible for monitoring the quality of the product by entering violations into the organization's discourse. The *topic* is always some violation of a quality product. The *purpose* of the drama is to maintain the station's communal standards for a high-quality, professional product. The drama reaffirms the shared identity of workers by upholding a degree of worker pride, station image, and social commitment to a quality production. Generally, the sequence of communicative acts constituting the social dramatic "fire" is interpretable in these four phases:

The Breach: Some activity occurs which has violated a cultural standard, as when the quality of programming is violated by audio problems.

The Crisis: Workers co-orient and attend to the violation by entering it into the organization's discursive life, or filing a "discrepancy report."

Redressive Action: For the most part, the redressive action occurs in one of two ways. An appropriate member in the organization may be motivated by the discursive force of other workers to repair or correct the problem wrought by the breach; and/or the breach may be recorded and filed in a discrepancy report along with the corrective action. In extreme cases, one that I know of, individuals who have violated the common standard are fired. As one manager said, "I'll tell them to get out of here."

Reintegration: Members reaffirm the high quality and professionalism of their product, or, a schism occurs until the problem is solved (or the problematic person —who is said to adversely affect the quality of the product—leaves).

The symbol of "the product," considered within this larger, dramatic communication form, enacts a regnant communal force, a shared and meaningful motive that lends a grand aura of unity to the workplace. As communicative drama, workers' speech coorients to violations in the quality of the product and provides an interactive form where workers not only repair and correct product problems, but also negotiate and reaffirm common standards of quality production. As a powerful, epitomizing symbol, "the product" represents a means of shared identification in the station's interactive life. Through it workers co-orient to a sacred organization symbol, constitute a regnant theme, and invoke a powerful grammar of motives in which *common* aspirations are expressed, respected, and celebrated.

CULTURAL TERMS AND TENSIONS

One substantive advantage of a cultural communicative analysis of organizational life can be illustrated with the following excerpt from my field materials. The comments that follow were made to me during a fifteen-minute interview about three weeks into the project, when I had few hints of their local force. They were spoken by an influential manager, and evoked—what I later recognized to be—a volume of grounded power. As the following is a typical statement, it represents a system of prominent terms in workers' naturally occurring speech. It also demonstrates the complexity and opacity of their communicative practices to outsiders.

> There are three different kinds of people, who are completely different types of people, that work here . . . and you've got all of those tensions which are exacerbated because they're all over there [in the Bundy and Administration Buildings] and we're over here [in the Rockefeller Building]. . . . I tell each of my people to forget about all of the others, don't worry about them. Just make sure your show is good. . . . And, there is one great equalizer in television. . . . We only communicate as much as it takes to get that product—which occurs on television—to be good.

Without the above analyses, or something like them, the particular sense and meaning of this person's communication is rather obscure. With such analyses, we can begin understanding what this particular person has "said," what the speech means. An insight into the "three different types of people," a particular meaning in "over there" and "over here," a sense of "all of those tensions," the limited and problematic function of "communication," and the unifying role of "the product" as "the great equalizer," all become more understandable. In order to unravel the meanings of organizational communication, communication practices such as these warrant our serious attention.

Moreover, one cannot fully interpret these practices without recognizing the presence in this communication system of considerable "tension." Among symbols, symbolic forms and their meanings, this tension exists at four discursive points: (1) through symbols of identity, between the "movers," "secure," and "administration"; (2) through "the buildings" symbol, among those deemed creative thinkers in Rockefeller, doers in Bundy, and financiers in Administration; (3) through the specific features of "communication problems," as when "information does not trickle down," meetings are closed, questions evaded, routine contacts made difficult, and casual contact lacking; and (4) between the identities of division through classes of workers, as those summarized above, and the unity for "everyone" through "the product." These cultural meanings of "tension" create in workers' practices three social consequences: workers speak of persons as three types, thus enacting social stratification and a degree of alienation, one from another; workers speak of work locations as supporting classes of individuals, each "very different" from the others; and workers experience the tension between stratification and unity, as their symbol system is used (Burke, 1937, 263–273; Cheney, 1991).

This kind of analysis thus has explored a spoken system that is prominent, intelligible, and commonly used among workers. But it has not yielded a view of singular purpose or likeness of mind. It has shown how cultural communication can create various types of people (divided and united), can create "tension" between and within those types of persons, with each type asserting its own properties and purposes, against others. Taken together, the types organize a system of social identities, where symbolic antagonisms are both prominent means and outcomes of routine communication.

Such a conclusion brings to mind Kenneth Burke's (1969, p. 115) comment: "mystery arises at that point where different *kinds* of beings are in communication." As noted earlier, this theme is explored by Goodall, Wilson, and Waagon (1986; see also Tompkins, 1993). In their study, the form of reports about the "appraisal interview" was interpreted within an external,

Burkean vocabulary. Their study produces insights about hierarchical relations among superiors and subordinates and themes of negotiation and conflict, and it raises a fundamental issue of "fitting into" organizational environments.

Note, however, that their study is based on three *reports about* appraisal interviews (rather than upon observations of the appraisal interviews themselves); it derives from three different organizations; and it is interpreted within a framework whose vocabulary is outside, above and beyond the workers' own. I point again to this example of recent research in order to make three points about the present study. First, the communication conduct of concern here has been studied primarily in the actual contexts where it was used. Second, specific forms of communication, such as staff meetings, were interpreted both relative to other forms, such as "communication problems," and within the terms of a local symbol system. An interpretation of a form was thus made contingent upon its place within local expressive practices. Third, these interpretations derive from an organization's cultural communication system. The approach, then, generates a theory of communication that is local, and of a community, and thus of limited scope, but it does so by applying and testing a general theoretical framework. Where Goodall, Wilson, and Waagon apply a Burkean vocabulary to reports about a general communicative form, the present study applies an ethnographic framework to discursive practices in order to discover a cultural vocabulary, which itself organizes symbolic codes of identity, communication, and the product.[3]

Part of the theoretical contribution of this study is the development of a vocabulary that enables one to generate cultural and social claims about communication. For example, at base, the essay suggests searching relations among the cultural order (e.g., symbols, clusters of symbols, forms, and their meanings), and the social order (e.g., the construction of various identities and relations among classes of persons). Each is reflexively constituted in the language persons use. The distinction warrants further discussion, which I will offer by way of concluding.

DIMENSIONS OF CULTURE AND SOCIAL IDENTITIES

The above analysis has explored a system of symbols, symbolic forms, and meanings, and analyzed the communicative codes that enact and create it. Importantly, each cultural term interpreted here resides in an intricate and interrelated *system of meaning*. For example, employees who gripe about "the building situation" potentially evoke not only their frustration with physical separation, but also with it, the division in "types of people," the heightened sensitivity to a "communication problem," a frustration with doing daily tasks (e.g., running from building to building), and so on. All are salient meanings in the hearing of such a term. All of these, of course, are complemented by the identification of "everyone" with a quality "product." Through expressions of "the product," workers' social divisiveness can succumb to a sense of shared purpose, a regnance and unity. The analysis, then, is not of one key symbol, or a set of symbols, but of a *system* of symbols and their meanings which, taken together, structure some workers' identities and lives. While the particular meanings of these utterances depend on the context and form of their expression, an understanding of the cultural system, or culturescape, can help one understand the range of symbolic meanings appropriate in their situated use. Thus, any communication system enacts and creates such a semantic system, and the symbols and forms that characterize it warrant further explorations.

One way to unravel the cultural meanings in discourse is with the *use of semantic dimensions*. This chapter has shown how workers' speech about "types of people" and "the building situation" operates prominently and intelligibly within a limited field of meanings. Thus, the complex, tensional, and polysemic nature of cultural terms can be interpreted by formulating semantic dimensions. This approach to talk provides a framework for interpretive research both by placing common expressions within a local cultural field and by showing how that field can support various types of social identities and relations.

Future cultural studies of communication could focus further on three *types of symbols*: symbols of persons (e.g., "the secure"), symbols of speaking (e.g., "the communication problem," "staff meetings"), and epitomizing symbols (e.g., "the product"). Each of these types is used in everyday communication; each is expressed through a local and limited semantic field; and each is related to the others. Thus, the following questions might be further asked: How do persons express a sense of who they are (in classes and in encompassing collectivities)? How do they conceive of and evaluate their speech with one another? Is there a symbol(s), and/or form(s) of expression that can unite the variety of persons? The local ways that express responses to these questions form a system of discursive practices, with each part being tailored to the demands of local scenes.

While the various expressions discussed in this study interactively coalesce, they serve fundamentally different *social ends*. One is stratified and divisive, the other, unifying. Taken together, however, they provide a tensional base, an agnostic interplay, that is apparently embedded in any communication system (Carbaugh, 1988/1989; Philipsen, 1987). The result is an inherent degree of discursive tension between the separation and union of people, between social division and integration (see chapter 7). Any sociocultural system of expression, however, makes sense of this tension, if in various ways; it provides a manner of speaking in which the moral valence of these axes is expressed and somehow balanced, or seeking balance. Thus, this study inscribes a particular expression of a *fundamental discursive dialectic in cultural communication practices* and describes its particular weighting and balancing in a way of speaking.

By discussing a fundamental tension in spoken enactment, I hope to have shown how it is not only the local (emic) speechways of a people that come to bear on this report, but also a general conceptual framework that enables their analysis (Pike, 1967; see also Carbaugh and Hastings, 1992). One simply cannot describe and interpret speech conduct *in vacuo*. At some level, there are always principles of selection which orient a description. This report has noted, and attempts to develop further, such an orienting frame. For example, as discussed above, the present report suggests a refining of the general (etic) framework-in-use. Additionally, the study demonstrates a formal method for interpreting cultural terms of identity along dimensions of meanings, and, further, suggests a tensional base that animates their use.

Of future importance in cultural analyses of speech is the comparative study of various ways of speaking. Conducting cross-cultural and cross-organizational studies would help test the adequacy of the (etic) framework in use, develop the analyst's ability to identify more fully the depth and richness of a phenomenon of current concern through such study, and lay an empirical base from which generalizations about speech conduct may be drawn. The present study seeks to contribute to the available fund of studies which move toward these ends.[4]

By uncovering and interpreting the communicative practices used in a workplace, I hope to have conveyed a sense of the richness and depth of insight to be gained from a cultural analysis of communication in human organizations. With this approach, one can reap the fruits of discovery by interpreting the discursive ways a group shapes and forms its identities in its routine communicative life. The analyst can thus be in a position better to diagnose and explain, or at least to articulate with, the people of interest. I have attempted to inscribe one such world, as a situated and common way of speaking and meaning. The intent has been, however, not only the description of that case, but also the further development of a perspective on communication and social identity. The study demonstrates a formal interpretation of cultural terms through dimensions, three types of symbols for further cultural and conceptual analysis, and an agnostic tension between divisive and unifying forces in cultural systems of identification. The study also contributes to the fund of ethnographies which describe how speaking and meaning help constitute institutional life. By gathering a corpus of data this way, we can understand the important particularities of sociocultural scenes, develop a general framework for such an understanding, and contribute to a literature that is eventually available for conceptual and comparative study. In this way, I hope not only to have described a particular case consisting of "completely different types of people," expressed "tensions," and a "communication problem," but also to have contributed to the potential and possibility that an analysis of organizing, from a cultural pragmatic perspective, offers the student of human communication.

SCENE THREE:
WEDDINGS AND MARRIAGE

CHAPTER 5

The Marital Self:
Styles of Names Used upon Marriage

One's name becomes a handle by the aid of which one gets hold of
oneself and acquires facility in thinking and speaking of oneself as an
agent, a striver, a desirer, a refuser.

—W. McDougall

While preparing for a wedding in the New England region of the
United States, several guests discussed what has become to them
somewhat of a puzzling situation. One said: "How do we address
the card? I mean, should we write it to Harry and Sally? That
seems a bit too informal. Maybe I'll write it to Harry Samson and
Sally McNeill. Are they going to share a name?" No one knew the
answer to that question. At the wedding, when the couple was
being presented to the congregation by the minister, the minister
smiled and said: "Ladies and gentlemen, Mr. and Mrs. Harry Sam-
som" (and the bride immediately winced). At a reception of that
same wedding, a female in her late thirties was being introduced
to a retired male school teacher. The older man had just met the
woman's husband, Tim Smith, and upon being introduced to the
woman as "Debbie," replied, "Oh, Debbie Smith!" inserting her
husband's last name after her first name. He assumed that they
shared a last name. The woman replied very forcefully, "My
Name is Debbie Miller. I kept my Real name."[1]

Consider, on the same theme, these other conversations and
comments: (1) A forty-four-year-old woman, married for twenty-
four years, was asked by her daughter, who was twenty-two years
old and contemplating marriage, "Can you describe for me the
process of choosing your last name?" Her mother: "Choosing my
last name? I didn't choose my last name." Daughter: "So . . . "
Mom interrupted: "I was born with Laskovich and married Powell." Daughter: (said indignantly) "Okay, so in other words, you
never considered anything else?" Mother: "No, I didn't." (2) A

sixty-eight-year-old woman, married for "over forty years," described a similar process: "Unquestionably you just assumed that your married name would be your husband's name. And there wasn't any challenge to that idea really. It was unheard of to do otherwise . . . that was the name of the game." (3) A thirty-nine-year-old mother, who has been married ten years, described the process of naming upon marriage: "I think the process was a . . . was a fairly uhm . . . uhm . . . quick one. I didn't really consider any other names. When I got married, I guess I did consider just dropping my own last name which was Godfrey and just going by Paula Chapman, but I wasn't 100 percent comfortable with uhm . . . sort of deleting my past roots and so I felt most comfortable with keeping the Godfrey and adding Chapman, but I wasn't real comfortable with the hyphenated uhm . . . part of it. So I left it Paula Godfrey Chapman, three separate names rather than a hyphenated name . . . because we chose to marry each other, I wasn't sure why I should kind of delete my uhm . . . social identity by immediately taking his name." (4) A thirty-three-year-old woman, married for three years, described the situation of her marriage and how the naming decision was made: "My husband's last name is Nobleton and I never thought of changing my name [Steiner] to Nobleton and neither did he. It was real clear that I would keep my name. . . . My mother-in-law calls me Mrs. Nobleton and occasionally I will be called Mrs. Nobleton, very infrequently. When I got married, they announced us as we were walking into the reception as Mr. and Mrs. Nobleton and I remember cringing, thinking, that's not my name! I don't really understand the custom of changing last names."

The purpose of this chapter, like that of some kindred investigators (e.g., Atkinson, 1987; Foss and Edson, 1989; Intons-Peterson and Crawford, 1985), is to explore some of the prominent styles of names that are being adopted upon marriage in America today (see also Fitzpatrick, 1988). Our goal is to try and understand why, as one of our informants put it, "it is a terribly perplexing and tense situation."[2] The primary cultural scene of concern is identified here not by a physical setting, but by a discursive scene, which we summarize with the cultural phrase "names and marriage." This scene can arise in almost any event but is especially salient in activities surrounding weddings as well as when people discuss the institutions of marriage and family. We ask of this discursive scene: What forms of names are being used when marrying? What motivates the selection of one form from among the available options? What sociocultural meanings do people associate with uses of each form? And, why is this phenomenon marked as a dilemma fraught with tension? What our study develops is this: a list of American forms for naming that are used upon marriage; a typification of these into three naming styles; a description of expressed motives for selecting from among the styles; the meanings prominently associated with each of these styles; and a summary of these various features into codes. The findings are then used, in the following chapter, to evaluate and extend the theories of personal address and person reference.

METHOD

The data which ground the study are of four general kinds: responses to a pilot questionnaire, intensive interviewing, field observations, and a collection of cultural texts where last names were used and/or commented upon. The collection includes moments of casual conversations which a research team heard, three excerpts from short stories, popular magazines such as *Ms.* and *Parade*, the "Dear Abby" advice column, segments from television shows, and a "Parent Worksheet for Birth Certificates."

The research was designed in two general phases. The first consisted of the pilot questionnaire, which was distributed to twelve female informants, three who were married and nine who were contemplating marriage. Of these twelve, six reported that they would adopt, or had adopted, the style of MN + HLN (retain the Maiden Name (MN) or birth name, as the middle name; and use the Husband's Last Name (HLN) as the last name, with no hyphen), three reported using the MN alone, two reported HLN alone, and one reported MN-HLN (with a hyphen between MN and HLN). The questionnaire also asked about the motives, meanings, and (actual or projected) consequences of the desired style. Based on these pilot data, in-depth interviews were scheduled. A total of thirteen intensive interviews were conducted (five MN, five HLN, two MN + HLN, one MN-HLN), amounting to a small stratified sample across what we found to be the three main styles (Honigman, 1970). For each style, both a married female and a married male were interviewed. If possible, a married couple was interviewed together (HLN, MN + HLN). The interviews were largely unstructured, but were also designed to elicit talk concerning three conceptual areas: naming styles (e.g., the process, if any, followed in selecting a name, and commentary on selections made by others), expressed motives (e.g., justifications and explanations for one's selection, and those attributed to others who made similar and alternate selections), and meanings-in-use (e.g., how and when the name is used, and what it, and the others, signify, when used). The typical interview lasted about forty minutes (with eleven of thirteen lasting between thirty and fifty minutes, and two lasting about twenty minutes each). All interviews were fully transcribed.[3] During this same second phase, the collection of additional field materials continued.

The analyses of our general corpus followed two general paths. First we asked, simply: From what variety of naming forms are selections being made? A catalog of naming forms was thus compiled. Second, and forming the main focus of our analyses, we sought to analyze each selection by asking: What are the motives and meanings participants associate with that form of name? We proceeded, then, to describe and interpret the "motive talk" which our informants presented to us. The description followed the framework presented in Mills (1940) and later developed by Stokes and Hewitt (1976; also see Ragan, 1983). Also, we interpreted the premises and dimensions of meanings associated with the selections as suggested by Geertz (1973), Seitel (1974), Schneider (1976), and Katriel (1986; also see chapters 3 and 4 above, and Carbaugh, 1988b, 1991). Eventually, these interpretive analyses culminated in what we take to be three principal styles of naming, with each being rather distinct in its motives and meanings, and each cued through some key symbols. After formulating our findings, we constructed the three *personae*, or identificational types introduced below.

NAMING OPTIONS UPON MARRIAGE

The Formal Options

In American English there is a wide range of name options available upon marriage, a number of ways in which one can choose to "fill" the name "slot." The principal selections have been mentioned already: HLN (husband's last name), MN (maiden name, or birth name), MN + HLN (maiden name plus husband's last name, without a hyphen), and MN-HLN (maiden name and husband's last name connected with a hyphen). But this does not exhaust all possibilities. We also found persons who reversed the typical sequence, using HLN + MN and HLN-MN. We discovered two persons (one couple) who created a new last name by combining features of each spouse's last name (CLN, or combined last names); for example, Miller and Singleton became Milton. We talked with one lesbian couple who created a new last name independent of their previous last names (NLN, or new last name). We also discovered a few women living a pattern of serial monogamy who, for example, upon their third marriage, readopted their first husband's last name (1HLN3, first husband's last name but the third marriage) (see Shoumatoff, 1985, pp. 161–171). This exhausts the options we discovered, a total of nine, but we would not hazard a guess that this list is comprehensive or complete.

Relational Combinations

Since the focus of this study is upon names and marriage, the options above are not conceived as selected *in vacuo*, but as cultural resources adopted at the moment of marriage, with the various uses of these, at times, saying something about persons, social identities, and social relationships. The necessity for this kind of thinking becomes apparent once one considers the complexity involved when the above options are brought together in a particular marital relationship. These are the various ways the naming combinations we found were put together in marriage: both spouses or partners used HLN, alone; H (husband) used HLN, while W (wife) used MN; H used HLN while W used MN + HLN, or MN-HLN; both used MN + HLN, or MN-HLN; both used wife's MN, alone; both used HLN + MN, or HLN-MN; W used MN professionally and HLN socially, while H used HLN (or, W and H both used MN among her social friends but HLN among his social friends); both used a NLN, or CLN; and so on. We have at least one case recorded for each of these options.

In this cultural scene, and basic to all of these last name combinations are these fundamental questions: Upon marriage, will the name be changed? Will neither, one, or both spouse(s) change his or her name? Will the name option for spouses be the same or different? These questions are responded to differently above. In some cases, neither person changes their name and they use different last names (e.g., H uses HLN, W uses MN, or a previous HLN); one person changes, and both share a last name (e.g., W changes to HLN, or H changes to MN); one person changes and they use different last names (e.g., W changes to a previous husband's last name 1HLN3); both persons change to the same last name (e.g., H and W use CLN or NLN). We found no case where both persons changed names, and both used different last names, although we speculate that somewhere such a selection has been made.

What is not immediately apparent in this listing, though, are the motives and meanings for making these selections. We shall see eventually, through characteristic personae, that responses to these issues (to change or not, and to share or use a different last name) carry undertones at some times of fairness and equality, at others of unity and loyalty; sometimes the matters are tradition and parental heritage; sometimes convention and marital identity; sometimes personal identity, sometimes professional identity, or familial identity; sometimes simply pragmatic; at still others status quo reigns; or at still others it is a matter of revolution. How can one reason through such a morass of meaning in this scene? Our effort to do so continues with a description of three typical styles of naming, with each providing identifiable responses to these complex issues.[4]

TYPIFIED PERSONAE
WHO ADOPTED EACH NAMING STYLE

Mr. and Mrs. John Powell: The Traditional Style

John and Mary Powell were married in November of 1965.[5] Mr. Powell is "in the automobile business" and Mrs. Powell is a "school teacher." They had a total of six children, who now live away from home.

When discussing marriage and their last name, Mrs. Powell did most of the talking. She began by saying: "Back then, we just assumed that the married name would be the husband's last name. Nobody challenged that idea." As far as she and her husband were concerned, "there wasn't a choice" involved. Getting married meant, by definition, that the woman adopted the husband's last name, and that was that. As she said: "When you got married, neither of us really thought about it. I simply changed my name."

When discussing the importance of their shared last name, Mrs. Powell said: "It is my identity. It's my connectiveness to my husband. It's the name we passed on to our children. It represents family." She continued: "The whole purpose of taking your husband's name is to become identified with your husband." Mr. Powell added: "You are also identified with the family. What is involved is the idea of ancestry and tradition." He went on to describe how when his family "first came from England and Italy, there were very few of us, very few Catholics."[6]

As far as the Powells were concerned, there was not a lot to say about their assumed name. They simply had followed a standard practice in what they considered to be the proper, customary way. What did however, rankle them, were some of the newer practices of naming, ones that touched their own family, and ones they tolerated but called "silly" and "cumbersome."

Upon discussion of these different forms of naming upon marriage, the Powells' expressed puzzled reactions, but added statements of tolerance for others' preferences. For example, when asked if she had thought about name changes since being married, Mrs. Powell replied:

> Only in the sense that I've heard younger people who hyphenate their names, which I think is sort of silly myself. . . . I think it gets very confusing. If you have a simple name, like Smith-Jones, it would be okay, but what happens with your children? If he is John Smith and you are Susan Jones, and then he becomes John Smith-Jones and you're Susan Smith-Jones, and then you have baby Sarah Smith-Jones. And when Sarah Smith-Jones gets married to Tom Brown, does she become Sarah Smith-Jones-Brown? That's why I think it's silly and cumbersome. But, to each his own. It doesn't bother me.

John added, in a rather exasperated way: "I mean, if everybody just keeps her name, if you do that, then actually you have only one generation connection instead of multigeneration connection. I don't know. That's the whole problem." Mary then told about her daughters, saying she did not care which style of name they used upon marriage: "It's their business." She described how two of her daughters "took their husband's names with no question." Then, she described her third as "the only daughter who maintained her [last] name [and her husband, his], but she didn't stay married. Amy and Jack, they are divorced. They were both going to maintain their own identities and not merge. And maintaining their identities actually has torn them apart."

As Mary discussed her name, marriage, and children, she expressed great comfort in being called "Mrs. Powell." In her playful words, "When you got six kids, you better be a Mrs." She became upset, however, when others refused to address her that way.

She described a similar preference of a friend of hers whose husband had died. That friend wrote cards to people "and clearly wrote her return address as Mrs. Jim Parsons." Her friend got "so angry" when "some insisted on addressing their cards to Jane Parsons" that she "drew a line through the Jane and above it wrote Mrs. Jim Parsons and returned it to the senders, explaining" that her husband's name had been "given, not loaned, to her." Mary understood, of course, that not all women who used HLN upon marriage would agree with Jane about this practice, but nonetheless she thought this way of addressing did represent "respect," family, and motherhood, and was something to be valued.

So the story was told by Mr. and Mrs. John Powell. But there are other voices to be heard, especially those adopting the newer practices which Mary and John Powell found confusing, silly, and cumbersome.

Ms. Beth Steiner, Mr. Larry Nobleton: A Modern Style

Beth and Larry were married in May of 1978, when Beth was twenty-eight and Larry was thirty-four. Beth is a "health administrator" and Larry, "an educator." They are the parents of one child.

When discussing name options and marriage, Beth compared her choice with others. "Sometimes I am disappointed that people change their names. But also it's arbitrary in that it's so much a personal choice. I think that's the nice part of it. You can decide what you call yourself." This general theme, of "having options," "choices," and "making decisions," was important to Beth, for it established premises of *voluntariness* about *her own name*, enabling her to *control* how her identity was expressed.

Beth went on to explain why she chose this option: It reflects

a certain view that I have about being married, that I am still my own person, that my life is not just created by my husband, that

I am a person with my own profession, my own friends, and my own values, and all that stays. So, while in some ways it reflects that, I'm not really making that statement. Mostly, I just feel like I don't know why you would just change your name unless you were [pause] It just doesn't make sense to me, which is mostly why I did it [kept my MN]. And it's a hassle to change social security and all. I just didn't see any reason to do that, but I do think it reflects a certain kind of marital relationship when I am fairly independent from my husband although we're intradependent with each other. But, I have friends that I go away with. I might go away with a couple of women friends by myself. I don't feel like I have to just do things with my husband. I can have other relationships so I guess it confirms that I'm still my own person even though I'm in this marriage that's intradependent."

Beth added: "My father is very happy that I kept my name, since he's very identified with it." She also discussed later that she did not like the "very ethnic" sound of Larry's name.

As Beth talked, Larry mostly listened. When asked about the process of selecting a last name upon marriage, he summarized his sentiments saying: "As an active feminist, I felt that my wife would be giving up her identity if she suddenly became a Nobleton. Besides, I was as much a Steiner as she was a Nobleton." So, to both Beth and Larry, the issue of naming was an issue generally of personal identities, and social equality, with their agreement on Beth's use of MN acting as an effort to maintain Beth's "own identity" and an "equal relationship."

According to Beth and Larry, there was a "most difficult thing" that resulted from their name choice. Beth explained:

The most difficult thing was what to call our child, and we decided to give my name as her middle name, and she has Larry's name as her last name. But very often people drop the middle name, so my name never enters into her full name. Sometimes I have to correct that. . . . We did not expect that my name would be dropped so easily from her name.[7]

The issue of "what to name the child" was expressed as a "difficulty" by others who selected this style of name. The issue derives partly from a lack of precedent or "obvious choice" for the child's last name. In fact, of our informants who selected this option, all discussed this as an "issue," and each responded with their own proposal of child-naming, which taken together created a wide range of options. Beyond the statement of the "problem" of what to name the kids, there is little convergence of opinion here. For example, one woman with two children said:

> It didn't bother me to have them keep my husband's last name, uhm, and I don't feel funny about that at all. In fact, my husband wanted to give them the middle name of [MN] and his last name, which I thought was too much of a mouthful, so I chose not to do that. I think it's fine that they have their father's last name. I don't necessarily think that they should have my name, y'know, I have my name because that's always my name.

Another woman, currently without a child, said she would make the same choice of husband's last name, and would even use the occasion of childbirth to change her maiden name to her husband's last name: "I'm dying to have a baby . . . and if he [husband] wanted me to change my last name now, if it was really important to him, I would."

For others, there is negotiating to do, especially when the husband and wife disagree on the name option. A woman contemplating having children described the importance and difficulty of naming:

> My husband and I are in the process of thinking of having children and one of the things that comes up for me is around names. What would we name the baby? I don't know if he's joking, but he thinks that if it's a girl, it should be my name and if it's a boy, his name. I think it should be a hyphenated name. . . . His feeling is that [the hyphenated name is] too cumbersome.

Later on, after further arguing for her proposal to use hyphenated names in their children's names, she expressed "surprise" at the degree of discomfort her husband had with her proposal, leading her to conclude: "My feeling is let the kids decide."

For still others (as below), the issue of baby-naming is nothing less than a "woman's issue," an issue tied to the social identity of women, where a voice of revolution should be expressed.[8] One woman, an avowed "feminist," put it this way:

> Baby-naming is a bottom-line issue, and it is probably one of the most difficult for feminists to talk about. A child's surname reflects our deepest feelings about how we define ourselves in relationship to the dominant group culture, that is men, and the degree to which our feminist beliefs are negotiable under relationship pressures. Baby-naming is the point at which even the most uncompromising feminists compromise.

She elaborates: "Giving up one's name, or keeping one's name and not giving it to offspring, is simply not an option unless one is a subordinate group member and behaves accordingly." The "excuses" for naming practices she most detests are, "for the child's sake," "because it was so important to him" (or one of the families), or "my name is just my father's name anyway." She adds: "Sure it's nice for everyone in the family to have the same last name. But it's still an excuse." To confront the naming issue, she feels women ought to speak in a distinctively woman's voice, in her words, "authentically," "without bringing in the apparent needs and wishes of children, in-laws, husbands, parents, or the world in general." What is at stake, for her, is "the strength and clarity" of "feminist convictions, and the personal risks" that one is "ready to take in order to stand behind them." So, rather than use "excuses," or "compromise solutions" (giving children MN + HLN), she suggests confronting the "real" issue, "the fact that patriarchal values may still run deep in our feminist bones."

As is evident from these few informants, naming the children, as Beth and Larry said, introduces a "most difficult" issue. While the informants who used separate names agreed that child-naming was a problem, they provided a variety of solutions. Many were discussed, proposed, and adopted. Consequently, as children and naming became topics in the discussions of this marital *persona*, its expression converged on child-naming as an issue, but diverged with regard to the optimal name option for children. In effect, they agree that there is no "one proper way" to name a child, and even enjoy the diverse "options" that are available.

Perhaps it is the sound of the "one proper way," and the motives and consequences attributed to it, that makes the traditional name choice, like the Powell's, so difficult for especially Beth to understand. In the course of our discussions, she puzzled over the traditional choice, saying, no less than four separate times, "I don't really understand the custom of changing last names." And again, "it doesn't make sense . . . , it just doesn't make sense to me." Beth disclosed that she "cringed" when she and Larry were married and they were announced as "Mr. and Mrs. Nobleton." She explained, with echoes of "the feminist": "I have a secret prejudice which is that very often in these relationships where women change their names the whole dynamics of the relationships are very different in many ways. I see some of the same traditional problems of male and female roles . . . women who give up their identity and give up their personal lives." She summarized: "I'm always a little disappointed in my friends who" change their names. "Most of my friends do once they have children." "I wish there was more of a matriarchal system where women weren't always the people who always lost their name." For Beth, the traditional choice was "disappointing," for it expressed constraining gender "roles" that she found problematic for her identity as a "woman." Like the "feminist" above, she hoped for a naming system more equitable, in which male and female identities were being equally preserved.

The drama in this cultural scene, according to Beth, involved the relative prioritizing of the identifications of "woman" and "wife." When her friends made the traditional choice of HLN, of "wife" and marriage, over "woman," Beth heard occasions of disappointment, like at her wedding ceremony when she was addressed as "Mrs." She said, "I am not a Mrs. anybody, I am my own person." She went on: "My mother thinks it's an insult to my husband that I don't use the *Mrs.* term or his name. He doesn't think so. We both know we're married and to whom." She recalls: "I remember when my mother used to write me notes in school and she always used to sign her name Mrs. David Steiner, and I always thought that that was real bizarre because it was like she had no identity of her own, and I never really wanted to be like that." She concluded: "I possess my name and my identity, not my husband's."

For Beth Steiner and Larry Nobleton, they have selected a naming option upon marriage in which both kept their birth names. This asserts Beth's identity, like Larry's, as an independent person, and thus expresses a "relationship" in which both are equal. While this presented a problem of naming their child, they have resolved that issue, and generally like the use of their two separate last names.

Paula Godfrey Chapman, Robert Chapman: An Integrative Style

Paula Godfrey and Robert Chapman were married in June of 1984. Paula is a family counselor with a private practice. Robert is a university professor. They have two children.[9]

Paula recalled the process of naming upon marriage as "a quick one." She "did consider just dropping" her "own last name, which was Godfrey, and just going by Paula Chapman," but she "wasn't 100 percent comfortable with . . . deleting" her "past roots." She "felt most comfortable with . . . keeping the Godfrey and adding Chapman," but she "wasn't real comfortable hyphenating": "So I left it Paula Godfrey Chapman, three separate names rather than a hyphenated last name." Paula liked the Irish ring to her name, and did not want to give it up for only Chapman. She laughed as she said: "[I am] a person who sort of tries to get along. Y'know, it's like even though you have a certain level of independence, you also chose your spouse's name." Using both names became important for Paula, especially when spending time with in-laws, where she was addressed as Chapman, and she did not force the Godfrey name. But also in her profession, she would use only Godfrey, the name she had first used in her counseling practice, and to which she adhered. What her name provides for her is, in part, flexibility, as a Godfrey and/or a Chapman. As Paula put it, the name "says I am a person, the same person that I've been since I was born. I'm also a married person. . . . I am a part of a family that I've chosen and, uhm, but I'm still the person that I always was."

When Robert was asked about the naming process, he explained it as

> her decision. . . . I knew Paula would decide which she would do, then tell me. I didn't want to press an issue. I was ready to live with any choice. I had been through a big disappointment in 1977 with another woman, who told me that if we were married, she was going to keep her maiden name. So, by now, I knew it was up to Paula, and basically just waited until she told me.

When asked about her particular choice of MN + HLN, he said, "Well, at first I just didn't understand why she had to have her maiden name in there, but in time I came to appreciate it, and her link to her family."

When discussing her "family," Paula described a consequence of her name choice that she found amusing. Her oldest daughter "considers Godfrey Chapman her last name." She laughed: "Even though she is not named that, if you ask her her full name, she'll give it [Godfrey Chapman] to you with her middle name." When discussing her social friends, Paula claimed that most of her friends have "their maiden name in the middle and their spouse's name at the end without it being hyphenated." She reflected on this practice of naming, saying, "I certainly see where the tradition came from, y'know, for adopting your spouse's last name." She considered it "romantic . . . a nice tradition of melding two people." But, she added, it is "sort of a patriarchal approach," since "it's the man's name that usually gets chosen." The adoption of the MN + HLN style then has some ambivalence associated with it for Paula, but all in all she said she "feels good" about her choice.

One practice which Paula can tolerate, but dislikes, is "the label *Mrs.*" She said, "It's like for some reason it seems like society has really valued women's being married . . . at a fairly young age, and if you're not married, it's like, oh, she's Miss so and so!" She laughed: "So I guess I'm real comfortable with *Ms.* as a label and then Paula Godfrey Chapman." The general statement this makes for Paula is: "We are from different backgrounds, and that that's okay, and we are related by marriage, and that I like that too." Other women who used MN + HLN expressed less difficulty with the *Mrs.* title (as one woman said, "it doesn't bother me a bit"), but there did seem to be unanimity of voice about first names. No woman of this style liked her husband's first name to follow the title *Mrs.* Unlike Mrs. Powell, all agreed that their first name was to be preferred over their husband's on all occasions, with Paula and others strongly preferring Ms. over Mrs., while others preferred either Ms. or Mrs.

Paula and Robert have then agreed both to share a last name, and for Paula to adopt her maiden name as her middle name. Their children officially adopted Paula and Robert's shared name, with their one daughter unofficially adopting her mother's maiden name as well. While Paula likes the "roots" expressed through her name choice, she also likes the "romantic" idea of "melding" people into family. It is this compromise, this ability to "get along" with others, to fluctuate between her expression of "core independence" and "marriage" that makes her style of name meaningful for her. We have seen how these forces tug and pull from many directions, through many motives and meanings, with each style of name typified here enabling easy expression in some ways more than others. What Paula and Robert have found indeed is a way to integrate some of these, a kind of integrative compromise between opposing social forces.

EXPRESSED MOTIVES FOR NAMING

Throughout the above discussions of names adopted upon marriage, we have heard several motives being expressed for selecting name options. Our purpose here is to present the vocabulary of motives used by our informants, and to discuss which motives correlate with the above three naming styles.[10]

We found seven kinds of motive statements that were used as justifications for a name choice. These consist of three general appeals: to convention, to identity, and to pragmatism. As we will see, the appeal to identity received the greatest degree of elaboration.

Appeals to convention consisted of references to tradition and the status quo. The selection was deemed customary, the thing done, needless to think about, valued, and generally accepted as a practice. As Mrs. Powell said, there was no "choice" involved. Another of our informants said, "At the time I got married, you just automatically took the husband's name." There was not much else to say. This justification consists of an appeal to a widespread standard of practice.

Appeals to identity consisted of references to important aspects of who one is. This was done by appealing to five common domains for identification: ethnic identity, family identity, self identity, professional identity, and relational identity. Being motivated by *ethnic identity* consisted mainly of statements about one's communal "roots"—as Italian, Jewish, Russian, Irish—and the unique denotative meanings of one's last name. For example, one person mentioned that her name meant "peace and tranquility," a feature she valued and did not want to forfeit.

Our informants also were motivated to choose a name based upon various aspects of *family identity*. The justification of name here, rather than appealing to ethnicity or other denotative name meanings, consisted of familial statements. As one woman said: "[I chose my name (HLN) because] it's my connectiveness to my husband. . . . It represents family." She identified mainly with her present family, as a wife and mother. But there are other motives expressed that invoke family identity in different directions. A woman said she chose to keep her maiden name because "names really do bind people. I did not want to lose the bind that I had with my family [of birth]." For husbands who keep HLN, these two motives, of a current and birth family, can coalesce, but for women, different naming forms can suggest different familial orientations: to one's past, or to one's present, or to both families (as demonstrated by Paula Godfrey Chapman).[11]

A third motive of identity is *self-identity*, an avowal that one is psychologically unique, independent, and separate from others. A woman justified her choice, saying: "I felt a strong identity with my last name. It was me . . . it's always made me feel special." Or, as Beth Steiner put it: "[I chose it because] I am my own person . . . with my own friends and my own values." Or, from "the feminist": "My personal identity was forged carrying my name, not my husband's. I do not assume a new identity because of marriage."

A fourth motive for name selection was *professional identity*, as a way of maintaining consistency in one's career, or as "a person with my own profession." And finally, some motives for naming appealed to a *relational identity*. In these cases, justifications were formulated as a matter of "equality" between "spouses." As one man (MN-HLN) put it: "I believe the name change made an important statement about marriage and equality that I was proud and willing to make." Examples included both spouses adopting the same hyphenated name, or neither one changing.

Appeals to pragmatism consisted of references to name sounds, length, and/or combinations. Some said they did not like the sound of their spouse's name, and thus would not adopt it; for example, it sounds like "whore" or "fart," or "it's too ethnic." Others would not hyphenate because of name length; for example Nancy Demerkowski refused to combine her name with Nick Popadopolous. Our favorite example of pragmatic concerns occurred when Jennifer Just was engaged to marry Corey Darling, with both saying the idea of being "Just Darlings" was too much to take. While they officially selected the modern style, a recent social invitation from them was addressed from "the Just Darling residence."

By abstracting this vocabulary of motives from our informants' speech, we are now able to ask: What motives were avowed by those making each of the three stylistic choices described above? Our findings were surprising, for we surmised initially that there would be a great degree of overlap between the motives of the different styles. But what we found, in our admittedly small sample, was, with only one exception (ethnic identity), a perfect correlation between expressed motives and stylistic choice. Those who made the traditional choice of HLN avowed motives of convention, ethnic identity, and/or current marriage/family identity. Those who made the modern choice (H: HLN; W: MN), expressed motives of ethnic identity, affiliation with family of birth, self identity, professional identity, relational identity, and/ or pragmatic concerns. Other than ethnic identity, there was no overlap in expressed motives between those making the traditional selection and those making the modern. But, among those who adopted the style of integration (H: HLN; W: MN + HLN), the whole vocabulary of motives was used.

COMMUNICATIVE MEANINGS OF MARITAL NAMES

While above we asked what motives were avowed by those using each naming style, here we ask what are the meanings that people associate with, or hear when using the naming styles. In response, we offer three semantic dimensions, separateness-connectedness, assertion-conciliation, and revolution-convention (Carbaugh, 1988b; Katriel, 1986; Seitel, 1974). Each was invoked by our informants in an effort to make their own and others' selections mutually intelligible. Taken together, the dimensions help us identify the ways the traditional and modern styles invoke a range of semantic oppositions, yet also how they operate within a limited semantic field. The dimensions also help in showing how the third style attempts to integrate these semantic oppositions.[12]

The semantic dimension of *separateness-connectedness* is used by our informants to respond implicitly to the basic identity question: Who am I? As our informants discussed their names and marriage, they spoke of their separate or their connected identities, their being independent or affiliative, and described the efforts followed to reconcile the commonly felt American tension between individual being and relational bonding (Carbaugh, 1988b, pp. 160ff). For example, at one point Beth Steiner talked about "having my thumbprint on the things that I do. It has to be me and my own thing." At another, she discussed her "marital relationship" and "intradependence," an interesting term that apparently said "we are separate and together."

The speech of these persons applies the dimension of separateness-connectedness to discussions of social and interpersonal life. But the semantic weighting of each pole varies with the naming choice. With the traditional style, the couple shares a last name, expresses motives including affiliation with one's current family, and perhaps even prefers an address as *Mrs.* The marital name itself, along with this motive and form of address, all point to meanings of sharing, connecting, and bonding, thus expressing a "linked" identity within an immediately identifiable social group. From this vantage point, to adopt a name is to add to one's identity, to gain expression as a member of a marriage and family, as a connected *we* over an independent *me*. As Mrs. Powell said, "It's my connectiveness to my husband . . . to our children. It represents family." Consider, on the other side, the modern choice where two different names are used, where motives for such a choice include self identity, one's family of birth, one's own career considerations, equal partnerships, and a general preference for the explicitly nonaffiliative *Ms*. With this style, one hears elaborated separate identities, individuation, and distinctive volitional beings. As Ms. Beth Steiner said, "I am my own person . . . , with my own profession, my own friends and my own values." To change a name, from this vantage point, is to "lose" parts of one's "own identity," perhaps through social institutions and forces. But to keep one's name is to express a continuity that is one's self, to present a steady *me* over the everchanging *we*. Thus, while any one person can (and does) orient to both of these meanings at any one time, the selection of name upon marriage, along with the motives expressed for the selection, carries semantic weight in predominantly one direction, more than the other (unless the integrative style is used). Part of the meaningfulness in name choice thus responds to this question: Shall my name express explicitly a separate, and/or a connected, identity?

The dimension of *assertion-conciliation* is used by informants —when discussing naming and marriage—to respond implicitly to the question: What actional force shall my name carry with regard to current societal institutions?[13] The power of this meaning dimension is demonstrated forcefully during the wedding reception mentioned at the beginning of this chapter. As the retired male teacher, who was not sure of the younger woman's last name, began inserting her husband's last name, she interrupted and exclaimed emphatically, "My *Name* is Debbie Miller. I *Kept* my *Real name*!" Similar stories are told by others of the troubles they experience when being introduced, when interacting with in-laws, coworkers, acquaintances, and so on. One's name, in these discursive contexts, whether intended or not, becomes a potent cultural resource that is *used* not only to assert one's own identity, but also is hearable as a directive about the ways marriage and society should operate. It is the prominent device used to say, as Debbie did, "I assert myself and my ideals quite counter to your expectations." While this mode of assertive action is used by some of the modern style with regard to their name—especially by Debbie and "the feminist" above—it is also sometimes attributed to them, even if such assertive actions are not endorsed nor characteristically done by them. This was the case as one woman described "construction workers" at her home who, knowing she did not use her HLN, made a big point of calling her "Karen [MN]," in her words, "just to shut me up." She said, "some people really have that attitude" that "you are just trying to be difficult, when I really wasn't." As is evident in these exchanges, there is a force of assertiveness, or a directive inferred—and sometimes intended—with the modern naming option that is relatively lacking in the traditional and integrative styles. With these other styles of naming, one is heard to act in a more conciliatory way, as Paula Godfrey Chapman put it, in an effort "to get along." While the modern option is spoken and heard relative to the others as an assertion, a form of resistance which sometimes meets resistance, the traditional and modern options carry a more conciliatory and assimilative tone. Thus, through the selection of name option, one is heard to respond to the question What is this person's preferred mode of action? with the modern option, at times, being heard as relatively more socially assertive in intent than the others.

The dimension of *revolution-convention* is used by our informants to respond to the implicit questions: How do I feel about the current social and cultural scene? and, How, if at all, do I identify with it? Two extreme responses follow from the above and could be put simply this way: At one end of the extreme is the modernist ("I am not a beneficiary of this society, am revolted with it, and thus must revolt over it"); at the other extreme is the traditionalist who is relatively pleased and comforted by present customs. The first position is anchored best by Beth Steiner and "the feminist" who expressed outrage "that our society remains a male-dominated one" and "patriarchal values still run deep." The modern style of naming thus becomes a "political" device expressing utter disappointment at an inequitable, unjust system. From this view, one does not "fit," and thus must fight against it, partly by selecting a naming form and motives that serve as correctives to the present injustices. The modern style of naming thus, at its extreme, can express and can be heard to express outrage and disappointment, reflecting a person who refuses to follow the more traditional ways and is thus acting against a "patriarchal society." The counter pole is anchored in relatively more contented expressions of conformity, family values, children, and motherhood. There is not much said other than: "this is the way it's done," "I'm pleased (or, at least, not displeased) with this way," and (at least to some degree) "I agree with it." Thus displayed, especially through the traditional style of naming and less so through the integrative style, is a person of the traditional society, relatively contented and comforted by it.

NAMING STYLES SUMMARIZED AS CODES

The above descriptions and interpretations of personae, motives, and meanings, provides a base for a more formal summary of the three styles of naming that are active in this cultural scene. We present each here, as a code, through a distillation of five cultural features: the stylistic choice made, and the key symbols, motives, meanings, and norms associated with each.

The traditional code: The traditional style of naming results when, upon marriage, the woman adopts her husband's last name, thus both persons share a last name. The traditional voice responds to last names and marriage with a vocabulary of "family" and "children." The key actors, in terms of this code, are "husband" and "wife," "mother" and "father." The title *Mrs.* is sometimes adopted as an expression of an affiliative identity. The motives for naming involve justifications in terms of convention or custom, ethnic identity, and the identity of the immediate marriage/family. The traditional marital name is meaningful to its adopters as an identity of connectedness, with an assimilative force, and a conventional placement of the persons within the customary arrangements of society. The normative judgment which orients the traditional system could be summarized as follows: Upon marriage, it is presumed or preferred that husband and wife should share the husband's last name. Such a name choice expresses marriage as a traditional connection, as an unseverable union. The traditional code thus foregrounds, in its discursive selection, one version of a central social institution, the nuclear family, with its attendant identities and relations.

The modern code: The modern style of naming occurs when, upon marriage, both spouses use their birth names, thus using different last names. The modern voice responds to last names and marriage with a vocabulary of "independence" and "equal relationships." The key actors, in terms of this code, are "spouses," most typically "woman" and "man," although this is sometimes not specified. "Children," and naming them, if discussed, can be called "an issue" with its attendant difficulties and "problems." The title *Ms.* is often adopted because it expresses an identity that is mute on relatedness. The motives for the modern naming option include ethnic identity, affiliation with one's family of birth, self identity, professional identity, relational identity, as well as some pragmatic concerns. The modern naming style is meaningful as an assertion of a separate and independent identity, in part, and is sometimes invoked as a way to change a suboptimal, or patriarchal, society. The moral and normative force orienting the system could be summarized as follows: Upon marriage, it is preferred that spouses retain continuity of their personal identities, thus keep their original last names. Such choice of names could be summarized as a union of dignified separates, or a separable whole. The modern code thus foregrounds, in its discursive selection, an individualized system of marriage, each with its own separate identities.

The integrative code: The integrative style of naming results when, upon marriage, and typically, the woman adds her husband's last name to her own, retains her maiden name as her middle name, with both partners sharing a last name and retaining their birth names. The integrative voice joins aspects of the traditional and modern codes. It is expressed through a vocabulary of "independence" and "family." Key actors and relations, in terms of this code, are expressed in a variety of ways from "wife" and "husband" to "spouses," with "children" often being prominent and central. Titles of *Ms.* or *Mrs.* may be acceptable to women, although the most favored is *Ms.* (with no one favoring *Mrs.* + *husband's first and last names*). Motives for the integrative code did *not* include convention but did include ethnic identity, the identities of the birth and current family/marriage, self identity, professional identity, and pragmatic concerns. The meaningfulness of the integrative code centered on its ability to express both poles of the dimensions expressed above. The integrative code is thus both polysemic (many meanings) and multivocal (used to express distinct types of identities and means of sociation): It enables separate and connected identities; it expresses degrees of assertion and conciliation; it is mildly revolutionary, yet also conventional. In its moral assessment it says: Upon marriage, it is preferred that both persons retain their original names, and share a last name, giving voice to the modern traditionalist, and its various motives and meanings. The integrative code thus foregrounds, in its discursive selection, varying degrees of personal and social systems, of distinct individuals and customary relations.

THE INTERACTION OF THE CODES

Because each of the naming styles orient to distinct, and overlapping, codes, it is illuminating to explore briefly how the codes are brought into social interaction. Recall how the styles of naming not adopted by informants were being characterized by them, and then how the characterization was used to account for some social problems. For example, some using the traditional style characterized the modern style as "confusing," "silly," and "strange." This view led another to explain her modern daughter's divorce from her husband: "They were both going to maintain their own identities and not merge, and maintaining their own identities has torn them apart." We repeatedly discovered this traditional account of a modern divorce in which "the different last name" was used as symbolic of a—if not *the*—marital flaw. On the other hand, those using the modern style expressed "disappointment" at those (of the younger generation) who "chose" the traditional style, implying that their "choice" of the traditional naming form was a "cop-out" being used as a mere "convenience." This practice, being denigrated as inappropriately conforming, created—according to some—an unthinking complicitous base that further perpetuated social "problems of [in]equality and power." Similarly, another woman explained that she felt "very suspicious" of the "traditional" style, assuming "the same traditional problems of male and female roles" would be apparent because those women "gave up their identity and gave up their personal lives."

From the standpoint of the traditional code, the modern is puzzling, even humorous. From their discursive view, it has failed to understand the bonds of family and marriage. However, from the standpoint of the modern code, the traditional has "sold out" to the patriarchy, failing to advance an equitable society which balances power between the sexes. But each such reaction is couched in terms of its own code, asserting its own coherence, and assuming its own preferences, problems, and plans. For the traditional, the value is connecting with others in family; the problem, divorce; the explanation of it, separate identities; the plan for action, a conventional union. For the modern, the value is the dignity and worth of persons as distinctive individuals; the problem, inequitable gender roles; the explanation, the tradition of patriarchy; the plan for action, a revolutionary one. The "semantic slippage" between codes accounts for those who say the other option "simply makes no sense." Given the different meanings, values, problems, and plans involved, there is little wonder that there are various perplexing dilemmas.

The conflicts and tensions can and do run deep between those using the different codes, especially when these arise within families or on other important social occasions when participants want to embrace common values and affiliations, but feel they have implemented divergent practices, with each in some way perplexing to the other. In such situations, the naming form for some can easily have "conflict potential," creating what Jackson (1975) has called a "disorganized state," at least as far as naming codes go, with different classes of people orienting to different—and, for some, mutually exclusive—codes. Clearly this is not a problem for all Americans in all social contexts, but when addressing and referring to others in any American context, these issues can become highly salient, for in these acts, persons and social identities can become quickly codified, in part, through the style of name they wear.

CHAPTER 6

Social Uses of Marital Names: Ethnography and Conversation Analysis

The last name has, of course, several social uses. Some of these include legal and administrative record keeping, such as in bank accounts, school credentials, social security files, credit card records, or professional documents. Other uses are more interactional and social, as in conversations when people in each other's presence are being addressed by each other, as when the retired teacher met Debbie Miller. Also, when trying to refer to someone who is not present, we often do so through names, with the form of last name sometimes carrying potential semantic weight on these occasions. One's last name, whether an adopted name or a birth name, becomes a principal means by which one is known, legally and pragmatically.

Studies of the pragmatic uses of names in social contexts have examined both *personal address* (focusing mainly upon occasions when people act as if they are present to each other) and *person reference* (when referring to someone not present). These studies suggest two general conversational "slots" which are filled with styles of last names. The classic study of American address suggests that the option of using a last name or a first name is "the principal option of address in American English" (Brown and Ford, 1964, p. 234). One's choice of last name, then, is nothing less than the "principal" resource by which one is identified, a handy linguistic means by which one is addressed and known. This resource becomes profoundly important in particular speech events such as introductions (e.g., of Debbie Miller and the teacher, or of the newly married couple to the congregation). However, if one is not present to others, and yet their conversation requires a reference to another, and interlocutors do not know or recognize the reference to that other by first name alone, then the last name becomes the next candidate for doing the person reference. This attempt to identify one by first, then last name is called a "try mark" sequence by Sacks and Schegloff (1979). In the contexts of personal address and person reference, last names thus can and do become especially powerful as conversational and cultural resources. They do nothing less than symbolize one's identity through a style and code of name choice. Thus the style of name one adopts upon marriage is not merely a legal matter of record keeping, but is a crucial source of identification within daily routines where it is used for purposes of address and reference.[1]

RECONSIDERING THEORIES OF PERSONAL ADDRESS AND PERSON REFERENCE

The findings of chapter 5 are particularly relevant to the theories of person address and reference. Both of these theories attempt to describe and explain, in part, the special place of last names in social interaction. The previous study helps develop these theoretical statements by introducing considerations of style and code. Generally, the study suggests questioning earlier correlations of name forms and semantic forces by further explicating the sociocultural variabilities of these communication practices.

In their classic study of American personal address, Brown and Ford (1964) explore the relation of forms of address, such as first name (FN) and title + last name (TLN). They explain the variation in such usage by positing "semantic dimensions" which "serve to relate to one another all of the members of the society" (p. 234). There are four aspects of their study of particular interest to us here. First, their study is based on the assumption that there is one style of a single linguistic form. Their formulation suggests treating the various styles of last name (e.g., Powell, Godfrey Chapman) similarly, as of one form (TLN). Second, their formulation suggests that a single form (TLN) carries a similar semantic force relative to another form (such as FN). Third, and more particularly, such an assumption leads to claims like: movement from an address of TLN to FN marks a progression in the meanings of social relations "from acquaintance to intimacy" (p. 236); and fourth, "mutual TLN goes with distance or formality" (p. 239). Let us explore each of these from the standpoint of our present findings.

First, we find several styles of the last name that are available, rather than only one style (see also Foss and Edson, 1989).[2] Further, each style has its own distinctive semantic force, or code, as it invokes a particular symbolic system, motives, norms, and meanings. Thus, of great cultural and pragmatic significance is the particular style of Last Name (or Title) being used. Put differently, there is great variation *within* a single linguistic form of address (TLN) as well as between them. This itself must become the substance of further cultural and pragmatic study. Without such study, we treat Mrs. Powell and Ms. Steiner similarly, as TLN, overlooking the particular meanings of each, and missing the important social identities that might come to bear when each is being addressed. Without exploring this *within-form variation*, we fail to capture some of the semantic potential involved when one form of address is used rather than another. For example, if our Mrs. John Powell met Ms. Beth Steiner, a decision is made about how to address each other, perhaps by using a mutual exchange of FN, "Mary, meet Beth," rather than another, a "mutual" exchange of TLN, "Mrs. Powell, meet Ms. Steiner." Our first point is this: Considerations of variety in cultural styles and codes of names can help account for within-form variations. Considerations as these are fundamental to theories of personal address, and when considered, suggest moving beyond simple correlations of a general form of address with its singular meaning. Which takes us to the second point.

Brown and Ford (p. 236) equate the movement from TLN to FN with a progression, although sometimes slight, from acquaintance to intimacy. Both their study and the present one discovered many contexts where people prefer FN over TLN as the form of address. In fact, many of our informants claimed to use their last names rather infrequently, preferring to be called by FN. As discussed in chapter 2, the same preference for intimacy is lamented by Sennett (1977) as a "fear of impersonal life." We could ask, then, why is this preference stated and followed? Brown and Ford, taken along with Sennett, suggest that speakers of American English prefer FN to TLN because it foregrounds meanings of intimacy (FN), over distance or formality (TLN). Because of this preference, American speakers prefer to use, as soon as possible, FN over TLN. Our study suggests, however, an alternate line of reasoning. People prefer FN as an address form, on some occasions, for these reasons: It is more neutral (than LN) in information value; it carries less potential for conflict (there is apparently in English less by way of potential semantic oppositions within the FN form than there is within the LN form); and, therefore, it (FN) steers away from the possibility of social tensions, division, stratification, or ideological debate, and moves more toward a comfortable common social ground. Thus, in American society today, because the styles of LN can carry more potent cultural information about the person than FN, and can introduce issues some prefer to be muted (are you a "real feminist" or have you "sold out"?), there is a preference for FN. It is not so much, as Brown and Ford and Sennett suggest, that people are driven toward intimacy, as it is they are moving away from potential conflict and discord, and toward a more common ground. Heard this way, a preference for mutual exchange of FN signifies a desire less for closeness than for commonality; with the dispreference for LN being associated, at times, less with formality than with possible division. From this vantage point, movement from TLN to FN, especially when very quick (Brown and Ford, p. 236), can and does signal a progression, but the progression can mark movement from an uncomfortable divisiveness to commonality, as much as from acquaintance to intimacy. After witnessing several shifts from the uncomfortable "Mrs. Powell, meet Ms. Steiner" to the more neutral "Oh, Mary meet Beth," the semantics involved move less clearly to intimacy, than they do to commonality, and equality (cf. Philipsen, 1989b).

Brown and Ford (p. 239) also conclude that "mutual TLN goes with distance and formality." Following the reasoning above, since the last name can carry more personal and impersonal information than the first, and since today LN is sometimes not even known by compatriots, it can signal more by way of solidarity than distance. For example, we heard one woman, who used her birth name after marriage, ask another, "Oh, Ms. Steiner, is that your maiden name?" (leading them to initiate and continue such mutual address, feeling united by the shared style of name and the code it symbolized). Also, such mutual use of TLN can sometimes be used to convey a closeness that FN cannot signal, "Why, TLN, I didn't know that you changed [or kept] your name, I did too!" (similarity leading to intimacy). Thus, mutual TLN, depending on the moment of use, the style of name used, and the interlocutors involved, can vary in its semantic force from expressions of distance and formality, to solidarity, even intimacy. The movement from TLN to FN does not any more seem simply correlated with a progression from acquaintance to intimacy, as it perhaps did in the earlier America of the 1960s that Brown and Ford studied.

Such qualifications of Brown and Ford's findings and framework hinge upon cultural pragmatic explorations of styles and codes as they infuse basic linguistic forms. Such study can be used to account for variations in the meanings and uses of names. Without considering these and similar features (e.g., ethnic names and forms), our theories risk silencing the differences that different names can carry. The same general line of reasoning applies to theories of person reference.

The theory of person reference as presented by Sacks and Schegloff (1979), and applied by Moerman (1988), rests on the assumption that conversation is "an orderly phenomenon [that] can be described by means of rules" (Moerman, p. 34). Two rules grounding the theory are "the preference for minimization" and "the preference for recipient design" (Sacks and Schegloff, pp. 16–17).[3] These two rules are of more general interest because they also ground the celebrated model of turn-taking (Sacks, Schegloff, and Jefferson, 1974). But based on the present study, we suggest that cultural codes and variations are inextricably tied to these robust rules.

Sacks and Schegloff (pp. 16–17) develop the minimization rule in this way: "On occasions when reference [to persons] is to be done, it should preferredly be done with a single reference form." While they acknowledge that "reference forms are combinable, and on some occasions are used in combination," they declare that "massively in conversation, references in reference occasions are accomplished by the use of a single reference form." They list a set of reference forms: "he, Joe, a guy, my uncle, someone, Harry's cousin, the dentist, the man who came to dinner." From such a set, a single reference form is preferred. They then list five examples of "single reference forms," all of which are single lexemes, two being FN, two LN, and one a third-person pronoun. This leads them to conclude: "Thereby a preference for minimization is evidenced." We must infer from their discussion that a "preference for minimization" involves a preference for a minimal reference form, such that monolexemic forms are preferred over multilexemic forms. The other basic rule captures the sequence of person reference, and is described by Sacks and Schegloff as follows: (1) that reference to person, if possible, follows a preference for recognitionals (the "recipient design" rule), with personal names being basic recognitionals, (2) if a recipient does not recognize the recognitional label offered, then (3) the preference for minimization is "relaxed step by step" (p. 16).

The findings of the present study, regarding person reference, enter with some force here. Consider that point in conversation when a first recognitional is not successful, and a slot is created for a second try at reference. For example:

A: Have you heard that Paula got promoted?
B: Paula?

At this very moment, following a "preference for minimization," one would expect further reference (to "Paula") to take the next minimal form, "Paula Chapman," since "Chapman" is both a recognitional (satisfying the recipient design rule) and a minimal reference form (satisfying the minimization rule). And this might do the job of reference quite well. But this form of reference is, to Paula, "too minimal." It is not her preferred form. She prefers, "Paula Godfrey Chapman," but that preferred form of self-reference is evidently not the most "minimal" of the possible "reference forms." If the conversational mechanisms Sacks and Schegloff describe are used, then one might—by using "Godfrey Chapman"—run the risk of relaxing the minimization rule too quickly. It seems that this is precisely the dilemma in which many women (and others caught at the moment of reference) find themselves. Their preferences for minimization may sound conversationally demanding to others, because they require more elaboration than others (or the routine mechanics of conversation) prefer. We heard repeatedly how "people will not use my full name," and much exasperation because, for example, "the boss addresses and refers to me as HLN, and refuses to use my preferred name, MN + HLN." Such commentary supports Sacks and Schegloff's description of the minimization rule. In such occasions, people evidently use a minimal form of name (e.g. HLN rather than MN + HLN). But this is a "preference" for only one class of participant, or for only some social scenes, because this generally preferred standard of practice is "too minimal" for others like Paula, and others who use the modern code. This raises an important empirical question: In the use of conversational devices, what constitutes a preference? What constitutes a minimization? And what constitutes a "single reference form"? Are these standards common across all conversation, and classes of persons, or do they vary by class, culture, and code (see Bilmes, 1988)?

Given our findings, we conclude that, at some level of actual communication practice, such preferences and sequences do vary, and may, because of that, be the site of important cultural information. At the level of cultural pragmatics, the matters are not quite as general, or simple, as the language of "single forms," "preference," "minimization," and "recognitionals" implies. Reference forms can occur in different styles and codes. Preferences do vary. Minimization can and does get constituted differently. Recognitionals can and do carry variant moral weight, especially, it appears, in moments when society is in transition or when one group is seeking transformation. Such commentary of course does not refute Sacks and Schegloff's theory. In fact, being able indeed to pose these issues hinges on their powerful prior work. What we call for, at the general level, is a refined conceptualization of "preference" and "minimization." In order to proceed theoretically, we must apply the ideas to actual scenes, with special attention to sociocultural variabilities in such matters (especially under conditions of change). Systems of reference, perhaps at the level of universal conversational structures, are all alike. But at other levels, in the pragmatic scenes of social living, particularly interesting in moments of reference (and address) are issues of agency and identity. Because reference systems are sometimes varied, differently designed through different styles and codes, and situated in their own preferences, in their own interactional motives and meanings, they need to be understood not just universally, but particularly as well.

A POTENT SITE OF COMMUNICATION AND CULTURE

Just one linguistic form, and three styles of its use, can operate in American events of address and reference to signal a relative positioning of social identities. The use of a naming style potentially signals an identity through a code, through a discourse of identification consisting of associated symbols, motives, meanings, and norms. People can use—affirm and resist—features such as these in order to express who they are, to address and refer to others, and to assess how their society is being organized. Clearly social harmony is not the only theme, although it is a prominent one. At other times, discord prevails, as tensions are aroused through the different styles and codes, and between and among social groups, families, marriages, genders. Through such styles and codes, social life can gain a coherent—if not wholly congenial—expression. That such diversity in social identities and relations comes to bear upon the styles and codes of naming upon marriage in America today, is evidence of the power that a single communicative practice can have in a contemporary cultural scene.

SCENE FOUR:
GENDER AND THE "TALK SHOW"

CHAPTER 7

The Gendered Self and "The Individual": A Vacillating Form of Identity Talk in the "Talk Show"

Every social interaction presupposes and creatively invokes social identities. Interacting with others carries with it messages, intentional or not, about the kind(s) of person one is (and others are), how one is (currently being) related to others, and what feelings are to be associated with this current social arrangement. Whether one immediately understands or agrees with the persons, relations, and feelings being shaped through social interaction, once caught by it, one will find oneself a subject in it, variously (often institutionally) related through it, and feeling from "good" to "bad" to neutral about it. Whatever one's intentions about conveying such messages, one will find that in effect one will have done so (Carbaugh, 1993a, 1993b; Goffman, 1967).

In this chapter, I want to explore how the above process works, by developing further this idea: Through primarily symbolic interaction, participants constitute public social identities (not necessarily "statuses") as moral agents in society. I build upon the main assumption of the introduction: that people identify ways of being, as a gendered self or other, through the symbolic practices of situated social scenes. Various symbols, forms, and meanings of social identity, then, are being treated as situated discursive practices (cf. Davies and Harré, 1990; Harré, 1991; Harré and Van Langenhove, 1991) with each of these being culturally distinct, socially situated, and individually applied (Carbaugh, 1993a, 1994). The general argument, as throughout the volume, is that social identities may be understood as specific communicative practices in particular social scenes, with these being immanent in rather durable cultural discourses (see Carbaugh, 1988b). More specifically, in this chapter I want to examine the specific social scene of the "talk show." Within this public scene, how do particular symbols of identity—of gender and personhood—get expressed? We will find that each creatively implicates the other through a vacillating communication form. Such a form, once understood, provides one way of understanding how multiple levels of identification can be active in a single cultural scene like the talk show.

Exploring social interactions and the social identities immanent in them can help us understand how different levels of identification are being conversed. For example, in chapter 3, workers symbolically identified on some occasions with a particular type of worker (e.g., as a "shaker and mover" or "paper mover") and, on others, with "everyone" in the station. Different levels of identification were active in an institutional scene. In this chapter I explore a similar theme: how symbols of gender differences are being played against an identity that is presumably common to all. In particular, I explore how the social identifications of "male" and "female" are played against a common identification of persons as "individuals." The communication practices of this scene demonstrate a rather robust play between these symbols through a vacillating form of identity talk.

THE AMERICAN TALK SHOW SCENE

The idea of a talk show, if not exclusively American, has been cultivated in a distinctively American way for at least three decades. The current plethora of offerings in this televised genre is truly mind-boggling. Part of the intrigue, I think, is that these programs showcase the audience and are thus built, largely, upon the performance of audience members. In the 1960s, the first popular show in the genre, *Donahue*, seized the day by placing a segment of the audience typically deemed unworthy of airtime (i.e., housewives and the unemployed who were home watching at 9:00 A.M.), right in front of the television cameras, and thus gave them the opportunity to speak to the issue of the day. While the topics being addressed over the years have changed, one fact has not: Whatever topic is addressed—from foreign policy to male born-again go-go dancers—it is the audience reaction to the topic as much as it is the topic itself, or the guests, that makes the talk show what it is.

Without this audience participation, without this display of the folk's "sayings," there would be no talk show as it has come to be known in America today.

This wide-scale display of participation in televised talk, and its captivation of a huge public, has cultivated certain ideational systems. Chief among these are the particular *beliefs being demonstrated about public discourse itself.* Put differently, the "talk" that is being "shown," that particular discursive formation, has itself assumed a public life of its own. Within this formation, it has become rather common for people to stand before millions and freely speak their minds (or "share their feelings"), for others to grant them the "right" to do this, and for many to believe that this is something important to do (to "talk it out"). That this is a rather recent accomplishment, that this is the particular workings of a particular American culture, and further that this form of televised conduct displays particular beliefs and values about public discourse itself (and proper uses of television), all of this warrants our vigilant attention (Carbaugh, 1988b).

In the process of "showing" on television this kind of "talk," and through the participation of the common folk in it, the talk show has also cultivated certain cultural *beliefs about the person.* One part of these beliefs about the person is sometimes evident in this talk, and can be put in this way: As one believes that "speaking up"—or "speaking out"—is important and valued, one also believes that being one who so speaks is important and valued. As earlier studies have shown, implicated in this televised discourse is a basic theme: One should "share feelings" and "be honest" in public, and these acts of "sharing" and "being honest" should accentuate the seemingly endless flaws of "society" (or its institutions or corporations) (Carbaugh, 1988/1989).

GENDERED DISCOURSE, AS AMERICANS

Within this televised game of talk is an occasional Burkean drama. Its dialectical forces play between a common identification and its separation into genders. The resulting communication tacks back and forth between a union among separates (as "individuals") and a separation of this union (into "men" and "women"). If we know who we are, in part, by the way we symbolize in social scenes, what does this social scene, and this play between these symbols, reveal about the communication of social identities in America today?

"Males," "Females" and "the Individual":
Translating between Gender and a Common Humanity

Consider the following social interactions. The first involves responses to a question about whether women in the United States should be permitted, or required, to engage in combat duty while performing military service. Speakers A and B are audience members. Speaker C is a feminist author. D is the president of the National Organization of Women. All are females.

Extract 1 (From Carbaugh, 1988b, p. 22)

1. A: Nobody wants to do it [combat duty] but by the same
2. token I think that a woman ain't made to do some of
3. the things a man can do.
4. Audience: I agree . . .
5. B: Some women are actually-
6. C: some women are stronger than
7. men.
8. B: That's true.
9. Audience: (Applause)
10. D: Some individuals are stronger than some individuals.

A second example arose after a discussion in which a few women with working-class, unemployed "husbands" implicitly blamed "the feminists" for crowding others, especially unemployed men, out of the job market. E is an audience member who described her situation to F, a panelist and female director of the Democratic National Committee. G is the male host of the program, Phil Donahue.

Extract 2 (Carbaugh, 1988b, p. 23)

11. E: Three years unemployed. No compensation, no nothin'.
12. F: That's what's happening throughout this country.
13. Especially in the industrial heartland. And it's
14. what's happening to families like yours. It is
15. happening to men and women. You and I are not opposed
16. to each other, we are not on different sides. We are
17. on the same side of individuals who are trying to
18. make it.

. . .

19. G: If a man and a woman are both out of work and there
20.   is one job opening and they are both equally
21.   qualified, who should get it?
22. Audience: The man. (Applause)

These interactions pose and respond to a fundamental question: How shall participants be characterized with regard to present issues? More specifically, through what terms shall agents be described as the topics of military duty and unemployment are discussed?

Note first the two levels of identity that are being proposed here. One involves speaking about "men" and "women" as the principal agents in the action (see lines 2-3, 5-7, 15, 19, 22). In both extracts, this motivates a response, with the term, "individuals" (see lines 10, 17). Social positions are being explicated here as terms of different genders (*men* and *women*) are played against another term of commonality (the *individual*).[1] The symbolic play between these familiar levels of identification occurs within what I will call a "general vacillating cultural form." The interactional process moves in a "back-and-forth," spiraling sequence, tacking between different gender identities and a common identity, with each identity (i.e., as gendered or "an individual") partly motivating talk about the other. Through this form, identities are being expressed, and played, one with the other.

Note further that by casting the scene with either agent, speakers risk (being heard as) neglecting the other. This can lead, on one hand, to proposals, acknowledgements, promotions, and so on, of gender difference, thus overlooking the commonality of "individuals." Likewise, by characterizing agents as "individuals," speakers can orient to this commonality, thereby promoting it, and thus risk (being heard as) overlooking the gendered differences.

If we listen a bit more closely to the meanings of the gendered agents developed in these segments, we find each is being built on specific premises of difference. For example, in lines 1–3 about combat duty, explicated is a gender-based, biological difference in physical capacity: "Women ain't made to do some of the things a man can do." This statement about gender differences in physical capacity is used to justify differences in moral positions (for men and women) and in institutional duties (as soldiers in the military). Similarly, in extract 2, regarding unemployment, the "unemployed" are being characterized as "men" and "husbands," leading in line 22 to applause. With their applause, some affirmed the belief that "the man" deserved the job (presumably because he is the primary wage earner in the family). This version of the gender difference (re)created a sense of man as physically stronger and primary wage earner, and thus implicated for woman, through this talk, a position that is either physically weaker and/or something other than a primary wage earner. This interactional process brings rather close to the surface a domain of institutional and family life with man's moral place being measured economically and woman's being measured relationally (as wife and emotional supporter of the unemployed husband).

In these segments, each gender is (talked as) distinctive (e.g., men being men and women being women). The distinction between genders is being based upon differing capacities (e.g., physically) and differing institutional responsibilities (e.g., in the military and family). Spoken this way, distinctive identities for man and woman are being created, as similar others are being symbolically derived from these (e.g., as soldier, wife, husband), in these human scenes and institutions. Cast this way, the scene implicates through a culturescape a conversationally based and historically grounded system, a way of speaking about gendered identities, human relations, and institutions.

This discourse of difference, like so many others concerning race, class, and so on, amplifies the sounds of social division (along gender lines) and divisiveness (e.g., disagreements over the nature, value, and application of this gendered discourse). For example, the gendered answer (line 22) to Donahue's question (lines 19–21), while applauded or ratified by many, was not unanimously endorsed. Presumably, others thought "the woman" should receive the job, or decisions should be based on gender-neutral merit. Similarly, lines 5–7 show how one belief of difference was co-constructed by an audience member and a feminist author: "some women are actually . . . stronger than men." The discourse of difference was exhausting to some because it not only cast participants through a basic (di)vision of social life (i.e., by drawing distinctions between men and women), it also created social reactions that were somewhat divisive (see, e.g., lines 4, 8). In other words, *as this discourse explicated gender differences, it implicated differences of opinion about that very difference, about how it should be conceived, and when it should be discussed.* Note how this difference of opinion, while an outcome of producing gendered discourse, is not necessarily a difference of opinion between men and women, but a difference in how the gendered discourse itself should be conceived, used, and evaluated.

These "sounds of difference" eventually ignited the other "pull" or pole of the vacillating form, a symbolic shift in talk that led to identifying people together, as "individuals." As a reaction to "difference," this counter-site of identity gave voice to a mediating, grandly inclusive model of the agent. For example, after the challenge on lines 5–8, the president of the National Organization of Women (NOW) said: "Some individuals are stronger than some individuals." Similarly, on lines 16–18, the female director of the Democratic National Committee (DNC) said: "We are on the same side of individuals who are trying to make it." In both of these examples, the language shifts the locus of agentive action from a gendered position to another that does not deny nor does it elaborate gender, but repositions the debate onto a different plane of identification, to a more inclusive cultural space, where all are deemed "individuals."

The language the director of the DNC uses is particularly interesting in this regard because it artfully builds a common "identificational space" (see lines 12–18). She prepares this position artfully through inclusive and centralizing geographic terms ("this country" and "the industrial heartland"), familial images ("families like yours"), conjunctive phrasing ("men and women"), explicit negations of difference ("not opposed to each other," "not on different sides"), pronominal shifting (from "you and I" to "we"), with the eventual "we" as "individuals" (line 16) functioning as a potently inclusive anaphoric reference that entitles all of the above-quoted phrases.

The explicating of persons as "we-individuals" thus carries an arbitral tone through the assertion of an alleged (and perhaps unquestionable here?) universalizing cultural premise: Each person, and all people (men and women, blacks and whites, rich and poor, and so on) are, at base, "individuals." Elsewhere I have referred to this potent symbol and premise as part of a political code because it derives prominently from the United States Constitution. Part of its creative force is as an "equivocal affirmative." Why? Because its use at once affirms, or asserts, something that is both radically distinctive to each person (as a uniquely particular individual or "self") and something that is universal to all persons (as an organismic embodiment of humankind). In an "individual" breath, these dual beliefs—about the distinctive humanness of each and the common humanity for all—are given voice (Carbaugh, 1988b, 21–39ff). These beliefs are elaborated through statements such as (with the words in quotation marks being explicated cultural terms): "We-individuals" as citizens in "this country" are "not opposed to each other" but are "on the same side." Statements such as this implicate cultural beliefs about person and its associated political institutions (e.g., the United States Constitution and the Bill of Rights). They also potently foreground, if equivocally, commonalities *and* differences in the legal, moral, and existential capacities of people (as "individuals"). The movement between gender terms and "the individual" is thus not a mere shift of words. It is a significant shifting in the cultural means of identification, from one plane onto another. The shift—(from a gendered social identity)—to the uniting symbol foregrounds, so it is believed, both the unique person (the individual) and the common identity of a common humanity (as individuals). This is a potently political and popularly American agent.[2]

Note a related consequence of the "individual" symbol. Because of its potent, equivocal affirmation of an "only one" (self) and an "everyone" (we-individuals), discourse of social-group difference is relatively difficult to sustain here in the televised format. Explications of identities that build images of difference based upon gender or ethnicity or class or social groupings, rather than those based upon commonality (or an everyone-or-only-one kind of talk), seem eventually to succumb to this "inclusive" language. In lines 11–18, domestic discourses of difference from unemployed family members got quickly talked over and supplanted by an other which was more "inclusive" and more broadly politically based. American public discourse, political language, consumerism, and some parts of television, being in a sense numbers driven—here's a little something for everyone—can easily assume this inclusive political identity as a common denominator, and thus mute, or quickly refract some of the more particular group-based discourses of difference (cf. Morgan, 1989; Scollon and Scollon, 1981).

The "individual" Has a "self":
From Relational Constraints to Independence

At times, some Americans hear role identities such as "being a nun" or "a wife" or "a husband" as containing unwanted constraints or impediments. When this is so, they can invoke a language of "self" liberation, and in so doing, reignite the vacillating form of identificational discourse. One aspect of the liberating discourse invokes the one cultural premise stated above: Each person is an individual with a uniquely particular "self." This is elaborated with cultural terms of *needs, feelings, thoughts,* and the closely associated terms of *rights* and *choices.* Uses of these terms and their meanings position participants as autonomous, uniquely independent sites of personal reflectiveness. What is deemed worthy of elaborate expression, from the vantage point of this discursive practice, premise and symbol system, is the highly particular, idiosyncratically distinct, world of the one (Carbaugh, 1988b, 41–86ff).

Consider the following story told by a nun about the effects of an "anger clinic" that she attended:

Extract 3: (Carbaugh, 1988b, p. 69–70)

23. Nun: Before that [the clinic] I was a people pleaser. I
24. grew up being a people pleaser. I'm fourth in the family
25. and that made a lot of difference. The only way I could
26. get along is really by pleasing my parents all the time.
27. I learned I don't have to please anybody else, I can
28. please my self. And once I became really convinced I can
29. please my self, I don't have to do what you're telling
30. me, then I became free and I was able to tell them
31. "hey, I don't want to do that!"

. . .

32. Donahue: Thanks a lot sister . . .
33. Audience: (Applause)

In lines 23–26, the nun is narrating a phase of life in which she positions herself solely within a relationship in which her primary task was to work for others, as both a "people pleaser" and "fourth in the family." So positioned, relational duties to others overshadowed senses of her self. In lines 27–29, she repositions her story through the term *self* as a way of expressing her newly acquired agentive standing. Now, she is one who is not solely in a constraining relation (as a "people pleaser"), but a "self" who is "free" from such constraint. Further, she is able to assert that this is so (line 31).

Stories such as this one again show a vacillating form of talk about social identities. Yet here, the movement is not explicitly from positions of gender difference to commonality, as above (although there are similarities), but from an explicit, constraining relatedness to an extricable, uniquely independent site of reflectiveness and expressiveness. The nun's story tells us why she went to an anger clinic: to learn to extricate her being from obligatory constraints and thus to discover her self. Stories of liberation, like this one, not without deep structural links to the *Odyssey*, the civil rights' and women's movements, and America's story of origin, demonstrate an identificational voyage. The drama charts movement from an identity caught up in an imperfect (Old World?), historical system of constraining relations, to a new territory in which one's uniqueness and independence is discoverable, discovered, and validated.

Yet, of what does this newer position consist? Consider the following metaphorical utterances (each in fact was made, but not within the following sequence).

Extract 4: (Carbaugh, 1988b, p. 79)

34. I filled myself up with drugs.
35. To be angry with a stranger or someone who only knows
36.   you a little bit is to reveal a piece of your self
37.   that you don't want that other person to see.
38. Now that I have a part-time job, I feel much more secure
39.   within myself.
40. The problem is that we never really learn who we are
41.   before we give ourselves away to somebody in marriage.

As is demonstrated here, the resources of "self" are *material* (the body, its parts, and what they contain, e.g., "drugs"), *symbolic* (e.g., information "revealed," feelings of "security"), or both material *and* symbolic (e.g., something "given" to another "in marriage"). From this position, all such resources (including one's physical capacities, thoughts, feelings, consciousness) are conceived as within a contained body, with a necessary and deeper awareness of these resources being a "right" of, and thus a popular motive for the journey of "self" (Carbaugh, 1988b, 77–84).

This particular drama, and these metaphorical utterances, show how the vacillating discursive form involves a play between a relationally constrained person (social deixis) and an independent self (personal deixis). Within this cultural form, the social task of "self" becomes the shaping of a uniquely extricable oneness, thus separating that identity from the harmful (gender?) constraints of the present and past.

The "self" Further Vilifies "social roles" and "society": Renouncing (Gender) Role Restraints

As "self" becomes celebrated in discourse, it runs rather uneasily into larger social arrangements that are also said to be unduly restraining. These are identified variously as "social roles," "society," "history," or "this country." Consider the following utterance, made by a woman during a discussion of gender roles:

> Extract 5: (Carbaugh, 1988b, p. 100)
>
> 42. While we're talking about men and women, if people would
> 43. just concentrate on themselves, and their goals, and
> 44. being individuals. Society says that you have to earn
> 45. money to be of any value. I feel that that's very
> 46. ingrained in men right now. That is what women are
> 47. fighting. I feel that I am fighting that right now
> 48. myself.

The form of this utterance is agonistic, or polemical; it plays two typical symbols of identity, one against the other, while preferring the one over the other. In particular, the playing goes this way: the terms "men" and "women" (42, 46) and "society" (44) identify historically grounded, socially differentiated, institutionally bounded notions of being; so identified, one's place is said to be duty-ridden, creating a sense of one's actions as enslaving, as a "have to" (44); this is deemed a cultural rut, or "ingrained" (46); and because these identities can be duty-ridden and enslaving, they must be fought (47). The position fought for requires "concentration" on "self" (43, 48), and "being individuals" (44).

Analogous examples of restraining identities can include "husband" or "wife" or any such term that implicates duties to another, or "worker" and "soldier" or any such term that implicates institutional ("stereotypical") constraints on one's actions. The nun's comments in extract 3 are partly constructed in this way as the roles of "child" and "people pleaser" are renounced because they hampered her "self." Extracts 1 and 2 likewise show how the more constraining positions of "man"/"woman" are played against the freer "individual."

Each of these are examples of how this form of identity talk vacillates between renouncing and celebrating identities. Each also is an instance of a larger meaning of the form. The cultural logic of this larger meaning could be put this way: Because "social roles," "this country," and "society," as cultural terms, largely constrain "self," they must be vilified and renounced. This motivates identification with the "free self." As the discursive form plays these identities against each other, it can renounce both smaller and larger sites of role restraint—from "men" and "women" to "this society"—and thus motivate the more liberating senses of "self" (Carbaugh, 1988b, 87–107ff; 1988/1989). In American folk terms, "if we could just be ourselves, and stop listening to society, we all would be better off." Or, so they say in some American scenes.[3]

CODING DIGNITY OVER HONOR

The particular symbols and premises of identity that are played within this vacillating form can be summarized as a coding of dignity (Carbaugh, 1988b; Philipsen, 1992). Through this communication code, the person, as an "individual" with a "self," is being celebrated. Treating these features as deeply coded is an effort to cast more generally clusters of belief (in existence and value) and the morals that are associated with those clusters in this kind of discursive action. Following the prior work of Philipsen (1992) and others, I call the code a "code of dignity" (see Berger, Berger, and Kellner, 1973).

One cluster of values captures an indigenous conception of the person. I refer to it as an *ontological dimension* of the code. The beliefs (and norms) of this cluster are: (1) Each person has (and should be recognized as having) *intrinsic worth*. One should recognize and support individuals as holding some socially redeemable value, even if this is difficult at first to notice. (2) Each person is (or should be) *self-aware*, or personally reflective. One should strive to know who one is and is not; to know what one can and cannot do; to know one's necessities, values, morals, abilities, capacities, and limits, independent of, as well as within, one's typical roles. (3) Each person is (and should be) *unique*. One should know how one's necessities, values, abilities, and capacities differ from others. And finally, linking to the pragmatic values, (4) each person should strive to be *sincere*, or authentic, or honest. One should be forthcoming and expressive about one's self, so one's outer actions coalesce with one's inner thoughts and feelings.

The above cluster about the person is associated with and overlaps another. This other cluster adds a more *pragmatic dimension* to the code, and thus refers to valued means of relating the person, so conceived, with others: (1) The basic social principle for action is *equality*. Conditions for action include the person's inalienable rights to being and acting, and should include (equal) opportunities for making "choices." (2) Favored actions that implement this basic principle include *cooperative negotiation* (saying who one is and what one strives toward, ably hearing who another is and what they strive toward, and conducting mediating action with both in view); *validation of personal differences* (acknowledging through cooperative conduct the unique qualities of each person); and *flexibility* (being willing to change one's sense of oneself, one's relationship with others, one's habits of action, and so on [i.e., "to grow"], as a result of cooperative conduct). (3) Evaluations of actions, if necessary, should be conducted on the basis of standardized criteria (and be applied to each equally).

In the above televised extracts, all of these values for persons and pragmatic action are active. Note however what motivates this coding of the person. What precipitates a coding in terms of dignity are discourses in which different, often stratified identities are being discursively explicated or implicated (e.g., with symbols of gender, family, the military, ethnicity, race, education). These alternate social identities bring into discourse a coding based not upon personal uniqueness but upon institutional and historical precedence, a positioning consisting of such dynamics as difference and hierarchy. These have been identified by Philipsen (1992) as elements in an alternate code of *honor*. This code carries an attendant emphasis on political connections, historical precedence, magnanimity, loyalty, and piety. From the vantage point of a code of dignity, these meanings of honor are often heard as relationally constraining or stereotypically obliged. Such a hearing can motivate expressions in terms of the code of dignity. This is nicely exemplified above as some women, through a version of the honor code, discussed "unemployed" men and the "man's" need of a job to support "the family." This discourse was countered through terms of the dignity code that emphasized equal standings, thus muting the gendered and familial scene the "wives" sought to describe. Thus the vacillating form in use here suggests not only a play between genders and a generic "individual" but a play between deeply different codes about what person, relations, and pragmatic action are (and should be). Displayed therefore is not just differences in overt social identities, but deeper differences between ways of culturally coding social interaction, persons, and public life itself.

How the Code of Dignity Hides Its Cultural Features and Forms

There is an irony built into the discourse of dignity. It consists in this general dynamic: As individualized meanings are being voiced, the cultural forms and moral imperatives necessary for the creation of those very meanings are being silenced. Put differently, discursively coding the person in terms of dignity amplifies meanings of individual and self, while muting the common cultural features that make those very meanings possible (Carbaugh, 1988b, 28–33, 57–59, 84–86, 109–112ff; 1988/1989).

For each discursive feature of the code of dignity discussed above, for each symbol, form, and premise, we can formulate a statement that must be practically necessary for the discursive action to take the shape it does. For each, the meaning the form promotes (i.e., individualized persons and actions) silences the form of those meanings (i.e., collectivized persons and actions). Consider the following summary of the ways the coding of dignity works:

1. The cultural construction of individuality.
2. The collective celebration of the unique self.
3. The communal rejection of social roles and societal identities.

For the first two, the common meanings of, for example, individual boundedness and uniqueness hide the vacillating forms of action (the cultural and collective) that are required for their promotion and realization. Similarly, in the third, the overt meanings—of obligation or conformity to a group—are renounced, just as the group conforms in being ones who so obediently renounce. In this way, each feature of the communication code both grants through its cultural contents, yet takes away through its cultural forms, the conditions of its making. Bateson of course reminded us that being agents-in-society is inherently double-binding, and here we have demonstrated in discursive practices just how this is so.

One possible danger of this coding to which I now turn—there are others—is its unreflective application, especially in intercultural contexts. This code is sometimes naively used to assert or to replicate its own presumably universalizing sense, that is, that all people are at base individuals, or constructable as such. This is especially troublesome in multicultural contexts such as some courtrooms and classrooms, where the coding of dignity confronts deeply different others, whose codes for being operate quite differently. Where issues of culture generally, or race and ethnicity specifically, are concerned, one often hears, today, the code of dignity being asserted and reasserted, without reflecting upon the particular cultural beliefs and values that are a condition for its production (e.g., Basso, 1979; Chick, 1990; Scollon and Scollon, 1990).

CODING DIGNITY IN CROSS-CULTURAL PERSPECTIVE: PERSONHOOD AND POLITENESS

Larry Wieder and Steven Pratt (1990) have discussed a psychology classroom in America's heartland that was convened on the topic of race and ethnic relations. The professor of the class had asked the students to get together in groups to discuss their own cultural heritages. For students tutored in the code of dignity, this presented no problem. One's unique background could be put into a disclosive form of action, thus positioning that person as an able discussant. For others, especially for some Native (Osage) people, this was not permissible. To position as an Osage first of all required a relational assessment of the situation, leading to a culturally salient condition for them: Being with tribal members previously unknown to them. If Osage wanted to display the Native "Indian" identity under this condition, they must orient to their cultural rule of modesty: Do not sound more knowledgeable than other tribal members, especially when discussing matters of the tribe's heritage. Under this condition, the most knowledgeable Osage produced appropriately vacuous comments about their cultural heritage, saying things like, "I don't know, what do you think?" Ironically, such statements explicated (but implicated much more deeply) to present Osage true membership in the tribe. Those Osage voluble on the topic performed, in effect, nonmembership as a Native (although at the same time aligned themselves with the position being presupposed and valued by their professor). The complexity in the situation runs deep, as those Natives highly disclosive on the topic displayed, in the special sense introduced above, some position of dignity, while simultaneously dishonoring another of their tribe.

Many other cultural agents and their other-than-dignity codes could be described. These range from conceptions of the person that include transindividual consciousness, as is the case in the Russian *dusa* (soul) (Wierzbicka, 1989; Carbaugh, 1993a, 1993b); dispersable particles and substances, as is the case among some Hindi speakers (Marriott, 1976); as well as others that are astrally projectable (see the reviews in Carbaugh, 1988b, 15–19, 112–119; Shweder and Bourne, 1984). Each such cultural agent, so acted and conceived, provides radically alternate cultural bases for being a person, different axes for social identities, relations, emotions, and actions. Such dynamics run deeply into many discourses and cultural worlds, even into aspects of Western worlds where parasocial identities are at work (Caughey, 1984). There are undoubtedly other general ways of culturally coding agents than the ones of dignity and honor discussed above.

Of special interest with regard to particular intercultural dynamics are differences in what constitutes "face" among these various peoples, especially the nature and value of likeness or difference among such cultural "faces." Ronald and Suzanne Scollon (1981), building on politeness theory (Brown and Levinson, 1978), have described how Athapaskans prefer positioning with cultural others on the basis of deference (thus asserting and assuming difference), while Anglos position with cultural others on the basis of solidarity (thus asserting and assuming similarity). They note how assertions of solidarity hold a kind of logical and often cultural power over others, as when the code of dignity presumes a common humanity for all (e.g., as basically individuals who can and should speak their mind). Coding persons and actions this way can lead easily to supplanting others' faces, those for whom real differences are presumed and preferred (see also Chick, 1990). The extent to which oral and literate discourse positions persons with culturally distinctive faces, and the extent to which the coding of dignity supplants others, perhaps even in academic theories (see Barnlund, 1979), in face-to-face interaction (Liberman, 1990), and upon mediated occasions (Carbaugh, 1993b) needs to be understood. Each such discourse activates particular cultural conditions of identification and social identities, largely through the vacillating form. How this gets played into particular scenes warrants our serious attention (see Brown and

Levinson, 1987, pp. 13–15). We can and must better understand the cultural pragmatics that are at play between and among peoples, genders, and ethnicities, for such dynamics, like those in the New European Community, increasingly animate the stages of our multicultural world.

CHAPTER 8

Cultural Agents, Social Identities, and Positioning: A Theoretical Interlude

Discourses of identity, as introduced in chapter 1 and noted throughout, can be explored by distinguishing the interrelated concerns of cultural identity and social identity. Where the concept of "cultural agent" highlights basic codes about being that are held in common across social scenes, "social identity" highlights the variety of selves enacted through those codes. In other words, some sense of cultural coherence about agent and agency is active (e.g., person as a psycho-organic container, or person as shared planes of subatomic energy) when various social identities are being effectively enacted (e.g., as a gendered organism, or as a gendered plane of energy).

Building upon earlier work (Carbaugh, 1988b; Harris, 1989), I use the concepts "cultural identity" and "social identity" to explore how agents-in-society are constituted in communicative practices. Based on ethnographic evidence, I presume that every communication system makes available agent positions that can be understood on these two distinctive but nonexclusive levels: (1) the cultural bases of personhood (e.g., Hymes, 1961, p. 335; Geertz, 1976, p. 225); and (2) a system of social identities that elaborates this basic cultural notion(s). When communicating in a scene, participants can be heard to invoke some features of their cultural and social selves, with each being positioned relative to the other (this was demonstrated in the previous chapter, as well as in chapters 2, 3, 4, and 5). This suggests the following: For the construction of cultural identity and its various social kinds there are various means and meanings of communication available, with each being distinctive in its rituals of entry, performance, evaluation, and departure. In the United States, for example, if one performs "being a mother" or "a wife," one symbolizes a distinctive social identity. Moreover, when one acts as such, one has symbolically implicated a system of social practices, relations, and properties. Doing "mother," in other words, does not just invoke a single social identity, but implicates many (e.g., father, husband, daughter, son, etc.). In so acting, or in being identified as so acting, a terminological system (of persons, relations, actions) is implicated that radiates, in some American scenes, cultural premises of sex, gender, and age status, as well as domains of meanings including the domestic, political, economic, and religious. Attending to the interactional accomplishment of social identities such as this "can show how members of various social kinds are reckoned to have differing agentive capacities and hence to be unlike each other as authors of actions" (Harris, 1989, p. 604). Through analyses of social interaction, the social kinds (if one starts there) may be eventually linked to deeper cultural premises and models, with the latter identifying the communal model(s)—or shared ontology—in which the social kind is sensible and appropriate. Possibly highlighted then are social identities of the person (e.g., as mother, woman, husband, man, student), as well as the cultural notions of what person is, can, and should be (e.g., as an American "individual" or as an East Indian plane of energy). Whether it is intelligible to be on a plane of energy, as some East Indians believe, depends both upon the cultural codes that render such a being commonly meaningful, and the social kinds for whom such a being is accessible and performable.

The communication of personhood and social identities, then, invites questions about a system of communication practices, tacking among social kinds and cultural notions, with elements of each being played with, or against the other(s). Exploring agents-in-scenes may help unveil how social kinds and cultural codes of being get interactively expressed and related. And further, through comparative study, the cultural distinctiveness and cross-cultural generalities for conceiving, evaluating, and acting personhood may be suggested (e.g., see Carbaugh, 1988b; Fitch, 1991; Philipsen, 1992).

POSITIONING:
THE PERSON AS COMMUNICATIVE PRACTICE

Communicative practices provide the primary resources through which agents-in-scenes can be identified. Through situated practices, participants make available particular—identificational—positions for each other to take up and address (and with which to hear others taking up and addressing) (see Hollway, 1984; Davies and Harré, 1990; Harré and Van Langenhove, 1991; Tannen, 1990). Such activity demonstrates the various interactional ways in which cultural and social identities are interactionally (de)legitimated. Through such activities there is an intricate and ever-present social playing of identities, each with its moral messages of rights and duties, from unquestioned cultural beliefs about "person" generally to the interactional accomplishment of the more specific social kinds. In short, each discursive practice simultaneously *positions*, within sociocultural discourses, its producer as well as the recipients of those messages (see Bakhtin, 1986, pp. 95–100). The focus on the communicative practice of *positioning* helps draw attention to these interactive dynamics.

Positioning occurs through communicative practices within scenes, and thus can vary systematically by context, participants, and occasions, with each symbolic scene locating and relating persons in particular ways (Bahktin, 1986; Hymes, 1972; Levinson, 1989). Conceived ethnographically, positioning occurs also in the culturescape of a community, with the ethnographer being as mindful as possible of the material, economic, religious, political (and so on) conditions of living in that community.

Persons as Variously Located with various Qualities

What is the nature of the positions being interactionally foregrounded and muted, or elided? The primary location (or place) of person positions varies by cultural scene and communicative practice. Some general locations of agentive activity, however, can be usefully identified. Each at different times becomes pivotal in positioning activity. A fundamental site of positioning activity determines, within an interaction, whether persons are deemed *present* or not, and are *addressed* as (if) present or not. If focusing on those deemed present, interaction can make a speaker, addressee, or audience the focal participant(s). If focusing on the nonpresent, these can be addressed *as if* present, or not. Regarding more specific qualities, person positions can be conceived from *material* to *immaterial*, *passive* to *active*, and so on.

The complexity of sites of positioning activity can be illustrated with an example. One might discuss a mutual friend ("Steve is a superb rock climber") thus identifying a nonpresent, material other and attributing qualities to him. In so doing, one also implicates something about oneself as a present speaker (one who would evaluate and compliment). Moreover, one is also positioning the present recipient of one's message (one allegedly interested in Steve and/or rock climbing and/or speaker's evaluation). As a second example, consider the Witches (men and women) of Salem, Massachusetts, who sometimes address "gnomes," "fairies," and other nonmaterial yet discursively "present" agents. In such discourse, an agent in a scene is being addressed, in an immediate present, although this agent is not a material presence (Mahoney, 1994). Such examples make apparent the need for discerning whether agents-in-scenes are physically present or not, the focus of interaction or not, material or not, and so on.

Further distinctions may be required to distinguish among agents, be they a site of consciousness and/or an individual member of an organic kind, a point to which I return below. For example, various forms of ancestor worship, and ancestral voices, demonstrate how the status of a valued agent-in-scene can be a site of consciousness, but need not necessarily coincide with a material presence, nor even a site of human consciousness (e.g., cows in India, alligators in Tallensi, an unconscious person, the "brain dead," etc.). While more could be retrieved from the examples (speakers' claims to moral positions, and so on), these serve to illustrate various locations and qualities of agents in the communicative practices of particular cultural scenes (see also Levinson, 1989, esp. 168–174).

Conversational Moves and Further Dimensions of Agentive Action

As discussed in previous chapters, identities are interactionally managed through various moves and dimensions of discourse. Sometimes a social identity is explicitly claimed ("I'm a basketball fan," or "I'm a shaker and mover"), a basic first order action that could be called an *explication*. This conversational "move" involves an explicit *avowal* of a speaker to being a particular kind of person. A basic move can also be in the form of a verbal *attribution* of an identity or quality to an other (e.g., "Keith is a paper mover"). Each explication of an identity, moreover, implicates others. To avow one (e.g., as mother) is to implicate another for one's recipients (e.g., as sons). To attribute a position to another (e.g., as excellent teacher) is to implicate others for self as utterer of that message (e.g., as gracious supplicant). Thus, much positioning work is done more subtly, through intonation and other means of inviting inferences about the identities of one or an other (see Gumperz, 1982). For this dimension of action, one could discuss the *implications* of identities, relations, actions, and feelings. If one explicitly takes up one position, one thus implies things about it, and about ways of being, acting, and relating with another. In a sense, to borrow Goodwin's (1990) descriptive term, there are "shadows" of identities being cast in all discursive practices. The implications are often very richly textured, especially as people metacommunicate, and thus convey messages about agents, social relations, institutions, and the nature of the social activity itself (Carbaugh, 1989a, in press).

Extensive explications or implications of particular social identities can be referred to as *elaborations*. This is simply a way to describe how a particular bid for agentive standing is developed sequentially, over time, and is perhaps being socially negotiated (explicitly or implicitly).

As further claims are being made about identities and how they are related, the moral grounding for each is (re)established or shaken. For example, a particular social identity may be explicitly avowed by one, or attributed to another, with further interaction negotiating the validity of this identity. For example, one might agree with another's attribution, saying, "My, yes, I agree, she is a remarkable scholar." As a result, we can hear, in the subsequent validation, the *social ratification* of a person as such an agent. If, on the other hand, a particular identity is avowed, or attributed, and subsequent talk (and symbolic action) ignores that position for that participant, or explicitly denies it (e.g., "That's not the way a professor acts"), we can claim the momentary *rejection* of that person as such an agent. Rejections then further implicate, through subsequent talk and inference, other possible identities for the one being so positioned.

ISSUES OF VOICE

Discussing various conversational moves and dimensions of agentive action can help us make various claims about the communication of identity. For example, it can help us hear how some social positions are explicated, immaterial, and socially ratified, such as in some seances. It can help us understand how others are being implicated, present, and denied, such as the blue-collar women in the previous chapter when they discussed unemployment. On occasions when a speaker explicates (or implicates) and elaborates an identity, and if further interaction ratifies that speaker as such, we could claim the speaker indeed had a socially efficacious *voice*. That is, the speaker was able to speak, spoke, was heard, and was socially validated as such. All conditions would be necessary for the constitution of voice. On the other hand, as one explicates (or implicates) and elaborates a social identity (for one and/or others), and if there is no subsequent uptake or ratification by others of that social identity, or if the identity is explicitly rejected, then one's voice, as such, has been refused, or denied. As a part of this communication process, another identity will be attributed, or implicated. And so goes the communication of identification.

Contested identities are also usefully disentangled as one hears, in contested communication practices, how each position is being explicated, implicated, elaborated, and/or evaluated (ratified or rejected). Current environmental debates, as the one discussed in the following chapters, provide a rich location for such · studies. "Developers" and "environmentalists" often elaborate one position while rejecting the other, with particular motives and meanings alternating between these agents-in-scenes.

The dimensions also can help unravel contradictory conversational messages. For example, speaker can explicate one social position while implicating a counter-other. During a recent gathering of academics at Oxford, where status games run deep, one participant said, with somewhat of a delightful irony: "I like to be modest about all of the things I've done. When I go places to speak, it annoys me when they introduce me by referring to . . . " and then listed several prominent accomplishments. The dimensions help unravel some of the complexity by pointing to an asynchrony between the identity of the speaker being explicitly avowed (e.g., a self-professed preference for modesty, a propensity for understatement) and the one being elaborated through the avowal (e.g., one somewhat vain, filled with pride by listing accomplishments). An ironic position is created which explicates modesty while elaborating pride. Similar dynamics occur in communication systems generally, as in some prominent scenes of American culture, where individuality is explicated while collectivity is implicated (see chapter 7), or in the work scene when workers explicate themes of unity, yet elaborately implicate dramatic differences among social positions (see chapters 3 and 4).

DIMENSIONS OF SOCIAL RELATIONS: RESOURCES, POWER, INTIMACY, SOLIDARITY

As agents are discursively located and interactionally negotiated, fundamental dimensions of social relations are being activated. These often involve symbolic messages about valued resources, including both *material* (e.g., economic) and *symbolic* (e.g., knowledge) currencies. Whether and how these are distributed, and discoursed, leads to various social relations from *equal* (i.e., the equitable distribution of resources) to *unequal* (i.e., the resource endowed and the resource deprived). Assessments about the design and distribution of resources may be invoked through social interaction as various identities and their differences—for example, in rights and duties—are conceived and socially arranged. A third general dimension of assessment, sometimes coterminous with the first two, involves the degree to which identities are construed as *close*, psychologically intimate, or more *distant*.

When the equal-unequal dimension is highlighted in discourse, the distribution of resources, relations of power, and issues of control get expressed. When the close-distant dimension is highlighted in discourse, relations of intimacy (high degree of closeness) or solidarity (relatively high distance, yet equal) get expressed. Taken together, all combinations are interactionally possible, though not always salient, such as relations of equality and closeness (e.g., some forms of spousal discourse), equality and distance (e.g., fan solidarity), inequality and closeness (e.g., workers as "everyone"; parent-child), and inequality and distance (e.g., "the movers" and "the secure"; or the CEO and the assembly line worker). Through communication practices not only social identities, capacities, and qualities are being expressed, but social relations and institutions as well.

POSITIONING AND INSTITUTIONS

On the relationship between identificational practices (or "lines") and institutions, Goffman (1967, p. 7) wrote: "The line maintained by and for a person during contact with others tends to be of a legitimate institutionalized kind." As Sapir (1931) noted early on, society's institutions, like social selves, are constantly being reactivated in the ongoing, everyday interactions among people. Elsewhere, I have proposed a communication orientation to the idea of "institution." This "implies a complex theoretical claim: that particular symbols, forms, and meanings are operative, that these are justifiable through a normative rule system, that this system of justification, or legitimation, solidifies certain social positions or identities for participants, and certain relations among participants, and that this configuration is robust socially, relatively durable, and stable" (Carbaugh, in press). Institutional communication—like that described in chapters 3 and 4—tends to solidify social identities and relations into justifiable practices.

POSITIONING, CONSCIOUSNESS, AND EMBODIMENT

Throughout the above discussion I have used the concepts of personhood and cultural agent rather interchangeably. I have attempted not to become too committed to either one. My purpose has been to suggest various cultural codes of the agent, from those humanly embodied (a more familiar sense of personhood) to others that are not *necessarily* embodied in human organisms at all (other cultural agents). As mentioned, examples of the latter include sacred crocodiles among the Tallensi that are considered to be persons because they "combine the human spiritual aspects with a living body" (La Fontaine, 1985, 127); the witch's "fairies" mentioned earlier that are not necessarily embodied; or still others for whom a human body is insufficient for granting the status of "person," although still implicating some agent (La Fontaine, 1985, 131). Some of these notions risk sounding rather fanciful or farcical because they challenge deeply held, cultural models of "person" in which the human body contains the site of conscious activity. This belief, that the body contains consciousness, is a strong and pervasive belief about persons and cultural agents, especially among "Western" societies, but it is no less cultural in its form and meaning because of that.[1]

For purposes of reflecting upon cultural agents and social identities, and for better theorizing, we would do well to distinguish the variety of claims being made about identity, and whether these are being assigned (1) to *an agent-in-scene* (to a socially explicated, implicated, and ratified being), (2) to *an ontological place* (to a site of consciousness, awareness, or reflectiveness), and/ or (3) to *an organic entity* (to an organismic entity, an individual member of humankind or some other species). The distinctions are important because they help disentangle the array of cross-cultural data being accumulated about identities and discursive practices. The questions here of course are not whether, for example, a nonorganic consciousness is "real," but whether and to what degree this kind of agent might be coded, explicated, elaborated, and ratified (or renounced) in the communication practices of a cultural scene.

PROSPECTS FOR A CULTURAL PRAGMATIC THEORY OF POSITIONING

The general distinctions introduced here can help cut into the sources of some public disputes that are very lively today, at least in some scenes. For example, many environmental discourses revolve precisely around the cultural status granted certain organic agents such as owls, plants, valleys, animals, and so on. Current U.S. vice-president Albert Gore has been criticized for granting "butterflies" the same status as "people." The issue, so presented, draws attention to the "butterfly" as a cultural agent-in-society, and suggests asking whether, and to what degree, this agent resembles other agents (especially "people") in terms of its social (and legal) standing. If a "California valley" is a "legal person," as a famous court case declared, then what about "owls," "butterflies," and so on. Which organic entities, presumably—for many—those without consciousness, can and should be symbolically ratified as agents?

Environmental debates are notable sites for exploring boundaries of identification. Alternate identities for agents, people, places, animals, plants, and so on, are being suggested and warrant our careful study. With regard to other court cases, the abortion debate rests heavily upon the question of what a "constitutional person" is. What status, if any, does (and should) a "result

of pregnancy"—a rather amorphous organic entity, capable eventually of consciousness, but not yet a full-fledged person—have as
a cultural agent? From the vantage point of legal discourse?
Moral, domestic, political, and religious discourses? What various
positions of agents and persons are being created in this debate?
Of what does each consist? Similarly, what of surrogate parent-
ing? What standing does a woman donor of an egg have regarding
the result of the egg's use? Is she more like a "woman" who gives
birth, or a "man" who donates sperm? Or is there another means
of identification needed? If a "child" is a fully fledged constitutional agent, able to exercise a legal proceeding (e.g., divorce from
its parents), what effect does this have on other institutions such
as the family, school, or law enforcement agencies? On another
front, some feminist discourse rests firmly on the explication and
assertion that female consciousness, or feminine consciousness, is
organically based and inherently transindividual, thus positioning
a kind of biologically based entity (but not necessarily a cultural
agent?) as distinct from a male one.[2] These practical issues and
cultural matters need to be further addressed, especially through
cultural pragmatic studies that relate cultural agents to social
identities and positioning.

    As these ideas are applied to these intriguing scenes, there will
be important theoretical work to do. The concept of positioning
adopted here needs to be further developed (see esp. Levinson,
1989; Harré, forthcoming). From the vantage point of ethnography and cultural pragmatics, I have developed two levels of positioning practice—the social and cultural (see also chapter 11)—
and drawn attention (in chapter 7) to these aspects of the communication process: (1) To the cultural premises, symbols, forms, and
meanings of communication that position persons, and their
sometimes unreflective use, especially in intercultural encounters
that involve an American coding of dignity. (2) To communication
practices in scenes as the site of agent activity, and treating the cultural discourses in those scenes *as if* activating social identities,
and not the other way around. (I shall return to this shortly.) (3)
To the various means of communication (e.g., a vacillating form,
symbols of gender) through which the positioning of identities
gets done. Particularly noteworthy was the way various identities
of persons occur as a response to others. This suggests a general
vacillating form of identification that occurs within a relationally
based, cyclical or spiraling process. Some questions this form sug-

gests are: What is the nature and function of this identificational form in various scenes? To what prior social identity, or cultural agent is this one responding? What does the play between or among these identities produce? (4) The positioning of identity thus consists in a *system* of terms (e.g., pronouns, nouns, conjunctions, etc.), forms, and their meanings, including a consideration of oppositional identities (and their terms, forms, and meanings). Considering one term of identity (e.g., a pronoun, or a noun), therefore, is deemed generally insufficient for locating social identities as agents in conversation. (5) Some positions suggest a code, or a deep structuring of beliefs and values that is immanent in various forms, terms, and meanings.

I mentioned that ethnographic studies of identity can treat communication practices as primary and culturally situated, then ask of it: What positioning of persons is getting done with it? Or, put differently, studies can hypothesize that social and cultural kinds of identities are getting demonstrated in discourse, then collect a corpus to discover if this is indeed the case, and if so, how so, and with what consequences? One begins, then, not by assuming a typology of persons, relations, or actions is present, as something prior to communication practice, but by assuming that activities of positioning indeed take place in communication practice, and then investigating the nature of that activity in those practices. This chapter (and the volume) provides a conceptual framework for such study. It suggests asking: What identities are getting discoursed here? What are their social locations, qualities, processes of ratification (or refusal)? What social relations are being constructed in these activities? The framework suggests ways to pose such problems and a vocabulary with which to address them. Beginning with a situated discourse, and questions about it, helps one construct a communication theory, and a communicative explanation of identity. One therefore does not begin with presumed grids of content to fill, but with parameters of positioning along which to look and listen (see Zeitlyn, 1993). Investigating this way enables one to describe a particular shaping of identity-in-scenes, and eventually to posit a system of cultural expression that accounts for identities being so conceived, and conducted. The resulting argument is: Social identity is immanent in situated, cultural communication practices, and conceptualizing it this way provides one account for social and cultural agents being what they are.

Different types of analyses are suggested with this basic vocabulary. Of special interest in future studies would be the continuing development of the interpretive theory being used here. Its main objective is to interpret communication practices with special attention to messages about persons, actions, emotions, social relations, and institutions (Carbaugh, 1989a, 1990b, in press). Parts of the theory have already been of some value in, for example, discursive studies of self (Harré, 1991a), with cross-cultural studies of the person being further recommended (Varenne, 1990; see also Carbaugh, 1993b, 1993c). Other investigators have used other parts of the theory, and demonstrated some of its considerable promise for understanding students' statements about communicative action (Baxter and Goldsmith, 1990), relations between oral and literate forms of classroom discourse (Gnatek, 1992), an indigenous form of Chinese talk (Garrett, 1993), various ritualized forms of actions in a community of witches (Mahoney, 1994), the speech codes of two cultural communities (Philipsen, 1992), and the discursive bases some Americans use to build a renunciative voice (Scollon, 1992). Of particular interest would be a move-by-move account of explications, implications (avowed and addressed), elaborations, ratifications, rejections, and so on. Thus, what are presented here, in the prior and following chapters, are only a few of the general possibilities.

CONCLUDING REMARKS

It is only appropriate that this chapter conclude with a bit of authorial self-explication. I cannot escape the dynamics I address. I cannot either, nor could anyone, address all of its implications. Yet there are two features of my authored position I want to mention here, feeling they are not yet elaborated quite enough. Each is a voice of criticism that I have discussed in detail elsewhere (Carbaugh, 1990a). One has to do with my discourse as a user and critic of academic theory. In particular, I have attempted to adapt and develop a communication theory that explores social and cultural notions of identity. My main objective has been to integrate a cultural dimension into interactional studies, believing as I do that the socially active *meanings* of social identity, including concerns more macro (e.g., culture, race, ethnicity, politics, economics), are at base at least partly the result of everyday communicative practices. By exploring such concerns this way, we can better grasp how the moment-to-moment living through everyday practices constructs identities for ourselves, others, and relations among us. Yet also, I adopt and advocate the approach and its related others not only for the study of identity and positioning, but indeed for the study of all social and even physical matters, such as studies of time (e.g., Brockmeier, 1992) and natural space (as in the following chapters). Part of my effort has been constructed, then, from an academic position with the development of academic concerns, theories, and methods in mind. Further, I draw attention to my discourse as an exercise in cultural criticism. I deem it essential that popular American discourse includes a reflective ability, an ability to see itself as a cultural artifact, an ability that I have tried here and elsewhere to develop. My tactic has been to select typical everyday discursive practices and describe some of the social identities they interactively produce. I also have tried to loosen their grip on us by discussing some implicit ironies and paradoxes in their use. Thus, my writings are caught in the vacillating movement described earlier, including my reactions to prominent theoretical *and* cultural concerns. My main proposal in these academic and cultural matters has been to conceive of social identities as situated communication practices that creatively implicate, produce, and develop cultural meaning systems. My main butt has been treatments of identity that rely exclusively on immutable psychological or biological endowments (with these being, from the vantage point of my proposal, the result of a potent discursive heritage). People do not everywhere identify in the same way, nor anywhere are they identified the same way in all social scenes. Needless to say, I believe our cultural practices, and our communication theories too, should recognize as much, and move themselves along as well.

SCENE FIVE:
A COMMUNITY'S LAND-USE
CONTROVERSY

CHAPTER 9

Decisions and Conflicting Selves: Dramatic Depictions of a Natural Environment

Mountains are symbols, like pyramids, of man's attempt to know God. Mountains are symbolic meeting places between the mundane and the spiritual world.

—Alan Hovhaness

Decision-making processes are sometimes conceived as individual activities. One popular version of the process goes like this: One reflects upon a current problem, and explores the various options one has available for solving that problem. One weighs the advantages and disadvantages of the alternative options, then selects the most desirable from among them. This process results in a decision. Envisioning the process in this rather cognitive way is perhaps to make this process a property of one's unitary self, a way of presenting and evaluating self's predispositions, a kind of internal dialogue radiating from what Harré (1991a) calls the "self-1." As Harré discusses, though, the resources that one uses in order to engage in this process can be thought of as fundamentally discursive. And further, what is intelligible—what is commonly sensible as a problem and what is coherent as solutions to it—can be thought of as largely cultural. If this is the case, then, responses to the questions "What is a 'social identity' or 'self'?" and "What, if anything, can (or should) one 'say' as such?" derive from the available discourses in one's cultural communities.

I am grateful to the Office of Research Affairs, University of Massachusetts, for a grant which enabled me to do the field work for this project. Also, I thank Gary Briere, Stephen Brown, and Dennis Regan for making various documents available to me. A half-hour video document about the following two chapters is available from the author.

157

The questions posed here are efforts to suggest that what a person (self or social identity) is, what a person can and should do, what a person conceives as actions—all such "things" or processes can be understood as deriving from the particular culturescape of particular communities. That one has a communal heritage, or contests one, or creates with some variety of it, and that it is constituted discursively—this is essential and presumed for the main processes of concern to us in this and the following chapter.

Moving the site of one's thinking about agents-in-scenes from the inside of the person outward suggests that one explore the social and cultural dimensions of this discursive process. With this view, the decisions of agents entail the personal, yet also move beyond the personal to larger interactional matters. This again emphasizes the relocation of thought (and models of identity) into discursive patterns, and moves these from an internal speech—which one also plays—to a communally based, sociopolitical conversation. Processes of decision making, and social identification, writ this way, tie into a complex matrix of social interaction, which is itself a part of cultural conversations.

In the particular case of concern to us here, what is suggested is a complex movement, development, and counterplaying between decisions and social identities, as each bids for social and personal standing within this community's system of action. As a large communal process, the communication involves personal and political interests, institutionalized resources, sacred ancestors, and government intervention, all of which leads eventually to the construction not only of a human sociopolitical scene, but moreover to newer ways of being and living in a natural environment. My hope here is to show the promise of a cultural pragmatic approach to decision making and social identities that can span this broad range of personal and social territory.

DECISION MAKING AS SOCIAL DRAMA

I use the concept of social drama to help organize the variety of discursive and cultural formations activated in the complex decision-making process explored below. The concept derives from Victor Turner (1974, 1980) and largely encompasses Goffman's (1967) idea of ritual disequilibrium. As a whole, it suggests that some processes of decision making, and some conflicts among social identities, begin with some sense of rupture, or a breach, or a violation. This realization ignites, then, a large-scale communicative process in four recognizable phases: (1) The event or incident of a breach or a violation occurs. (2) This is followed by a discourse which publicizes the violation, thus ratifying it socially as a crisis, with various social identities and relations being forged in the process. (3) The crisis is responded to in some ways, with the responses involving various types of remedial discourses as efforts to redress the violating incident(s). (4) The redressive actions may suffice, resulting in some sort of social reintegration, or they may not, thus recycling through violations, creating further social division or schism. For each phase of the form, there is a distinctive rhetoric, style, and mode of discursive action, with the redressive phase being crucially important, for it is in this phase, through cultural communicative forms, that attempts are made to repair the violation and bring contesting factions and interests together. From the vantage point of decision processes, it is here that attempts are made at drawing the competing alternatives and options—that arise during the crisis phase—into a conjoint plan.

The following case of decision making revolves around a land-use controversy. The land-use debates of concern here followed one version of this social dramatic process. Through the use of particular discursive patterns within this larger communicative form, particular configurations of social identities, social actions, motives, and a natural environment were being played into a larger-scale cultural scene. In the process, particular models, or identities of the person, or "selves–2" (to use Harré's [1991a] term), were constructed and subsequently associated with publicly contested actions and motives (see Mills, 1940). The drama thus demonstrates how communicative practices such as these carry great psychological consequences, for as the discourse gets produced, so too do social *personae*, competing motives, and conflicted relations. And further, in this case, the consequences flow in two prominent directions. In one way, the discourses carry inward, as the discursive process subjects persons to bodily anguish, dissonance, and considerable consternation. In another, the discourses are materialized outwardly, as they carry designs for living-with-the-environment, and with each other, through two contesting ways of inhabiting a natural landscape.

The dynamics in this process thus demonstrate a decision making drama, a movement among social selves, between an inner and outer world, from the personal outward and back again. Through this dynamic process, one can hear in participants' own words not only individuals speaking but social identities, not only internal thought but communal conversations, not only dyadic dialogue but socially dramatic action. The exploration of this discursive and dramatic dynamic contributes, I hope, to a thoughtful reflection on human and humane living, a sometimes delicate dance *between* the inner and the outer, a dialectic of discourses that creatively constructs the personal and cultural conditions of life. At its base, it suggests that the large-scale processes of deciding and identifying can be conceived as discursive, as a communal conversation that penetrates personal and cultural worlds with persons creating senses of themselves, their motives, and their relations by creatively playing the dramatic discourses of communal life.

METHOD

Intensive field work for this report spanned a nine-month period from March through November of 1990, with subsequent periods of data collection still ongoing. Primary data included eight intensive interviews, averaging about seventy-five minutes each, all of which were fully transcribed. Participant observations included attendance at several public meetings, several informal conversations, and various social gatherings. Also included, but less central to the present study, were seven and one-half hours of audio-recorded and fully transcribed public hearings about this land. Additional data were collected during a unique set of field observations made while "Scrambling" with two thousand others up the massif, Mt. Greylock, to which the disputed land is attached. Other data included newspaper accounts about Greylock, an archive collected by the Appalachian Mountain Club pertaining to Greylock, files and reports of the development group, a book about the mountain and its cultural history (Burns and Stevens, 1988), and two televised broadcasts about this land. Harder to specify as data, but equally important to the above, were the hours I spent wondering about the disputed "Greylock" land during all four seasons.

Data were analyzed largely within the social-dramatic form, and further refined by attending carefully to a particular communicative form, *verbal depictions of the land.* Eventually, I discovered how listening to different versions of this form would help me "track" the particulars, in this case, of the decision-making process. This focus was chosen, then, because of the potent meanings this kind of depictive practice carried for this community (see Carbaugh, 1992). My eventual claim should, if effective, show how—in this case—decision making involves depictions of the land, and illustrate how each depiction consists in local terms, their meanings and uses. More generally, my claims should demonstrate how dramatic uses of these practices construct various social identities, social relations among these, and distinct sets of motives, as well as conflicting proposals for living with nature. The dramatic process of deciding, in this case, involved nothing less.

THE SCENE AND HISTORICAL ROOTS
OF THE DISCOURSE: GREYLOCK GLEN,
MT. GREYLOCK STATE RESERVATION, AND ADAMS

Greylock Glen is a 1,040 acre parcel of land in northwestern Massachusetts. The land consists mainly of wooded mountainside, some rolling pasture land, a series of ponds, hiking trails, and dirt roads. The parcel is immediately to the east of Massachusetts' flagship state park, the Mount Greylock State Reservation. The reservation was formed in 1898 with the state purchase of 400 acres on the summit of Mt. Greylock which, at 3,491 feet, is the highest mountain in the state of Massachusetts. The reservation has now grown to over 11,000 acres. On the other side of Greylock Glen, about one mile from its center, is the town of Adams, with a population of about 11,000. The geographic relationship of Greylock Glen to the Mount Greylock State Reservation and the town of Adams is shown in figure 9.1.

Since the early 1940s, Adams and much of northwestern Massachusetts has experienced deep and relentless economic decline, including the closing of many manufacturing industries with an attendant loss of employment, population, and tax base. Because of these general economic woes, and because the Greylock natural area was and is such an attractive parcel of land, it was sought by many, becoming, it seems, a site of continual struggle. In the 1940s, clear-cutting was begun, yet protested, then halted. In the early

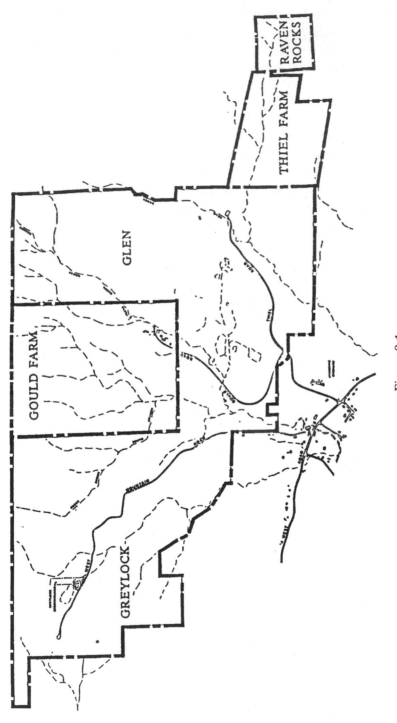

Figure 9.1
The Greylock Region

1960s, the Mount Greylock Tramway Authority was formed, with some state support, to plan a "highly commercial $5.5-million downhill-ski resort project, including four chair lifts, 11 miles of ski trails (some of them hundreds of feet wide), restaurants, cocktail lounges, a dance terrace, swimming pool, sauna, motels, fountains, riding stables, an amusement park, an international shopping center, and a 1,000 car parking lot. The centerpiece of the resort [was to] be 'the world's largest' aerial tramway, transporting passengers to a 100-foot tower on the summit of Mount Greylock" (Burns and Stevens, 1988, p. 77). After news of the full proposal got public, and this took from two to three years, a public reaction was spearheaded by the Mount Greylock Protective Association. This group was able to raise $18,250 from 1,300 members to delay, and finally defeat, the proposal. In the early 1970s, when a private developer began to piece together several private properties totaling 1,040 acres, the area became known as Greylock Glen. This development proposal—more modest than the earlier Tramway idea—involved a condominium complex, convention center, golf course, and ski area. Despite some groundbreaking and foundation pouring, financial backing for this resort idea began to fall through. In 1980, as a last-ditch effort to save the project, the developer proposed bringing Las Vegas–style casino gambling to the area, but the state legislature refused to consider the bill, and then-Governor Dukakis opposed the measure.

An Economic Breach:
Unemployment, Business Failures

In the early 1980s, when much of Massachusetts was experiencing, as Governor Dukakis put it later, "a miracle" of economic growth, the northwestern corner of the state was not. Companies were leaving the area and unemployment had reached double-digit figures. The northern Berkshire area earlier, during the Reagan era, had seen no money "trickle" its way, nor during the Dukakis "miracle" had it been "saved."

An Attempted Redressive Act:
Massachusetts State Legislation

> Many social goals . . . require partnership between public and private groups. Though government should not seek to replace local communities, it may need to empower them by strategies of support,

including revenue-sharing and technical assistance. There is a great
need for study and experimentation with creative use of the structures of civil society, and public-private cooperation.
—The Responsive Communitarian Platform, p. 10

Because of the economic doldrums in the Greylock region, the history of development failures, and the conflict of interests, the state
in 1984 decided to intervene and solicit a private developer who
would appease the various interests. The general idea was to propose for this land, with the input of state officials, environmental
leaders, area residents, and business leaders, "a public-private
partnership." The main objective was to provide—as worded in
the developer's Final Environmental Impact Report—"a recreational facility of regional economic impact." Specific goals of the
Massachusetts' Commonwealth in the legislation were:

1. To ensure continued protection of Mt. Greylock State
    Reservation and the unique scenic, natural, and historic
    resources that it encompasses; and
2. To facilitate the diversification of the Northern Berkshire
    economy through the development of a four- season desti-
    nation resort/recreation area at Greylock Glen.

By 1985, the "Massachusetts miracle" still had yet to reach the
Greylock environs, but with this legislation passed, help seemed
on its way.

Back to the Future:
Potential Redress Leads to . . .

As time passed, the immediate euphoria among many Adams' residents upon passage of the legislative act could not help but wane.
As the specifics of the development "partnership" became known,
the bubble of excitement began to burst, as some environmental
horns sounded, and the state economy began to crumble. By 1988
and 1989, two environmental groups—Massachusetts Audobon
and the Mount Greylock Protective Association—had gone public
as opposing the project. The main items of dispute included the
number of dwellings to be placed on the land (from 1275 "condos"
to 850 "mountain homes"), the size of a pond/lake to be built (from
twenty-five to thirty-five acres), money issues (how much money
should a state, now experiencing economic difficulties, put into a

partially private development?), to questions about the proposed "public-private" ownership of the land itself (why is this a public-private partnership, when this land could be annexed by the state to the public reservation?). In mid-October 1990, the place hit the headlines again. This time, however, for undisclosed reasons, the Massachusetts' inspector general was "investigating the proposed construction of a state-backed $220 million vacation home resort on Mount Greylock." The investigation occurred amidst much political activity: Then-Democratic-Governor Dukakis, the original proponent of the plan, was about to leave office, with Democrats and Republicans worrying the project would, respectively, die out, or be secretly finalized. So, as one group attempted quickly to ratify a land-disposition agreement on what parts of the land would be state-owned and how profits would be divided between the state and private developer, so development could begin, the other filed a bill prohibiting development on the land. Finally, the land disposition hearings were held, but not until Republican Governor Weld entered office. After the above investigation, and hearings, Governor Weld's early (1991) administration decided to halt the agreement between the state and the developer, and to reassess the fate of Greylock Glen.

Further Violations and Crises

At this point in the discussion, in the wake of the legislative act, one could hear various alleged violations. One vilified the attempts to develop the land, casting "development" as a violation by the government of the "commonwealth's" land and landscape. These allegations were stated through a rhetoric of environmental destruction that motivated certain parties, mainly self-avowed environmentalists and some who live adjacent to the land, to publicize this fact and form alliances with like-minded others. The other alleged violation involved the government's withdrawal of the state plan, which precipitated discourse from many in the town of Adams, especially those in the Chamber of Commerce, who felt that "the rug was pulled from under us." On this front, one heard a rhetoric of abandonment. Crises ensued as the earlier attempt at redressing the region's economic situation through the state's legislative act was now being undercut by the economic decline in the state, which resulted in further complications of economic, environmental, political, and personal sorts.

Let us enter this conflicted conversation a little closer to the ground, as people in this community discuss the land-scene, and with it their current lives and livelihood. As a result of listening more closely, we will begin to hear in their discourse their concerns and their motives for decisions they are making, and eventually to identify the relations this discourse creates among the various people involved, and between them and their natural environment.

CRISES AND THE CONFLICTING FACTIONS: TWO DEPICTIONS OF A NATURAL ENVIRONMENT

> Conflict seems to bring fundamental aspects of society, normally overlayed by the customs and habits of daily intercourse, into frightening prominence. People have to take sides in terms of deeply entrenched moral imperatives and constraints. (Turner, 1974, p. 35)

Simple turns of phrase can get read into ongoing cultural discourses in ways that are puzzling to outsiders. I experienced as much early on when I would ask townsfolk about "Greylock" (thinking of the 1000 acres of land) and receive a long narrative about "Adams" (the town). A way out of my confusion arose as I began to understand that people in this region of Western Massachusetts could refer, in short, to this land as either "the mountain" or "the project," with these phrases implicating larger motivational systems through a communal sense. By using these terms, even if unwittingly, a social position is forged by them with regard to decisions about this land. Caught in this discursive process, persons and competing factions are being constituted, with relations among them and their world assuming a dramatic quality. In other words, these two main discursive references to the land are coding this drama—in Turner's terms—into a "conflict" between "deeply entrenched moral imperatives and constraints." In the process, each is creating a rupture between themselves and those who "see" (or speak?) the scene differently. Each position, from the vantage point of the other, carries with it an associated sense of violation, a continuing of the crisis, and different ideas about what is proper as corrective actions. Consequently, each way of speaking about the land has associated with it conflicting beliefs about who people are, their actions, and their ways of living with nature.

I will call the one discourse a "coding of economic needs," and the other a "coding of natural ecology"—following the issues being foregrounded with each. As each solidifies a particular rhetoric, style, and mode of discursive action, it further accentuates its own senses of violation and crisis. As a result of each being played *against* the other, a conjoint decision, an integrative redressive action, is made more distant and difficult—if not downright impossible—to attain.

"Up on the project": Coding Local Economic Needs

On a hot summer afternoon, in an office suite in downtown Adams, I sat down with "the developer" (his term for himself) to discuss "Greylock." Surrounding us were detailed and attractive diagrams which showed the vision of what "the Greylock project" would be. After showing aerial photographs of the land, and how certain features of the project (e.g., cluster housing, golf course, ponds, ski trails, etc.) would be situated upon it, he described several past projects in Adams which were "stalled"—housing projects, real estate businesses, a color photograph laboratory, a furniture store, several attempts with restaurants—and contrasted these with successful ventures further away, both to the north (in Vermont) and south (in "Southern Berkshire"). Against this backdrop, he described "Greylock" as "a catalyst" for Adams, an energy boost for the town (with "busloads of people going to Boston to lobby" for it). He described the considerable efforts taken by the town to prepare itself for "the project" (rewriting zoning ordinances, getting public aid grants to redo Main Street, hiring a town planner). All of this, according to him, showed how eager the Adams' people were to "try to get the economy back on track." Because the development would bring others to the Adams area, rather than to the outlying areas which are relatively well-to-do, he reasoned, the project would "provide demand for the businesses that are here, to prosper and grow." He went on:

> This project is perceived as more a catalyst than anything else. . . . The business community is not so much concerned about how many and exactly what kind of jobs we can create up on the project, even though that is clearly an important issue, but they are mostly concerned with whether this project is going to bring X numbers of warm bodies here with money to spend,

and we need that. Our economy desperately needs that. . . . We have a thousand acres of land up there that until this project came along had always been a private ownership and was never public and was never part of the Greylock Reservation, so it's been privately owned. One of the benefits of this project is that it has forced a master plan upon the land, a four-season recreation community on a large piece of continuous acreage in a way that's responsive to the land and to the desires of those who use adjacent lands. . . . It's a magnificent piece of property. It can be a hugely successful project if done properly.

Others depicted this piece of Greylock land similarly. Each used a discourse—of coselected symbols and meanings—which depicted the land as an "up there," thus suggesting symbolically to listeners that they view—or portray, or sense, or feel—the land from down below, as a member of the developmentally minded segment of Adams. By using this discourse, the developer has also created a symbolic sense of this "Greylock" land as a "project" and "catalyst" that could transform Adams' current dismal conditions into a better place. He also has created a sense of himself, his motives, and relations to others with his words. There is much getting said here. Let us look in a bit more detail at some of the prominent meanings in this depictive form.

Notice again how the developer described the land, as *above*: "We have a thousand acres of land *up there* that was never public and was never part of the Greylock Reservation, so it's been privately owned. Anything could happen *up there*." The use of phrases like "up there" in the developer's speech carry great symbolic weight in this cultural scene. Uses of the preposition, "up," plus an indexical locator, like "there," "on the project," "on the Glen," "on the site," or "on the property," create phrases which refer to the land as an "up there," "up on the Glen," or "up on the project." This phrasing portrays "Greylock" as a place above, and suggests symbolically that participants view the land from "down below" in Adams, looking "up."

This symbolic location of one down below looking up at the land, it is important to make clear, is not a simple verbal artifact of a speaker's physical situation when speaking, such as down below the land. While such usage is prominent down below in Adams, I also heard it up higher when I was above the disputed land, on top of the mountain; that is, this usage appeared also above the land, where it makes no literal sense. Similarly, I heard it away from the base of the mountain (in other nearby towns). This depictive usage does invoke a spatial dimension, but it is more than a simple literal reference to a physical place.

This "locational" usage is a socially based moral claim as well. Depicting the land this way invites participants into a physical *and* moral space in which the land and its people should be conceived in a very particular way. Through this symbolic location, specific ways of thinking, acting, and feeling are evoked which are prominent down below in Adams, implicating *that* town's particular historical, economic, and political concerns. By depicting the land from this symbolic vantage point, interlocutors are invited into that town's physical *and* symbolic space. The land, then, rendered as an "up there" above Adams, is not simply a reference to an external reality, although it is that, but it is moreover a socially based moral move within a cultural game, a move which creatively evokes a complex of associations, a discursive invitation to see, hear, feel, and act upon "this land" in particular ways.

The complex of meanings specifically associated with this coding of space are geographic, economic, and political. Cultural geography is being implicated when the parcel of land is symbolized as "up there," physically above the town center (e.g., "a thousand acres of land up there"). Solidifying this view is the hearable claim that "this land" is also, "officially," a part of "the town." As a prominent resident asserted: "It's our land. We'll win any lawsuit if it comes to that." Speaking "the land" this way draws it into the town's boundaries, thus drawing a verbal map of a cultural geography which includes Adams and this piece of land within a single geocultural-political space (see figure 9. 1). As such, it becomes a site which is included in the town's municipal boundary, is a part of that town's history, and is the location of its most recent civic "project."

Included within this geosymbolic space, the land becomes a distinct part of a town and its activities, thus positioning participants to see/hear this land from the standpoint of that particular town and its concerns. To interpret the full meaning, then, of Greylock within this system, we must have some sense of the concerns of this town, especially the very real economic and political conditions which town members see as their own, and which create further the larger symbolic scene within which this "land" plays its distinctive role.

The economic climate of Adams in 1990 was avowedly dismal. As several townfolk put it: "The business climate is really suffering"; "In this month of July in the year of 1990, yesterday it was announced four hundred jobs are leaving Adams"; "Last week they announced that we're beginning the reduction of 22 percent of the work force, 550 people leaving good paying employment." This theme of economic deprivation runs deeply into the recent past: "We lost 3,000 jobs in the last five years"; We never experienced any of (then-President Reagan's) "trickle down in the early 80's" nor of (then-Governor Dukakis') "miracle" of the mid-eighties. In fact, the only economic heyday for the region seems to have been short-lived and occurred around 1875 when the Hoosac Tunnel was blasted through the Hoosac mountains to provide for the cheap and efficient transportation of manufacturing goods to Albany and Boston.

It is rather ironic that what has been the main attraction of this area to so many (outsiders?)—the scenic geography—has also been a key source of its economic problems. Placed between mountain ranges in a valley, Adams is relatively inaccessible. The remoteness created by the geography has had, so town members say, its further economic and political consequences.

The town-land is also symbolized as economically bypassed. When the discourse encompasses the larger cultural map, as the developer mentioned above, Adams is contrasted with its surrounding areas. These adjacent regions provide symbolic counterspaces where things and people are deemed better. One such place is called "Southern Berkshire" (a distinction common throughout Massachusetts), which has its associations of wealth, stability, and upper class. "Southern Berkshire" is the location of Stockbridge (a popular tourist destination, former home to the artist Norman Rockwell, summer home to the Boston symphony, Tanglewood, and several summer theaters), and Sheffield (the place of second homes for many wealthy New York and Connecticut residents). The "Southern Berkshire" space thus connotes—from the vantage point of this economic coding—greater affluence, upward mobility, a different and higher class of people and activity. Similarly, this discourse identifies the region to the immediate north as "great ski country," which includes the major ski resorts of southern Vermont, Stratton Mountain, Bromley, Haystack, and Mount Snow among others. Associated with both of these adjacent regions is the wealthy and upper status that Adams' people so desperately seek.

The full discourse of which this depictive code is a part thus positions the land as a place and the speaker as a vested person within a general geocultural scene. It invites one to locate within a historical and current site of economic deprivation (i.e., the town of Adams), and thus to promote its main symbol of economic opportunity (i.e., "the project up there").

Promoting the land "up there" counters not just these economic deprivations, but also the image of the town as politically marginal. The larger cultural map introduced above, when extended another direction, to the east, amplifies this meaning, with the symbolic movement in this direction introducing not just economic but political deprivation. As an informant put it, importing a phrase from another region of the United States commonly portrayed as marginal and deprived: "The perception of Berkshire County, in particular Northern Berkshire in Eastern Massachusetts, is very bad. It's like the dreary Berkshire County backwater." During a public hearing about "Greylock," an older man from Adams' described how "a Boston newspaper" referred to Adams' as "the boondocks" and "a cultural nowhere," and to its people as "millrats" and "Joe six-pack." It is the Appalachia of Massachusetts.

A similar symbolic reference to Adams' relative political impotence occurs as "environmental groups" are mentioned. Although somewhat implicit, when introduced within this coding strategy, the point is made: From the vantage point of this economic code, the people in the east—including some "environmental groups" like Massachusetts Audobon whose headquarters are close to Boston—are given much more public press and power than the Adams' Chamber of Commerce, or the project developer. These "eastern others" are thus portrayed, in contrast to Adams, as "outsiders" and sources of political power, especially the state officials way over in the capital of Boston.

The frustration of being "marginalized" geographically, economically, and politically is shown in this comment, made by a successful native son of Adams: "Let [the head of Massachusetts' Audobon] sit in somebody's living room who just lost their job and explain to them why he would oppose something like this [the Greylock project]. . . . He wouldn't have the courage to go in and tell them." His potent symbolic message contrasts Adams' people, actions, and needs (i.e., as geographically peripheral, economically deprived, and politically marginal) with potent distant forces from the east (i.e., as geographically central, economically endowed, and politically efficacious). Through their code, people speak and are heard not just as personally invested, but—as is typical during phases of crisis—as *representatives* of the town and its woes, as ones who are motivated to become champions of the town's "project."

The Redressive Act Associated with this Economic Coding. Because many members of Adams see themselves as deprived of essential political and economic resources (as contrasted with virtually everyone around them), and because they see Greylock as a part of their town and its most valuable resource (e.g., "the last developable land in the town"), they advocate the land "up there" as a "project," as a chance to transform their dismal present and past into a promising future, as a chance to make something more of their community and themselves. "The project," within this system, takes on what Kenneth Burke would call a God-term quality, a cure-all for past and present social ills. What specifically is it that town members envision with this "project"? When "the project" was mentioned, I would sometimes ask if it could be described to me. Most typically, it was described, as one person put it, by mentioning "some cross-country skiing, a golf course, and some housing." This quick coding of "the project" was elaborated by the developer on a "fact sheet." Quoting from that sheet: "recreation facilities include nordic ski and hiking trails (46 km), a norpine ski area (1 chair lift; 80 acres of trails), an 18-hole golf course, a 1,000 seat outdoor amphitheater, 10 tennis courts, 3 swimming ponds, 2 swimming pools; community facilities include a 150–200 room village inn, a retail commercial center, a fitness center, a golf pro shop and nordic center, a country club, 850 units of cluster housing, and a 150–200 room conference center/health fitness resort." The developer goes on to explain that all of the project is adjacent to, not on, the state reservation: "of the 1,040 acres of land, approximately 300 will be utilized for development of the village, country club, conference center and all housing. Approximately 740 acres are devoted to open space and public recreational uses." The developer predicts, by the year 2010, the "cumulative municipal benefit to Adams" will be 45 million dollars.

"The project" is thus seen from, and inextricably linked to, Adams. When mentioned, it signals what former President Bush and some Adams' residents described as "one giant ray of light" for the community. Within this cultural scene, it will help transform what those from the east portray as, and those from Adams sometimes agree is, the "dreary backwaters" of an economically deprived, politically usurped, and geographically bypassed region. Coded in this way, a parcel of land "up there" becomes a promising "project" and presents itself as one giant remedy to the town's considerable economic and political ills.

"At the Foot of Mt. Greylock": Coding Cultural Ecology

An alternate coding of this "same" land positions participants in a very different physical and symbolic place. One prominent environmentalist is the leader of a local land trust and conservation fund. When asked about "Greylock," he began by saying:

> Well, Greylock Glen . . . well Mt. Greylock, maybe I'll start with the reservation. It is wonderful. It's a wonderful reservation. It's the oldest [state park], has great dignity, has great character, has great historic presence. And it has a warm and loving constituency who feel strongly that it should be preserved. Greylock Glen, that troublesome property to the east of the Greylock reservation has been subject to any number of ill-conceived proposals . . . by a succession of scoundrels [he excepts the above developer from this label]. . . . It's right beside Mt. Greylock. It's an attractive piece of land.

Others depict the area similarly. From a naturalist on the state reservation:

> I'm a naturalist and emotionally attached to the mountain, so seeing anything like this [the Glen project], you look down like now and it's a pretty area. It's open land and lakes . . . and just to think that it's going to be developed into more houses . . . would make me feel sick to my stomach looking down on it.

The land is being symbolized here, literally, as part of the Mt. Greylock massif. Similarly:

> Greylock is a unique, natural resource, the best one, and probably the most famous one in Massachusetts and we ought to keep it that way. . . . I have visited all of the meadows and farms at the foot of Mt. Greylock. . . . While it [Greylock Glen] is a beautiful spot for a few condominiums, that would virtually destroy

the scenic aspect of the lower portions of the Greylock land-scape.

These depictions symbolically place participants in a very spe-cific physical place ("up") on the state reservation, most likely from the summit viewing area, looking down. Note the first speaker above, who audibly fluctuated between the two available depictions, deliberately anchoring his position above (starting with "the mountain" and "reservation"), rather than below (on "the glen" or in "Adams"). Greylock, depicted this way, is viewed not from the town below but from a different geographic angle, from up above. Coding the land this way draws it into the borders of the state reservation, associating it with an alternate discourse of symbolic meanings, elaborating themes not explicitly of local political economics, but of Massachusetts' highest natural envi-ronment and its inspirational effects upon contemporary Ameri-cans and their ancestors.

This depiction of Greylock Glen from above looking down creatively evokes symbols of wildness, a refuge of nature. The depiction is sometimes even elaborated with descriptions of the natural environment: "It's scenic land. . . . There are bears and bobcats and things coming around . . . and an occasional sighting of a mountain lion or cougar." From a biologist:

> Massachusetts doesn't have much in the way of mountains, compared to other areas of the country, but this one mountain is pretty impressive. It's the one highest mountain. It's unique. It's a monadnock in the geologic sense. It's isolated and it's pretty spectacular. . . . It harbors a lot of scarce or rare flora that we ought to be concerned about. One species I know of has only two individual plants growing on the mountain and both of them are very close to foot and vehicular traffic. . . . I'm con-cerned about things like that. Lower down in the area of Grey-lock Glen, there's unique crayfish, the Appalachian crayfish.

Another described the Glen as "a marvelously quiet and tranquil area."

The symbolic sense of Greylock as a pristine natural environ-ment is associated with another that is more historical, an Ameri-can literary tradition, and as such, this land is even considered to be a generative force for some classic American literature and poetry, such as some of the famous writings of William Cullen Bryant, Nathaniel Hawthorne, Henry David Thoreau, Herman

Melville, and Oliver Wendell Holmes. I did not fully appreciate this symbolic link upon first hearing it. After climbing a rugged ridge to the summit of Greylock, I was more than a little puzzled to discover that regular gatherings were held at the rustic summit lodge for "tea, poetry, and literature." I eventually was told by patient others about the great Americans who were associated with Greylock, who had walked and hiked there. Many claimed even today to sense their presence. In fact, appearing in the summit lodge during the summer of 1990—and periodically since— was a proud display of the great American figures who are linked to Greylock (see the summary in Burns and Stevens, 1988, 42–50, 93–100).

The early American poet, William Cullen Bryant, wrote numerous poems about Greylock's streams, peaks, and natural features. Nathaniel Hawthorne was the first to refer to the mountain in print as "Graylock." He was reportedly fascinated by the local scenery, especially relations between mountains and clouds. He hiked often on the mountain and wrote of it as "a most romantic and picturesque country." In his story "Ethan Brand," his title character spends his last night on Mt. Greylock. In 1844, Henry David Thoreau climbed Mt. Greylock, spending the night on its summit with a board as a blanket, and wrote extensively of the experience in *A week on the Concord and Merrimack Rivers.* Thoreau's mentor, Ralph Waldo Emerson, dubbed Mt. Greylock "a serious mountain." Herman Melville finished writing *Moby Dick* in the nearby town of Pittsfield, and dedicated his novel *Pierre* "To Greylock's Most Excellent Majesty." Oliver Wendell Holmes wrote many poems that mentioned Greylock. Perhaps most salient for present purposes are the following lines penned by Holmes as a tribute to the Berkshire Mountains in the last year of his life (1894).

> Oh how I should love to look on Pittsfield again! And yet I have always dreaded the rush of memories it would bring over me, and dread it still. But there lie buried many of my dearest and sweetest memories of my earlier middle age; and, if I cannot look on Greylock and Pontoosuc with these eyes which are fast growing dim, I can recall them with infinite affection and delight.

Upon being exposed to these well-known American writers, and their association with Greylock, I began feeling, seeing, and hearing this land anew, as a most majestic, historically evocative natural environment and culturescape. The literary history integrated into this depiction renders Greylock as a generative force in American literature and lives. Foregrounded in the depiction from "above" is not just a physical location, a mountain park and forest, but a whole multifaceted tree whose branches span widely over a vast natural refuge, and whose roots run deep into America's past.

So informed, one begins to see, hear, and feel this natural place through an alternate discursive coding, being placed differently (up above, in a heavenly? space) for viewing, highlighting natural features of its environment, and evoking its own natural and cultural past.

The above depiction of this land is activated with potent local phrases, such as "at the foot of Greylock." Speaking the landscape this way places interlocutors in a very precise physical place, up above on the mountain, and suggests looking down at a natural environment that is linked to this mountain. Verbally portrayed is a place that is (and should be) a part of the state's first park ("the foot of Greylock"). This communicative placing—of interlocutors in space—invokes two additional sets of cultural meanings, with one elaborating the uniqueness of this specific ecological system and the other identifying a specific literary tradition which is associated with it. So positioned, "Greylock Glen" assumes status as a part of Mt. Greylock, on or "at its foot."

The redressive act associated with this ecologic coding. This verbal portrait conceives the land as a natural refuge that is public (in the broadest sense of a state and national property), and should *stay that way*, because its particular ecologic and literary meanings would benefit the larger common good, rather than enhance just one community's economic and political power. Those who portray the land this way thus display an identity (often heard as an "environmentalist"), through a motive of preservation, which contests those more developmentally minded.

Is it possible for these two depictive codes, the ecologic and the economic, these two ways of conceiving people, projects, and place, to work together? Can these contesting codes move from battle and competition to cooperation and collaboration?

CHAPTER 10

Dueling Identities:
In Search of Common Political Ground

There are two solutions being proposed through the two coding strategies described in chapter 8. The one is to preserve the pristine; the other is to promote the project. These are sometimes invoked discursively through a quick mention of "the mountain" or "the project," suggesting that "the land" is (and should be) the one rather than the other. Here we will explore just how these proposed solutions to a community problem operate interactionally, one with the other, to create antagonistic identities and conflicted relationships between participants. Forging a decision—an efficaciously integrative action and identification—between these contesting codes seemed, for a long time (and maybe forever?), nearly impossible.

Three interactional messages are being foregrounded when these two depictions are brought together into one discursive occasion. One involves the symbolic presentation of social *identities*, or typical *personae*, which are affiliated with each depiction; a second, introduced above, involves the advocacy of a redressive *action* that is associated with each of these positions or personae; the third are the *social relationships* that are constructed between the two general personae, and their advocated actions. This complex of dynamics is perhaps most pronounced when participants praise one code, thereby asserting one identity, position, or action over the other. Similar to the vacillating form discussed in chapters 7 and 8, I call this dynamic "dueling identities," or "dueling depictions" (see Carbaugh, 1992). Within one forceful version of this process, when one code is in use, the other looks—or is rather said to be—downright preposterous. I write "said to be" because it is also abundantly clear that whenever one of my friends, or informants, used one of the above codes, or a feature of it, they also demonstrated, generally, an awareness of, or familiarity with, the other. So, it is not so much that each depiction or persona is unintelligible to the other, but rather that they are treated as such, interactionally, in order to make the moral claim that the one is better than the other. In the discursive process, participants thus engage in deeply coded battles through the local communicative practices of this scene.

These dramatic messages are shown here in an excerpt from an interview with a naturalist, who lived in Pittsfield, and brought the codes together as follows:

> When I've talked to the folks in Adams and I've talked to a lot of them about this project, it's a sense of "How dare you as an outsider tell me how to run my town. What I'm doing is in Adams, it's for the people in Adams and why should you who lives in Lennox, Pittsfield, or Williamstown be concerned with this?" It's a real sense of local rule and local entitlement that drives these arguments, and when I say "Wait a minute, I've got people from across the street who care about this reservation of Mt. Greylock," they get mad and say, "It's always the outsiders. It's the people from the east who are telling us what to do."

In this instance, the depictive codes are played one against the other in this way: "this project" is mentioned and associated with "the people in Adams" and matters of "local rule and local entitlement"; this cluster of symbols is contrasted with "the reservation" or "Mt. Greylock" and those "outsiders" who "care about" it. By invoking the symbolic meaning systems described in chapter 9, we can hear the "Adams' people" promoting the "project" to bolster their economic and political standing, while the "outsiders" champion "the mountain" and its cultural history as a natural preserve. This illustrates a way the codes are played against one another, with the proposed solutions of each being further separated and solidified in the process, just as the motives and identities of each party are also being separated and solidified.

From the standpoint of the economic code, as it is used here, local people have made up their own mind about the project and don't want anyone from the outside meddling in their own affairs. From the standpoint of the ecologic code, the locals are so insular and provincial that they can't even hear an alternate view even if just "from across the street." The identificational work getting done, by the naturalist here, maligns the local economic code. It is discursively cast as one promoted by a provincial, perhaps even selfish, persona who, by means of a symbolic contrast with the

ecologic code, "cares less" about "the mountain." Associated
with the ecologic code is a persona who may not live immediately
in the town of Adams (the common sense suggests he's an "outsider"), but cares nonetheless deeply about its "mountain."

These dynamics sometimes become more intense, leading in
some cases to name calling, with discursive attributions being
made about others' personae. Those promoting the ecologic code
were called, from the standpoint of the local economic code,
"environmentalists," "outsiders," and "intellectually dishonest"
(because they first seemed to support, then later antagonize, "the
project"). Their actions were said to be "insulting" (because as
outsiders they could not hear nor consider local issues) and condescending ("who are they to tell us what to do?"). As one put it:
"Our view is, you don't live here, we live here. That property and
that land is part of a functioning community and that community
has, should ultimately have control over it. And I look distaste-
fully at the folks who come in from almost everywhere and tell me
what I should and shouldn't do with my property." The most
intense hostility and anger was expressed by those promoting the
local economic code against "outsiders" (see Lange, 1990, 1993).

By playing the depictions in reverse, valuing ecologics over
economics, proponents of the natural code portrayed the others,
especially the developers, as "scoundrels" (those from the earlier
Tramway-gambling era), "land speculators," and "rapists of the
land." Their activities, or desired activities, were said to involve "a
commercial enterprise" which was "evil," a "real estate misadven-
ture" which would "destroy the scenic aspect of lower Greylock"
and "sacrifice bird and animal life."

Constructed through this dynamic of dueling depictions are
two sets of personae, each maligning the other. Each is aligned
with a primary motive and strategic action. When a "town member" says, "I'm for the project," she or he is heard to be motivated
by local (primarily economic, but also political) needs and meets
those needs through advocating "the Greylock Glen development." The "environmentalist," on the other hand, is explicated
as one who is motivated by ecologic problems, and a literary aes-
thetic, and claims to act in order to preserve or conserve "the
mountain" for the "common" good. During this drama, each such
avowal can be used as a basis for attributing to, or implicating for
the other a suspect persona, strategic action, and motives. From
the economic code, the ecologists are implicated as "outsiders"

who want town land as a site for their playground (their motive) and are condescending and meddling in local affairs which they don't understand; from the ecologic code, the locals are profit-driven, provincial, and self-interested (their motive) and don't understand the more general environmental consequences of their "project." The social relationships thus created through these dueling depictions derive from these competing identities, while the competing proposals each is heard to have made is creating— through these dueling codes—an antagonistic, intractable, and strained social drama.

The above discursive formation has a firm grip on these participants. The discourse is robust. It is conducted so often *as if* there are two extreme, mutually exclusive, diametrically opposed personae and patterns for action. When keyed this way, the features of this "talk" presume, and recreate, the very dilemma being discussed. When discussing "the project," it is assumed that development should proceed as planned; with regard to "the mountain," the land should be annexed to the state reservation. Generally, in a nutshell, this land-use controversy is spoken as that cut-and-dry.

HINTS OF AN INTEGRATIVE REDRESS:
A COMMUNITY SEEKS COMMON GROUND

Rarely, in 1989–1991, sometimes in a back room, in quieter moments, with few people listening, one could hear in rather hushed tones—as some put it—some "middle ground." These cautious proposals began to moderate the antagonisms by scaling down the degree of development, suggesting more "low-level development," or "limited development." In the other direction, the hard-line ecological code was being "scaled up" to include some very modest development. Mentioned here during these times were several rather undeveloped ideas, such as fewer housing units, or a small public campground on the northeast part of the Glen (the Thiel Farm area). This would have minimal impact on "the foot of Greylock," but would provide modest economic benefits from "up on the project." Still other proposals involved channeling economic development toward other parts of the Northern Berkshire area, thus abandoning the Greylock Project altogether. That these ideas were rarely mentioned, and if mentioned, were done so largely in private, demonstrates the dramatic grip the economic and ecologic depictions have held on this communal conversation. At base, it shows the difficulty of depicting "this land" in economic *and* ecologic terms. The community was having great difficulty adopting both terms of the original legislation: They wondered, how can we depict this land as a protected preserve which diversifies the local economy?

With the January 1991 change in state government administrations—from the Dukakis Democratic to the Weld Republican—came a period of reassessment. The government plans for this land were being reevaluated. Creative ways of resolving, or mediating between, the divisively different factions needed to be found.

A key move in this reassessment was the eventual formation of a widely representative "Advisory Committee" by the state of Massachusetts' Department of Environmental Management (DEM). This currently ongoing planning committee consists of twenty members: six from state agencies, six from the town of Adams, four from various environmental groups (i.e., Sierra Club, Mt. Greylock Protective Association, Audobon Society, Appalachian Mountain Club), and four from more-local governing groups (e.g., community and regional development offices, Berkshire Visitor's Bureau). The essential task of this committee has been to generate a mediating "concept," a broad-based consensual plan for this land that could meet the ecologic and economic criteria of all involved parties and the original state legislative act.

The formation of this committee was extremely significant for several reasons. First, the government was acting as mediator among the various interests, a position not adopted by others or by the other available institutions in this case. Second, the formation of the advisory board put into one setting people who had been advocating opposing decisions. As a result, the members of the board could not simply rely upon the solidified codes outlined above and be socially productive in this group, given its purposes. The committee, acting as diplomatically as possible, was being charged with generating newer, integrative "visions" that could weave its various interests into a single cloth. In short, the competing groups were being "welded" into an official government group, and as members of that group, together, they had to create a discourse that both represented their own interests while incorporating the interests of the others. The formation of the board then created a significant shift in motivational exigencies. Speaking simple vested interests would not be sufficient to this task. Could this group move itself—and help model for others how to so move—from insular and competitive enclaves, from identities of difference, to an integrative community?

As a part of the committee's considerable task, they commissioned outside consultants' advice about this land. After receiving the consultants' reports, the committee met in September 1992, and not surprisingly, at that meeting, the proposals made by the consultants largely fell prey to vested interests in terms of the two codes outlined above. The one was being labeled "an Environmental Education Center" and the other, "a Conference Center." The former plan was of a small economic scale, ecologically focused, and largely motivated by "an educational agenda." The latter was of a larger economic scale and foregrounded a "profit motive." Introducing these plans from "outside" consultants, however, enabled significant symbolic movement by the committee, if ever so slight. It helped begin weaving the two codes into an integrative "concept" that could create, possibly, the bases for a decision that the committee sought and the wider public—and the state government—anticipated.

The process of attempting to forge such a vision out of these earlier codes and consultant plans has been, and continues to be a long and tedious one and has produced—what the advisory board has called—the "Greylock Center Concept Plan." The committee noted in a recent (1994) document: "The concept plan is the result of an eighteen month consensus building project." Neither the language of the document, nor the process that produced it, can be analyzed here in any detail, but I can mention that the concept is now referred to as the "Greylock Center" and has "three main components." These are "a conference center, an environmental education center, and a variety of recreation areas and facilities." These "will attempt to creatively integrate recreation, education, and sustainable approaches to development" (p. 16 of the August 1993 "final draft"). In a 1994 letter to prospective developers (recall this is a "public-private partnership"), Governor Weld captures the idea in this way:

> The development of the Greylock Center is a public-private venture melding economic and environmental interests. As envisioned, the Greylock Center will contain a full amenity confer-

ence center, a residential environmental education center, and a network of year-round recreation areas and facilities, including a championship 18-hole golf course. All development companies are encouraged to utilize state-of-the-art energy saving and environmentally sensitive technology.

The "concept plan" created by the committee, then, is not so much the invention of a new idea as it is the bringing together into one "plan," a "centered plan," ideas—and identities—that were previously kept farther apart. This is by no means a meager accomplishment. The plan presents, and subsequently requires a discourse that affirms historically antagonistic codes, in various degrees, and thus attempts to carve into this social and natural scene some common ground. The process—if evolving ever so slowly, and in short—seeks an integration of the traditionally competing factions. Representatives of groups which the community cast as antagonists are now working together in the hope of producing such a joint decision. These current efforts are interesting in their attempts to forge for this public—at least for some period of time—a community-wide plan. Whether this can be done, and for how long, and whether this social drama has played its last major crisis, or will again rupture into a social schism—all of this remains to be seen.[1]

DECISIONS, DRAMA, DIALECTICS, AND DEPICTIONS: THE WORK OF DISCURSIVE FORMS

Decisions undoubtedly involve individual predispositions and judgments. Yet, in order to formulate them, we draw from a complex discursive formation, and as we implement parts of it, we are drawn to some degree into that formation and the social identities it makes relevant. As I began inhabiting the symbolic world reported here, I soon realized my own initial "senses" about "the mountain" were only part of the picture. As mentioned earlier, I was deeply perplexed when I would mention "Greylock" (thinking, myself, of "the mountain") yet find others responding directly to me with a sometimes lengthy narrative about Adams' economic or political woes. I wondered: How can a mention of the "mountain" create a grand discourse about Adams, its history, and its political economy? By now, the reasons for this discourse, and the associated proposal for this land, should be clearer. From the one view, I had asked about "Greylock . . . the town's project"—not about the "mountain"—and was simply being instructed in a local way to understand it.

This exploration of a large discursive system can help us understand the ways decisions and depictions like these are not simply our own but are perhaps more like evolving ships upon a shifting communal sea. Given the state of the sea, we select—or realize in retrospect that we have selected—a vessel (a depictive discourse, or position of self) that is at least familiar, and perhaps to our liking. We ride it along and see how it navigates the waters through which we are moving. Eventually, we get some sense of our vessel both as we move in and with it, and as we begin seeing others—in other vessels—traveling along. We may learn, sooner or later, more deeply about our vessel, or that another vessel may serve us better, or that this vessel we are on, itself, has changed (or should change) its shape and its means (or motives) of propulsion. Traveling like this, our depictions as our identities are *part* of a shifting discursive scene, with its own geography, its own history, its own constraints upon what we can (and should) do, upon what indeed we "are" doing. As we move our lives along, deciding as we go, we realize similarly that our social identities are not simply in our hands, but are more largely a part of shifting seas and scenes, symbolic spaces that move through and sometimes engulf us. In each sea and scene are discursive practices, and they are instrumental in making us what we are, just as we struggle to make what we will of "them." Cultural scenes span the vessels and seas that individuals inhabit, by spanning the personal and cultural conditions of life.

Some such geographic metaphor is particularly apt, I hope, at least for the case examined above. Each proposal that participants advocated earlier responded to its own storm of violation, thus forming both alliances and conflicting factions. Later, the grip of each vessel was loosened, with each moving slightly closer together, and eventually together into calmer seas, but also into uncharted territory. The more hostile scene had been recrafted with a more conjoint—if still strained—climate being somewhat in the air. This general process—the movement from violations, crises, and factions to attempts at redress and integrative efforts—demonstrates the social dramatic flow of this discursive process. Each phase of the drama carries with it its own rhetoric, its own plot, its own mode of enactment (Turner, 1974, 1980). Reflected upon generally, the rhetoric of violation and crisis temporarily gave way to a rhetoric of redress and integration, only sometimes to precipitate further crises; the plot turned from antagonistic to cooperative actions, with various ebbs and flows between these; the modes of enactment were sometimes official and governmental, including legislative acts and advisory committees, and at other times were more informal. The drama is, then, in this case, of a large and particular discursive scene, with its various ships and terrain, its shifting rhetorics, plots and subplots, and modes of enactment.

The large-scale, dramatic process consists of discursive practices that create nothing less than various ways of being, relating, and living-in-environments, of inhabiting social scenes and material worlds (bodies included). Our senses of being, and of being related, and of how we should act, and so on, are being crafted from discursive systems—like these seas—and from discursive codes—like these vessels—that we can more or less select from, and create with. Which discourse is being used is partly a matter of habit, but is also possibly a matter, at least at some times, of individual choice. And thus it was for those in this case who consciously decided, for example, to purge "the project" from their vocabulary, and thus to fight on for "the mountain," as a matter of principle, knowingly recreating a conflicted and contentious scene. Others made decisions about the issues more privately, unwilling to talk much about them, knowing a few words would say much more than they desired. If people would talk, they often expressed their concerns more in one code than the other, somewhat bewildered when the dramatic contest played out, yet again, and again, and again in a seemingly unstoppable process. As they'd say: "I wish people could just get along on this." To "get along" and bring people together meant, in this case, that one be willing or able to understand not only one's own code, but moreover to speak in terms of both codes—and to create hybrid codes—forcefully, in order to give each its due, and possibly identify each together. Indeed, the tide of the debate has been moving this decision mostly between these conflicting vested interests—with little common ground—for at least two decades now. It is time, many say, to pull something together.

Understanding how this depictive process is working, and being able to embrace its considerable importance, suggests then that we envision decisions as discourses, and further hear how these discourses are not only locally tailored, socially forceful, and individually applied, but are moreover consequential for our senses of identities, social relations, motives, and material living. Decisional discourses can thus be understood as being guided partly by our own rudders, with these helping to navigate particular vessels, seas, and terrain; that is, our decisions are partly our own to make. Yet also, these inevitably are part of the larger communicative climate and territory of our times. An ethnographic approach can thus help us understand not only our ruddered wills but also our contemporary worlds, and thus, to enable thinking of our discourses and identities with both the personal and the cultural in mind.

Focusing more upon the discourse of this community, we can see and better understand not only the general forms of decisional and dramatic processes, but a more specific one as well—in this case, verbal depictions of nature. In concluding, I will briefly elaborate the constituent features of this depictive form, mention several of its dialectical qualities, and discuss prospects for its use in future studies. The ways these dramatic and depictive discourses create identities of selves, motives for acting, and social relations among people will be, I think, of some future use (see Carbaugh, 1994, forthcoming).

The references to nature which are made by these people during this land-use drama demonstrate how a small communicative form—the verbal depiction of nature—is sometimes a very powerful symbolic expression. When this form is used, it can ignite a potent complex of sociocultural messages. First, with regard to a referential function, depictions make reference to a very specific physical place in a very specific way through the selection of a particular term(s) of reference (e.g., of "mountain" or "project"). To make reference to a place is to suggest to one's contemporaries that some place is worthy of attention (that physical place), that it can (and should) be attended to in this way (through this term of reference), and that it can (and should) be viewed from this physical location (the way the term physically places one for viewing). The communicative act of referencing nature thus invokes a complex of geographic messages: a place at which to look, a way of living with that place, and the optimal place from which to view it; all of this is getting said. The use of a depictive form(s) then, generates claims that are both about and from a physical place, positioning one to see from a particular vantage point, into that place, and to live with it in a particular way (see Basso, 1988).

Communicating about natural space further invokes a *system* of social personae through particular meanings. For example, the way "nature" is turned into an expressive means says something about the people who express it in that particular way. As a result, these expressions help construct not only typical personae, but also—when a part of a social drama—political factions, counter-actions, and the disparate motives deriving from each. Put differently, each social dramatic depiction of nature is heard as an avowal of some identity, while implicating another for others. *Developers* want a "project" in order to better the town's civic life; *environmentalists* want the "mountain" preserved in order to better the eco-life. Created through this dueling of depictions is a complex of identificational messages, of how the land (above or below), and people (outside or inside), could be and/or should stay.

Dialectical meanings are perhaps immanent in social-dramatic depictions of nature, as they powerfully integrate, through competing forms, a referencing of a physical world, a complex of cultural associations, including contesting personae, political factions, modes, and motives for action. This potent communicative process seems a prime candidate for what Basso (1988, p. 123) has called a "mini-maxing" phenomenon (the mini form being "the project" or "the mountain"), a cultural discourse in which "a few spoken words . . . accomplish large amounts of communicative work." Most noteworthy, as well, in this case, is the way in which a single depiction within this larger dramatic form can radiate, in a saying, two deeply dialectical codes (e.g., of cultural ecology over local economy).

The dialectical complexity of the particular political issues involved here can become particularly convoluted for American audiences. The contemporary, two-party political scene is often cast, on a national scale, as a drama between the "liberal Democrats" and the "conservative Republicans." Typically, the liberal left is heard to be champions of rights for the disadvantaged, the poor, and the environment. The conservative Republicans are heard to be champions of small government and private enterprise. In Adams, however, the dialectic between the political left and right worked in alliances that do not neatly fit these grand political images. The "environmental left" argued for preservation of the land as a common good for the people of the state.

They antagonized the local private business interests in the process. But also in the process they argued for "preservation" of a common good (the land) and a national heritage (the literary tradition). A perhaps unintentional consequence of this argument was the further muting of the disadvantaged: the economically deprived townsfolk of Adams. Stepping into this American picture from afar, one cannot help but puzzle over finding the liberal left arguing in ways that favor preserving tradition at the expense of disadvantaged locals! The conservative right, on the other side, argued for development of the land in order to help the local economy. They antagonized the environmentalists from elsewhere in the process. But in so doing, they argued for change of a local good (the land) and transformation of deprived people (the poor). The conservative republicans arguing for the disadvantaged, for change and transformation!

The typical sound—to many American public ears—of these alliances and arguments demonstrates how general, cultural political images can shed very little light on local circumstances. One wonders further if general cultural slogans (e.g., "thinking globally") mitigate against or confuse subsequent local actions and interactions. Some of the most difficult dynamics in the above occurred when "global thinking" spoke over and above the local scene, making local circumstances almost impossible to hear. Abstract dialectics, and political discourses, and academic theories, untutored by local discourses, at times tower over such debates, and in the process do little to help us understand them.

While the symbolic meaning systems of primary concern in this essay are deeply local and conflicted, as part of a larger culturescape they also ignite other traditional American dualisms and dialectics. Some of these include the relative weighting and conception given to classic counterforces, such as (1) the impulse to transform versus the impulse to render permanent and stabilize; (2) the locus of the decision-making process, whether local, inside (of the town), or elsewhere, outside (by others); (3) the scope of the decision, whether short-term, or longer-term; (4) the site of the problem, whether of a community, a region, or a larger natural environment; (5) the different valuing of the political agents of village or town versus national or state government; (6) the ownership and use of land, whether private or public, conserved or preserved (see Oravec 1981, 1984); (7) the dialectic between motives for public policies, be they economic or ecologic, and whether these can be simultaneously met. All such large concerns are woven into the fabric of the above conversational cloth. With each single thread, one weaves a hearable, potentially robust dialectical design—whether one wants it or not. One's heritage often speaks louder than one's will!

Running through all of these dualisms and tangles is some *cultural* version of a nature/culture distinction, some vacillating relation between the order of nature (or wildness) and the order of culture (or cultivation). How can one address and redress this apparently robust, bipolar categorization in *cultural* thought and action? Here, I think, is where further developing an approach to the study of cultural pragmatics, social identities, dramas, processes of decision making, and verbal depictions of nature can hold great promise.

First of all, to know people—who they are and how they are related—and the places they inhabit in a holistic sense—that is, to know how life is experienced *and* expressed in its place—is to know both a physical space and a cultural place. Knowledge is needed of the emphatically material *and* symbolic "there," of how each people plays its settling role. Not to recognize this is to blindly impose one's own symbolic orientation onto a "peopled place," where others are currently living. Focusing upon a "here," though not necessarily staying only "there," commits one to some degree of local knowledge—of people and their place—to knowing what is indeed there, both the local terrain and the ways that place is currently known to its people, or discursively coded by them. This point of departure is crucial not only because indigenous people and places, like the Hopi (Johnson, 1991) and others (Mitchell, 1991), have fallen prey to outsiders' foreign interests, but also because all living is of some region or place, and is to a degree unique unto itself, and its people. To know, then, is to go "there" to that peopled place and experience it. It is to discover, while there, the cultural space which that place holds for those who inhabit it.

To know the local system, one needs a framework for discovering, describing, and interpreting it. Through ethnographic field work, one can come to know the discursive ways in which a people inhabit and play out dramas about a place, the space that place holds in their lives, what they see in it, with it, and seek from it. By listening to the ways places (including bodies) are depicted, and their geographic positioning through a complex of cultural associations (historical, economic, political, and social), one can gain access into local places and lives. Depictions of nature thus help bring into view the relative weighting, and potential antagonisms between the experiencing of nature's space and the cultural expressions of that place, exploring what both permit. By exploring depictions, we can see and hear with an integrative double allegiance, asking of this natural place and space what it permits, *and* of this people what they have made of it and themselves. Assessments, such as decisions, depictions, and cultural pragmatic studies about them, would be grounded, then, in natural and cultural discourses, permitting knowledge which is in, or seeking, balance.

PART 3

Conclusion

CHAPTER 11

Social Identities, American Community, and the Communal Function

The chapters included here cover a wide range of social identities, diverse communication practices, and a variety of American scenes. Together, I hope, they give some sense to some of the multiply variegated terrain that is in America today. Further, I hope they illustrate the thesis that social identities are immanent in situated communication practices.

Reflecting upon these studies together, one might rekindle some of the fire set by Sennett (1977) as he lamented the lack of public play in contemporary Western scenes. While we do have playful scenes, like ones for being a fan at basketball games, perhaps setting a scene aside for play like this is symptomatic of the problem he describes. Rather than incorporating a playful dimension across the scenes of public life, scenes and selves are being cast quite seriously. This application of Sennett's point—that play is not incorporated easily into public life but set aside only for special moments—gains some force when the playful fan is examined alongside the more seriously keyed scenes following the basketball game, scenes of tension-filled workers, diverse models of naming and marriage, differences of gender, and virtually interminable battles between developers and environmentalists.

From the vantage point of what is predominantly accomplished socially across these scenes, we find communication practices that model—or encourage, or cultivate—not play but competition, and stratification. For example, the land-use controversy is recreating decades of deeply divisive political interests, with each finding it difficult to cooperate with the other. A similar dynamic, perhaps a condition for competition, is the discursive division among workers into social classes, creating through these practices social stratification and division. The various preferences for names and marriage invite people to recognize the range of options and expressed lifestyles that are available, and to make a selection from among these, saying something about one as preferable to the others. Even being a fan through a communicative ritual that is largely playful, ventilative, and integrative, also encourages one to identify as one against others. These parts of social scenes, and the identities in them, show how communication can cultivate serious competition, divisive identities, social stratification, and strained social relations.

By foregrounding these competitive and divisive features, we can remind ourselves of the importance of "identity" to Americans, and acknowledge, in many scenes of social life, that the competition and division among social identities is not largely a laughing matter. Although there are some scenes set aside for play, the stages of social life considered here are largely keyed in a rather serious way.

Why is this so? We would do well to remind ourselves that "identity" and "identity politics" (in the cultural sense) is a peculiarly American preoccupation. This is itself taken very seriously. Part of this seriousness, I think, is based on the unrelenting belief that "identity issues" go to the "natural" core of persons, and thus these become personal differences that are somehow permanently hard-wired into the biology and psychology of each person. Shoulders shrug and we are told: "I am what I am." Conceived this way, around a stable "core," identity cannot easily be altered, or played with. Based upon these beliefs that identity is personal, important, relatively permanent (as with gender and race), and should be expressed, casts social life upon a rather serious identificational stage. Watchful eyes and carefully tuned ears strain to capture the revelations of identity. People are left, therefore, to the serious task of digging deeper into their own and other's "core" selves, for this is deemed the site of what is "really important" to many in the American scene today.

Without denying such a core feature of "self" identity, and acknowledging that it is important at least to some Americans on some occasions, perhaps we can be freed from this cultural self as a necessary, serious concern for all social scenes. This becomes possible if we treat social identities, as we have done here, as communication, and focus upon communication as a primary, situated, and variable practice through which identities are socially negotiated. As evident throughout our discussion, this kind of thinking suggests focusing less upon the durable internal psyches of persons, and more upon the palpable pragmatic scenes of communication in which selves and social lives are being conducted.

As mentioned in the preface and part 1, the approach I have taken to explore self—as a situated symbolic activity—involves theoretical, descriptive, interpretive, critical, and comparative modes of inquiry. As a result, I have adopted a particular communication theory and turned it, here, to the problem of identity. I have used it in order both to *describe* how communication shapes a variety of scenes, and to *interpret* some of its meaningfulness for participants in those scenes. As the communication in those scenes expressed suboptimal social conditions for some (e.g., workers, marital partners, women with unemployed husbands, a nun, local developers, environmentalists), it was subjected to a kind of *critical* inquiry (Carbaugh, 1990a). In the process, attention was drawn to the way communication (re)creates social stratification, competing systems of legitimation, and the different allocation of differently valued cultural resources (see Thomas, 1993, p. 36). The *comparative* mode was used primarily, in these studies, to highlight contrasts across the American scenes, and less so to contrast cultural models of identity and communication (see Carbaugh, 1990b, 1993b, 1993c). This general approach, then, to the communication of self is descriptive and interpretive; it is also theoretical, critical, and comparative (Carbaugh, 1993a). Further, it was used to address issues of concern not just to interpersonal and organizational but also to mass and political communication.

VOICES OF IDENTITY, A HOLLOW COMMUNITY

If we extend our focus for a moment from these particular studies and theoretical concerns to the American scene of which they are a part, perhaps we can broaden the scope of our cultural concerns. In the conversations of America today, we can find further that "core identity" is being urged in a variety of directions, with each contributing in its own way to a refracting of what could possibly become, in various ways, strong American communities. For example, we are urged through a kind of globalism to become participants in a "new world order," or, in general, to "think globally." Such slogans encourage us to turn our eyes and ears (and mouths) elsewhere, to identify those elsewheres as proof we are abiding by this dictate, and thus to ably show our concern for this everywhere-else. Identity, as a result of this relevance to the global everywhere, ends up being displaced, because it is being located in a nowhere-in-particular, a self for all scenes.

We are also being encouraged through a version of individualism to be ourselves, to reflect upon our own personal beings, our limits, and to express our selves. As Michael Walzer (1992, pp. 120–121) puts it: "Every individual member of society is self-associated, primary in his own eyes, secondary in everyone else's." Identity, as a result, ends up being located inside individuals, in an only-one-in-particular.

At the same time, and more frequently today, we are encouraged through a kind of identity politics to champion a cause, and thus to affiliate with an enclave, to become part of a particular political faction that is concerned for example with the environment, crime, or the poor. Identity, as a result, because it selects one or some set interest over and above the others, ends up being affiliated with that one group and its interests, and thus adopts a tunnel vision of this one, and loses sight of the many with whom it lives together in the community or society.

Each of these bids for identity creates singular forces that are at odds with the creation of strong communities. Why is this so? The "global horn" sends people out of their particular place and gets them thinking—and thus acting—out of context. As a result, some Americans know more about the rainforests of Central America, or labor conditions in Mexico, than they do about the woods in their own backyards, or the workers in their home town. The "horn of individualism" sends each person in search of self, hoping to discover its own personal qualities, and if not found, to "work" on them. Know self, and as a result of this preoccupation, one loses sight of the rest. The horn of "identity politics" sends people in support of a cause, very worthy ones at that. But as a result, that cause and its supporters compete with other such causes, with whatever is gained in its name, creating a loss for someone else. A cause gained is an alliance lost.

As a result of these various sounds of identity in America today, centrifugal forces are set in motion that send people off into an ill-defined global everywhere, into their individual minds, or in support of a particular political cause. While each of these is not of course entirely wrong, each alone is not quite right either. Taking the group together, and *situating them all in some particular communal scene*, it seems to me, can offer something by way of a corrective, with each providing a partial remedy to the excesses of the others, each becoming more cognizant of the specific community scenes in which lives are being lived.

Such a learning became apparent to me as I conducted the studies included here. I could not understand very well what people were saying, or communicating to me, until I explored the deeper particulars of their "sayings" in their specific social scenes. In the television station, I could not quite understand "the secure" until I got to know "the paper movers" and "the shakers and movers." With regard to marital names, I could not understand the "modern" selection until I understood "the traditional." In the land-use dispute, I could not understand the "environmentalists'" concerns about "the mountain" until I took the time to understand "the developer's project." Cast at a different level, I could not hear (or know) the individuals I met along the way very well until I listened within (or understood) their particular social and cultural scenes. This is all by way of introducing a final point: *Interpreting the communication of identities requires a theoretical attitude that willingly and openly explores those worlds of identification, ably hears the ethos of each, and is ever mindful of the social relations they create together.* Individuals, social identities (or social classes), and cultural agents are not isolates. They are thought of and acted together in the specific scenes of particular communities. Each can be understood as an always situated part of a wider system of identities, with each acting, in turn, in relation to those others (Schneider and Smith, 1987, p. 219; see also Cohen, 1985). Our social practices, and our theories about them, must learn to ably incorporate this communication practice of interrelatedness. Without it, we cultivate a doughnut model of a hollow community, with practices constantly cultivating the global, individual, and political periphery, with no one tending the interrelated (w)hole.

Our theories of communication, and our communication theories of identity in particular, must strive to productively integrate knowledge of such differences in social identities, with special attention to the local scenes in which they are played together (Carbaugh, 1993b). A key condition for creating such productive knowledge and action is building into our theories of communication, culture, and identity a dialectic that is at once cognizant of commonality and difference.

THE COMMUNAL FUNCTION:
A DIALECTIC OF IDENTIFICATION

Gerry Philipsen (1989b, p. 79) has written about "the communal function of communication . . . communication as a means for linking individuals into communities of shared identity." In an earlier programmatic statement, he wrote about "the cultural function of communication, the use of communication in the creation, affirmation, and negotiation of shared identity" (1987, p. 279). Given these quotations, and the larger conceptual system of which they are a part, one might ask, what are "communities of shared identity"? Or, what is a "shared identity"? Would "fans" constitute "communities of shared identity"? Would "workers," or would the subgroup of workers called "shakers and movers"? "Men" and/or "women"? I think questions such as these are important to pose because the theoretical response to them is not immediately evident, at least on the face of it. But there is more. I think the questions are important also because responses to them carry proposals or visions with them about communities and the relative weighting of commonality and difference within them. This issue is a vibrant issue, culturally, in America today, because it forms a central theme in what many—like NEH Director Sheldon Hackney—are calling a "national conversation," a renewal of interest in discussing "American" values and "American identity."

Based upon the above studies, I want again to suggest that we integrate into our views of communication two typical enactments of identification. Both are being played into the various social scenes examined above, and thus we need to build our thinking about communication and community by being attentive to each. One enactment of "shared identity" is evident as people place an explicit accent upon commonality of codes, upon common premises for being, acting, feeling, and dwelling. Here, the forms, symbols, and meanings of communication display membership as a cultural agent in a common group. At least people are willing, for now, in the scene, to talk, or act symbolically, in this way, as if they were—at some level—alike. This was the case as people together stepped into the identity of a fan at a basketball game, or as they became a worker "putting out a fire," or "an individual trying to make it," or a committee member working on a "centered" proposal for a parcel of land. Communicated in these scenes was a shared sense of self, the features of which were acted *as if* held in common, enabling all in the scene to gather as such, and to identify their actions in a mutually meaningful way. For shared identities like these to be forceful, a common code for so being, acting, and feeling must be presumed, realized, or conversed in the scene. When so, this demonstrates, if this follows Philipsen's statements, the "communal function of communication," an enactment of "shared identity."

Yet also, there is a particular use of cultural codes within "communities of shared identity" that the current studies suggest making a bit more explicit. Sometimes communication is conducted such that the "communities of shared identity" give way to *different identities within a shared community*. Communication can be conducted coherently, and membership in group-life demonstrated, through this communication, not by amplifying the "shared identity" of those present, but by knowingly accentuating the different "identities" which different people in that community knowingly, for now, communicate. In this process, through their symbolic activity, participants place an explicit accent upon diversity and difference in identification through an application of their cultural communication codes.

Within this process of—what I will call—social identification, only some of the present members can (or should, or will) symbolically affiliate with any one particular identity. In the process, others present will be knowingly implicated into another social position. Presumably, if all goes well (i.e., coherently), those present in this kind of scene can find the particular differences in identity to be mutually intelligible. And further, presumably, they will know how to align their actions on the basis of these differences, as did the developers and environmentalists, or the shakers and paper movers. In so doing, actors identify agents-in-scenes as different, and thus accentuate, and knowingly affirm, for awhile in a scene, the differences in their social identities. At least people act, for awhile, as if these differences were significant and important to them. Other examples include those symbolic occasions in which a traditional "husband" and a modern "spouse," a "man" and a "woman," or promoters of the "mountain" and the "project," engage one another.

What is being explicated through these communication practices, in these scenes, are differences in social identifications, with each being enacted only by some in the scene. As any one particular identity is being explicated, it also addresses others as knowingly different, thus implicating a larger social system of different identities, and arranging the present social relations accordingly. This kind of communicative dynamic, I think, encapsulates what might be called "the social function of cultural communication."

The general play between cultural and social levels of identification is immanent as communication amplifies, on the one hand, commonality of identity through cultural codes, and on the other, differences among identities through various social uses of those codes. Cultural codes are, therefore, in this sense, a condition for and a dimension of all communication, when it proceeds coherently, or intelligibly. Also, some version, even if a shallow version, of the cultural is necessary for different social identities to operate efficaciously together.[1]

To explore further the relations between the cultural and social levels of identification, we can focus for a moment on *the cultural*. Cultural communication involves deeply common codes about persons, actions, feelings, and dwelling that operate for a people across various identities and scenes. Conceptualizing at this level helps us identify deep sources of commonality among people, or among cultural "contemporaries" in Geertz's sense (1973, pp. 365-366). This also helps us understand the deep differences between people, through their codes, like for example the differences between American conceptions of the "individual" and Hindu conceptions of persons as "dividuals." The cultural bases of communication and identification provide deeply coded and unquestioned premises that are evident in each case across scenes, institutions, and agents in society. The cultural, thus, penetrates and underlies agents-in-scenes and provides bases for cohering various of their social identities and situations. Put differently, any social identity, if it is to be efficaciously performed, and coherently related with others in a social scene, must implicate cultural codes in its communication, that is, it must implicate common beliefs about the person (what person is and should be), actions (what agents can and should do), feelings (how agents can and should feel about the present scene), and dwelling (how agents live with nature) (see Carbaugh, 1993b, forthcoming).

How cultural and social identifications operate together can be seen in the television station as socially stratified worker "types" were played against each other in ways that all workers found deeply intelligible. Different social identifications were being accentuated through common communication codes. The reverse dynamic was also evident as the social divisions among the worker types gave way to the shared identity of "everyone," those who monitor the "product" and "put out fires." Social and cultural identifications thus worked together to coherently structure social life. Also, the play and counterplay of the cultural and social was evident as symbols of gender—a cultural means of social identification—played against "the individual"—a cultural means of cultural identification—through a vacillating form. The consequent was the deep discursive rendering of both social differences, *and* a cultural commonality. Similarly, in the land-use controversy, as the deep codes of economy and ecology were being forged into a centralizing proposal, a discernible sound could be heard as the social accent on difference gave way to another enabling common identification.

Each enactment of identification, be it a cultural coding of commonality, or a cultural coding of difference, is ever-present in all systems of communication, like two sides of the same coin. Yet, at any one moment, in any one scene, through any one communication practice, perhaps one accent can be heard over the other, with each, in turn, through the vacillating form, motivating the other. This is the communicational life of the basic identificational dialectic, an alternating between the cultural coding of commonality (a union of a possible separation) and the cultural coding of difference (a separation of a possible union) (Carbaugh, 1988/1989).

This basic identificational dialectic can be summarized as follows: The basic cultural function accents commonality of code or, as Philipsen puts it, "communities of shared identity," with communities (in the plural) being linked to a shared identity (in the singular). The cultural function is thus a condition for coherent and appropriate communication, derives from shared resources, and serves to unify people through common cultural symbols, forms, and their meanings. These common symbols, forms, and meanings provide the basic communicative ingredients for "membering" or for "realizing" a shared identity (Philipsen, 1987, 1989b). The social function of cultural communication places the accent upon differences within a code, "a community of shared identities," with community (in the singular) being linked to shared identities (in the plural). This social dimension, if interactionally coherent and efficacious, presumes a deeper cultural code, but applies it in order to accent social differences, to symbolicaly place people into specific social positions. This process creates social identifications within cultural communication.

The cultural, I think, is fundamental, analytically, and must have some of its features operative, expressively, for social differences to be felicitously communicated. The resulting performance of difference thus can be conducted in a coordinated and mutually meaningful—if hotly contested—way. But the ways identifications are being performed culturally through a presumed code of common identity, and the ways the communal function is being performed socially, through a presumed code of different identifications, needs better understood. Keeping these in view will help us explore the communication of commonality across communities (e.g., symbolizing as "an individual" in America), and social differences within cultural identifications (e.g., symbolizing developers and environmentalists, or "man" and "woman" in America). It will also help us understand di-verse "communities of shared identities," such as the cultural differences in social identifications (e.g., symbolizing Finnish "woman" and American "woman"), and of course cultural differences in cultural identifications (e.g., symbolizing Finnishness and Americanness). While the former has been the primary focus here, the latter two warrant our future attention.

Sharpening this difference will help us respond more forcefully with a vision of community that is attentive to both commonality in communication codes, and their social differences. This idea of community, I hope, has been evident throughout these essays, for it is presumed in the general ethnographic approach being espoused. As much could be summarized using Hymes' basic idea: that we model community not as a bland replication of uniformity, but as "an organization of diversity." A monolithic vision, as a result of theory or other practices, will not do. Thus, the spirit here is to embrace the diversity of communicative resources available in the various scenes of actual communities, be they competitive, divisive, or integrative in tone, or global, individual, or political in focus. Whatever the case may be, and however people employ the cultural and social dialectic of identification in communication, we can reflect upon their various situated uses, so to better create knowledge not only about communication and various social identities, but also about the particular cultural communities of which each is inevitably a constituent part.

APPENDIX
SOME PARTS OF ONE
ETHNOGRAPHER'S
INTERPRETIVE KIT

FORMS, SYMBOLS, AND MEANINGS OF IDENTITY

The angle of vision, or the way of hearing social identities as communication, that I have adopted throughout this study has drawn attention to the ways identities are being "symbolized" in situated scenes. The "situated" nature of communication has been *described* largely through Hymes' conceptual system (Hymes, 1972; also see Carbaugh, in press). The norms for *interpreting* that communication have been conducted, throughout, by explicating various *symbolic forms*, *symbols*, and their *meanings* (Carbaugh, 1991). A more detailed summary of the concepts used in order to generate the latter, interpretive claims is provided here.

The focus in this appendix is on the interpretive mode of ethnographic inquiry. To reiterate, interpretive claims are theoretically guided, and formulated on the basis of descriptive data (primarily audio and/or visual recordings, and transcriptions or notational systems that derive from these recordings). Data such as these are used, subsequently, to generate arguments about *patterns* of communication practice (e.g., that nature is verbally depicted). After establishing that communication is patterned in particular ways in particular scenes, those patterns or features of those patterns can be interpreted. As I have conducted them, generally, the interpretations involve treating a communication pattern, or parts of that pattern, as a particular *form*, or *symbol*, of communication, *and* interpreting the common, accessible, and potent *meanings* of that particular form or symbol, when used in that scene (Carbaugh, 1988a). Sometimes, differences in communication practices and/or interpretations can eventually be formulated as *codes* (e.g., coding nature as cultural ecology, or as local economy). Comparative and critical assessment, then, derives from and contributes to these basic moments of theoretically guided, descriptive, and interpretive inquiry (Carbaugh, 1990a, 1993a; Carbaugh and Hastings, 1992).

The main *cultural communication forms* discussed were of at least four general types: rituals, social dramas, a vacillating form of identificational talk, and verbal depictions of nature. Chapter 2 analyzed a scene of college basketball games through a *ritualized form* of communication that is used in that scene (Carbaugh, 1988b; Katriel, 1991; Philipsen, 1987). Participating in that form, in that scene, is part of what it means to be a fan of college basketball. Similarly, in chapters 3 and 4, I discussed a ritualized form used by workers in a television station. Called a "staff meeting" by workers, it showed how a boss's status is being elevated and celebrated through a communication practice in that scene. Both the fans and the workers show who they are, in these scenes, by symbolizing through a ritual form of communication.

A *social drama* is a communication form that responds to violations by publicizing them, and motivating actions in response to those violations (Carbaugh, 1993c; Katriel, 1986; Philipsen, 1987; Turner, 1980). In chapters 3 and 4, we heard how workers employed this form and identified it with the folk phrase "putting out fires." Similarly, in chapters 9 and 10, a large-scale drama over the use of a large parcel of land was examined. Here we found a very complex communication process in which the contesting identities of "developers" and "environmentalists" and the political interests associated with each were being played one against the other. How identities arise and are created in response to social problems, indeed what constitutes a proper identity and problems worthy of public address, these are the themes foregrounded through the form of social drama. We find, in these cases, that the workers and the community members know who they are, in these scenes, partly at least by symbolizing through a social dramatic form of communication.

A *vacillating form* is an interactive sequence in which at least two contrastive sets of identity symbols—and their meanings—are being played with, or against, each other. For example, in chapters 5 and 6, we found this form of communication as some women "played" the address form "Mrs." and the use of their husband's last name against others who preferred both the title "Ms." and using the last name given to them at birth. Playing these symbols of identity together, and exploring the motives for selecting one rather than the others, showed how identities gain a sharp sense through contrast within this vacillating form. In chapters 7 and 8, we found a similar, yet complex version of the vacillating form as the symbols of "man" were played against those of "woman." Moreover, this gendered identification was being played itself, through the vacillating form, against another. By casting gendered agents against "individuals," the dialectic of identification was being shifted from social differences in gender to a common cultural denominator. The vacillating form can thus play various versions of social and cultural identities, together. This dynamic is further developed in chapters 9 and 10. We found a dueling of identities as different political interests got played against each other in a particular community scene. In each of these cases, married persons, men and women, individuals, and politically involved citizens all showed who they were (and were not), at least for a while, by symbolizing through a vacillating form of communication.

A final form we explored was the *verbal depiction of nature*. This form involves a linguistic appropriation from nature, thus turning nature's materials into expressive means. Each such means, then, carries particular meanings about nature generally, or a particular natural site, with each such means and its meanings, in turn, suggesting a way for people to think about, live in, or live with the natural world. In chapters 9 and 10, we found how various expressive means were being used to create a sense of a natural environment, and how these means created sense differently of social identities and political actions, thus straining social relations. As it turns out, people in this community, and those involved in its debates, show who they are, partly, by verbally depicting nature.

Symbols of identity are basic words, phrases, or images that identify persons as a participant in an identificational category or as a member of a social group. For example, in chapter 2, we examined a rather unusual image—funny-looking mascots—and asked how that image related to the social identity of "fan." Among workers, we found a rather detailed vocabulary that is used to identify, as they put it, "completely different types of workers," thus placing workers into social classes. These symbols of identity created identities and relations among workers that are often tense and strained. In chapters 5 and 6, we found various symbols of identity, including styles of last names chosen upon marriage, address terms, and significant symbolic shifts between sub-sets of these terms such as between *Ms., man, woman, part-ner,* and *Mrs., husband, wife.* In chapters 7 and 8, we found significant shifts between gendered symbols of identity. In chapters 9 and 10, symbols of identity revolved around two key terms—*environmentalist* and *developer*—with the selection from among these two carrying great weight for one's social identity, social relationships, and political activities. In each such scene, these people show who they are, and know who others are, partly by the way they symbolize through these terms of identity.

The *meanings* of these communication forms and symbols were interpreted with the aid of various concepts. The ones most used drew attention to the *cultural premises*, the unquestioned assumptions that participants presumed in order to symbolize through these particular communicative forms, and symbols (Fitch, 1994, esp. pp. 116–117). Exploring *semantic dimensions* was a way of interpreting meanings as continua along which sense was being made, with two sets or domains being implied by the work of each semantic pole. This concept was especially helpful in making sense in chapter 3 between the social classes of workers (see Seitel, 1974). A similar concept, the *dialectics* of meaning, was used to interpret the conversational play between different symbols and premises, such as in chapters 3 and 4 between separation and union. It also captured the flow between different semantic premises, such as in chapters 9 and 10 between political potence and impotence, economic endowment and deprivation, regional and local entitlement (Carbaugh, 1988/1989). Finally, it captured a basic dynamic through the social and cultural dialectic of identification discussed in chapter 11. The concept of *norm* (or rule) was used to interpret moral imperatives that are stateable and granted legitimacy by participants (Carbaugh, 1987). Normative claims about the way people should act are evident throughout the book, and the formulation of them, of specific "ought" statements, helps identify a potent moral dimension of each identity in each scene (Hall, 1988/1989; see also Carbaugh, 1990b). Finally, the concept of *code* was used to help formalize ways communication implicates basic beliefs and values about persons, social relations, communication itself, and nature (Carbaugh, 1989a, in press; Philipsen, 1992). This concept was especially helpful in chapter 5 when interpreting the different preferences for choosing last names upon marriage, in chapter 7 when interpreting an American code of dignity, and in chapters 9 and 10 when interpreting different orientations to dwelling in a natural environment.

Taken together then, and in sum, social identities have been conceptualized as situated communication practices, with the interpretations of the meanings of those communication practices being explicated through the general constructs of forms, symbols, and meanings.

NOTES

PREFACE

1. The form of the following statement follows closely the one composed by Basso (1990, pp. xii–xiii). The perspective I formulate is a version of the ethnography of communication as discussed originally by Dell Hymes (e.g., 1972); and a variant of cultural communication as explicated by Gerry Philipsen (e.g., 1987).

CHAPTER 1

1. Note that I am viewing "culture," here, from the vantage point of communication. Hopefully, this provides some balance to the vantage point described above, of viewing communication from the vantage point of culture, thus making culture the sole base upon which communication plays. This approach is of course quite robust, important, and interesting, as analysts posit "culture" as an explanation of communication (e.g., Why do people do, think, feel that?—"It's their culture"). However, it is also possible to posit communication as an explanation of culture (e.g., "It's their communication"). It is this latter, more neglected point, that is developed here, not to supplant, but to supplement the other view.

2. It is important to emphasize that social identities are identities that individuals apply (Carbaugh, 1991). There are of course differences in individual's abilities, physical stature, vocal qualities, particular background, forms of socialization, and so on. These differences between individuals can be very important, but they are not being foregrounded here (they are ably dealt with through a kindred theory of communication, see Cronen and Pearce, 1991/1992). Of primary concern here are the particular symbolizing practices through which individuals perform social identities in situated social scenes.

CHAPTER 2

1. Yet, elsewhere, and earlier in America's past, as one entered scenes of impersonal and public life, personal meanings waned. A parallel argument is formulated by Berger et al. (1973) when they argue that

Western life's honorifics have declined in the face of a creed for personal dignity.

2. Sennett (1978, p. 323). The relationship between the public sphere, and the idioms of childhood and adulthood has been taken up recently by Katriel (1991). As implied here by Sennett, and on the basis of Katriel's Israeli data, and the following analyses, the main thesis of Joshua Meyrowitz's essay (1984) needs some qualification.

3. The following analysis stands at the nexus of two distinct philosophical traditions, ordinary language philosophy and hermeneutic phenomenology. See Ricouer (1981, esp. pp. 101–128), Gadamer (1977, esp. pp. 59–68), and Apel (1977, pp. 292–315). For a review of hermeneutics see Stewart (1981). For a philosophical taproot of the ordinary language perspective see Wittgenstein (1958). Situated here, and developed ethnographically, the analysis explores naturally occurring, social interaction among speakers.

4. Are there other scenes where this salutation is as forceful or common?

5. When a player is hurt the fans also grow silent. This appears to function in a unifying way as all fans hope the player is not badly injured. If the player can leave the court under his own power, a round of crowd applause recognizes his efforts and his health.

6. The analyses presented here reflect the influence of Paul Ricouer (1981, esp. chs. 3–8, 11).

7. I thank Chuck Braithwaite for drawing my attention to this snippet from a column by Dave Barry.

CHAPTER 3

1. See, for example, Schwartz and Davis (1981), Silverzweig and Allen (1976), Whorton and Worthley (1981), Corporate Culture (1980).

2. See Hiemstra (1982), Pettigrew (1979), Rodrick and Beckstrom (1980), and Smircich (1983).

3. Early on, there were several theoretical discussions of the concept of organizational culture and its use in communication inquiry. For examples, see Jelinek, Smircich, and Hirsch (1983), Pacanowsky and O'Donnell-Trujillo (1982, 1983), Pettigrew (1979), and Schall (1983). More recently, Everett (1994) has reviewed and developed aspects of Weick's (1979) influential theory. To date, however, there have been few empirical studies that apply the concept to communication research in organizations. The present study attempts to make such an application as a test of one specific interpretive framework (see below, note 4). It is time to see what fruits are gained from the approach.

4. The present study uses the theoretical framework detailed elsewhere (Carbaugh, 1985, 1986, in press).

5. Case descriptions such as this, however, not only inscribe an indigenous way of speaking, but also contribute to a fund of ethnographic research that is designed (1) to facilitate the continuing development of the general theory for describing communication that grounds the approach taken here, (2) to generate certain hypotheses about communication, (3) to test extant theoretical claims against such localized communication patterns, and (4) to examine these accounts in comparative study or cross-cultural analyses. This is not an exhaustive list, but it is representative of the general research goals to which empirical studies like the following contribute. The ethnographic base is drawn from the programmatic essays of Dell Hymes (1962, 1972), Gerry Philipsen (1977), David Schneider (1976), Clifford Geertz (1973, 1976), among others (Carbaugh 1990c, in press). For specific studies see chapter 4, note 4.

6. The use of recurrence and regnant force to identify "the central themes" reported here is analogous to the method of identifying "interpretive themes" reported in Owen (1984).

7. Communicative practices such as these display a distinct and communal meaning that (1) is enacted in a particular sociocultural context, and (2) constitutes such a context in its spoken performance. This point is nicely illustrated by Dore and McDermott (1982, p. 375). In their "interactional approach to utterance interpretation" they present analyses, like the ones in this study, which "are descriptions of the behaviors which people use in organizing each other, and accounts of the various kinds of contexts which they organize together." For a complementary study of "talk" and an administrator's use of it to interpret, define, and organize "work," see Gronn (1983).

8. The analyses presented here were not officially commissioned by the organization studied. However, I presented them to several members of each level in the formal organizational hierarchy. Sometimes the presentation was a verbal summary, sometimes station members read this report. In each case, reactions could be summarized with the paraphrase, "Yep, I hadn't thought of it that way but that sure sounds like this place." Most members were very excited and wanted to show the report to others who worked there. In fact, one worker referred to it as a "hot item" that everyone wanted to read. It helped them, I was told, to realize ways their working lives were patterned and thus helped them move along better. It prompted several workers to make proposals to change their work lives for the better. One high-level manager, however, I should add, did not like the report, but considered it an accurate and valid one. The dynamics presented below have also changed since the writing of this report. Several top-level managers have moved to other jobs, and the station has moved to a consolidated facility.

9. The analyses performed here followed a procedure of analytic induction. For an explication of the method see Bulmer (1979) and Robinson (1951). A rough form of triangulation was also used in the descriptive and interpretive analyses. When possible, I would attempt to use an inferred pattern in discourse with workers. For example, early in the study I inferred that the atmosphere at the station could be described as "politically sensitive"—following a phrase used by an informant which seemed quite descriptive of the organizational dynamics. I was repeatedly informed that this phrase was not "that apropos" to this station, and an elaborate account was given of more appropriate ways to speak of "political sensitivity." The resulting reinterpretation linked my phrase "political sensitivity" with their theme of "the communication problem" discussed below. Similarly, the understanding I had gained of "the building situation" was validated discursively at several points through knowing nods and smiles. In this way, my analyses were subjected to discursive tests, with these always being the final arbiter of any conflicting interpretations. For discussions of triangulation which inform this procedure see Smith (1978), Ketner (1973), Dawson (1979), Mishler (1979), and Campbell (1975).

10. A framework for analyzing cultural terms through semantic dimensions is proposed and illustrated in Seitel (1974), Katriel and Philipsen (1981), and Carbaugh (1988b). The general procedure builds through a general process of "abduction" (see Sebeok, 1981, esp. ch. 2).

11. The effects of physical setting on workers has been previously studied by Oldham and Rotchford (1983).

12. The use of focused observations as "theoretical leads" is discussed in Schatzman and Strauss (1973, esp. 53–63) especially pp. 53–63. This procedure involves a process dubbed "strong inference" by Platt (1964). See also Ketner (1973).

13. These codes for Rockefeller and Bundy were used by one employee as she expressed keen excitement about her move, her shifting of identification from Bundy, where "things are done," to Rockefeller, where programs are "dreamed" and "created."

14. I am using the concept of "ritual" as in chapter 2, to refer to a communicative form: a structured sequence of acts, with each phase of the sequence holding some symbolic significance, and the whole form having a general, identifiable function (i.e., paying homage to some sacred object). Thus, the data of concern here is rather routine communication, but it is interpreted through this ritual form. See Philipsen (1987) and Katriel (1991).

15. The "staff meeting" is accompanied by a system of address consisting of mutual first-name exchanges. This use of informal/intimate address suggests a degree of openness and closeness among workers, while the ritualized enactment of the speech event maintains a type of

rigid distance between "staff" and "the boss." As a consequence, workers' discourse of address creates a tone of intimacy, just as the speech event and managerial style enact a degree of distance. Thus, in this meeting, the form of address and the social function of the speech event carry contrastive meanings as the participants address in a close and equal way, but enact the event through an unequal form. See Brown and Ford (1964), Brown and Gilman (1960), and chapters 5 and 6 below.

16. Note how this lack of "casual communication" renders the daily performance of "work" problematic. Workers' complaints, then, suggest a need for scenes in which "chit-chat" can be effectively accomplished. A detailed documentation of the effective use of such scenes in managing the definition of a work situation appears in Gronn (1983). For a different view on the assumed "damaging effects of idle talk," see Killingsworth (1984). For more current comments on how formal communication is no longer "deemed more significant than informal communication," see Eisenberg (1986, p. 88) and Baxter (1993).

CHAPTER 4

1. One Friday afternoon during my field work, I had arranged an appointment with a top-ranking manager (in Rockefeller). I arrived for the 1:00 appointment about five minutes early, prepared to talk about my project. I waited about an hour for the manager to arrive, and feeling rather unimportant, I went to visit with others I knew better in the station (in Bundy). It took only a few minutes in Bundy until I discovered a "fire" was burning. The station was full of frantic activity, searching for "crew" and tapes, calling sister stations, etc. After watching the rapidly paced activity, and sensing the importance of the activity to the station's articulated image, I began to understand the manager's absence. Later that evening, the manager called me at home, his explanation consisting of "a fire" that needed to be "put out."

2. The following discussion builds on the field work of Victor Turner (1974, 1980; also see Philipsen, 1987).

3. The approaches are not, of course, mutually exclusive. In fact the ethnography of communication owes a special debt to Kenneth Burke, which is explicitly acknowledged (e.g., Hymes 1972, pp. 51, 54, 62; Carbaugh, 1990c). It is nonetheless important to distinguish different uses of the Burkean conceptual system, especially as these differently formulate (1) problems of study (actors' common symbolic meanings, or meanings attributed to actors from another vantage point), (2) data for study (e.g., enactment's of the event, or reports about an event), and (3) scope conditions of study (e.g., an intra- or cross-organizational study). Such dis-

tinctions should be made in order best to evaluate the nature of each study and the kinds of claims each is making.

4. For examples of comparative analyses of communication see Basso (1970), Braithwaite (1990), Carbaugh (1990a), Brown and Levinson (1978, 1987). For a sample of studies of communication and various processes of organizing, see Baxter (1993), Gordon (1983), Gronn (1983), Manning (1982), and Tway (1975). Of course this is not an exhaustive list. But case studies like these that attend to speech-in-action in a sustained and intensive way, and that resist the immediate tendency toward generalized abstractions, can contribute to the general research objectives outlined here. See also Cheney (1991) and Tompkins (1993).

CHAPTER 5

1. As I am writing these words, I am overhearing another relevant episode. Our six-year-old twin boys are trying to address end-of-year cards to their teachers. Both teachers are known to be married. However, one prefers to be called "Ms." The other prefers to be called "Mrs." My one son asks: "Why are they different?" In a nutshell, what can and should be said?

2. Several people deserve mention for assistance during the course of this study, forming a research team valuable as much for conversation about naming phenomena generally as for helping with data collection and analyses. The plural pronouns throughout refer to Amy Chorost, Lisa Coutu, Rebecca Drake, Debby Kelm, Myoung Hye Kim, Sarah Kitchell, and myself. For taking the time to read and react to this and the following chapter, I thank Lisa Coutu and Kristine Fitch. Of course, where good sense does not show through, I alone am responsible.

3. See Schatzman and Strauss (1973, pp. 57–58) on the use of "theoretical leads." The transcriptions of each interview total 6–7 pages of single-spaced text.

4. I use the concept "style" to capitalize on three technical senses: (1) following Ervin-Tripp (1972), style implies a selection from among alternatives (in this case, one style of naming has been chosen over others); (2) following Katriel (1986), style is linked to cultural ethos, igniting clusters of affective meanings, motives, and normative actions (in this case, differing selections of name carry different meanings and motives for acting); and finally (3) following Hymes (1974), stylistic structure implies organizing expressive linguistic resources into larger units (in this case, by treating names selected at marriage as styles and codes). Using this concept of style, we discover two which are opposed along three dimensions of meaning, with each invoking contrastive motives and

norms, and one which mediates between these contrasts. Thus, style, as used technically here, involves a selection of one communicative resource rather than others, with each selection being culturally loaded with its own distinctive motives, meanings, and norms. The major conceptual tide, then, flows from one linguistic device (last names), to three styles, and their respective codes.

5. The personae sketched here weave our data into a set of representative expressions which are associated with each of the three naming styles. All sayings that are presented for each persona ushered forth from persons who made the general type of selection under discussion. The general method derives from Aristotle through Weber, where typifications of social phenomena are constructed. More recently, such typifications have been conscientious in melding abstractions and particularities, such as the union of abstract properties of social roles and the unique personalities of individuals into "characters" (MacIntyre, 1984, pp. 26–29), and the combining of ideal public images with personal traits into "representative characters" (Bellah et al., 1985, pp. 39–41). In our present case, the communicative practice of last names at marriage is analyzed on the basis of the sayings provided by our informants. In other words, the sayings presented in the typifications recurred with prominence across informants. The sayings are thus taken to be at once particularized instances of generalized types.

6. Comments are portioned here, as below, to reflect roughly the quantity of time each spouse talked during the interviews.

7. A key question suggested here, and overlooked in the theory of person reference, is: What constitutes "minimization" in person reference? Discussion of it is taken up in the following chapter.

8. The quotes in the following paragraph are taken from the brief essay by Harriett Lerner, "Feminist Kids: The Hyphenated Generation," *Ms,* December 1983, 98.

9. There are two rather prominent options for naming that fall between the more traditional style adopted by the Powells, and the more modern style adopted by Beth Steiner and Larry Nobleton, one being the unhyphenated MN + HLN for the wife, and the HLN for the husband, and the other being some combination of hyphenated names for wife and/or husband. These options carve out the middle ground between the more traditional and modern styles discussed above. For our purposes, we will describe the option of Paula Godfrey Chapman and Robert Chapman, since we found it to be the most frequently expressed "middle position" in our data. In some ways, as we will see, it falls somewhat closer to the traditional naming style than do several hyphenated options.

10. The procedure for inducing motives followed two steps. First, we culled our corpus for every utterance which responded to the ques-

tion: why was a last name adopted upon marriage? We abstracted all avowed and attributed motives for selecting a naming option (Mills, 1940). These utterances were then typified following the procedure of analytic induction (Bulmer, 1979). The resulting taxonomy thus reflects the motives expressed and attributed—as justifications—for adopting a style of name. Second, we returned to the corpus to ask: which motives are avowed by those making each stylistic choice? This led to our finding—as we discuss below—a high alignment between the style of name selected and the motives used to justify that style.

11. But for some the sequence of MN + HLN privileges the latter over the former, thus reintroducing difficulties of "equality."

12. The semantic dimensions were derived inductively by examining speech where "last names and marriage" were the topics of discussion. Each dimension provides a "two-valued set that is used to conceive of and evaluate" last names upon marriage (Seitel, 1974, p. 51). We asked: What prominent and recurrent meanings do speakers express about their naming option? The following dimensions respond to that question and offer an interpretation both of the meanings distinctive to each style, and sharpen the points of contrast between styles. There is precedent for this type of semantic analysis of names. In some societies in Central Brazil, Maybury-Lewis (1980, p. 7) reports, naming systems enact "a common set of contrasting principles" which carry the great burden of identifying social persons and relationships.

13. R. Rosaldo (1980) has examined how naming practices lay bases for identifiable forms of speech. Thus, children's names, among the Ilongot, are associated with characteristic acts of speech such as teasing, commanding, and witty repartee: "Naming people not only designates unique individuals and discriminates social categories, but it also shapes the qualities of social interactions" (p. 22). A similar path of analysis is followed here, with the modern naming option associated with a relatively assertive force, and the traditional and compromise options carrying a force more conciliatory and assimilative.

CHAPTER 6

1. Our study contributes to the literature on address and reference by pointing to cultural resources (last names under the condition of marriage) used in these processes. This leads us, eventually, to reexamine some of the extant theoretical claims about American address and reference. Our contribution is built by expanding the notion of "semantic force in address and reference," with special attention to the style of name adopted upon marriage, and its cultural coding into communication practice.

2. In the course of our study, however, we found a few women who adopted the integrative style of MN + HLN over thirty years ago, at the time Brown and Ford formulated their theoretical framework.

3. Bilmes (1988, p. 172) presents a refined argument that the use of "preference" by Sacks and Schegloff here is unlike its use in Sacks' earlier works. Bilmes claims that its use in the theory of person reference is more folk psychological, and is thus drawing attention to something more on the order of a communal imperative. He argues that this counters the explicit purposes of the authors, which is to formulate an analytical ordering principle, or a formal method for explaining the conversational action that is getting done. The current discussion bears directly on this point (cf. Murphy, 1988).

CHAPTER 7

1. The language being introduced here, of "explicating" social positions and, later, of "implicating," etc., others, is developed in the following chapter.

2. I hasten to add that, in the extracts presented here, some tensions are possibly discussable, but significantly not taken up. We can not claim to know exactly of what the phrase "our side" or "those trying to make it" consists (because this was not explicated). While the cultural and political beliefs just cited provide one possible account of "our side" (i.e., we-individuals), there are possible others—for example, of women against the patriarchy. In fact, using the principle of the vacillating form, we can expect the sequence to turn yet again back upon itself, as the mentioning of "our side" might precipitate perhaps yet an "other side." That such a position was not taken up here attests, I believe, both to the robustness of this kind of identification and the difficulty of formulating a position "other" than "individuals who are trying to make it." If we were to speculate about possible "other (third?) sides" on this occasion, those being brought close to the interactional surface by these speakers are perhaps "Republicans" (for the director of the DNC) or "men" (for the president of NOW), with neither being pursued by these speakers on this occasion. The vacillating form, it seems, can play itself out.

3. That "self" is no less an historical and institutional practice tends to escape the common cultural sense. Further, that each individual's self-concept is in its way subject to constant symbolic explication, elaboration, and ratification/rejection also escapes the common cultural sense. As discussed in the introduction, this is the result of cultural conceptions of persons based more upon biology and psychology and less upon social and cultural communicative processes. Some of the ironies and dynamics of this belief are taken up below and elsewhere (Carbaugh, 1988b).

CHAPTER 8

1. The resurgence in "spiritual" matters, spiritual dimensions of persons, and alternate conceptions of these in contemporary, popular American discourse shows a fascinating counter-discourse in response to this robust materially based conception. Also, the resurgence of popular interest in Native peoples, and the union of the spiritual and natural, is particularly noteworthy.

2. See, e.g., Gilligan (1982) and Tannen (1990) for descriptions of moral traits and conversational styles, respectively, attributed to gender. Also see, e.g., Goodwin (1990) and West and Zimmerman (1991) for social interactive bases of these gender assessments.

CHAPTER 10

1. The preceding paragraph was read by the Greylock Center Project Manager at a public meeting in Adams on August 5, 1994, a meeting attended by the Department of Environmental Management's Commissioner. Having read parts of this report, the Project Manager thought it nicely captured the charge of the "advisory committee." At this meeting, the committee officially approved the current "Greylock Center Master Plan."

CHAPTER 11

1. Of course, actions that avow a positive identity and attribute a negative one to others can involve a kind of interactive, if self-sealing symbolic game. This kind of communicative action often involves, to a degree, a coordinated and coherent production. Like the deep symbolic play among developers and environmentalists, or similar dynamics between races, or religious groups, such communication can structure rather intractable social relations, and do so in rather coherent and mutually intelligible ways. In turn, as previously separated social identities (of ethnicity or whatever) begin working cooperatively together, social differences may be woven more deeply, if delicately, into common cultural codes.

REFERENCES

Apel, K.-O. (1977). The a priori of communication and the foundation of the humanities. In F. Dallmayr and T. McCarthy (Eds.), *Understanding and Social Inquiry* (pp. 292–315). Notre Dame: University of Notre Dame Press.

Atkinson, D. L. (1987). Names and titles: Maiden name retention and the use of Ms. *Women and Language, 10,* 37.

Bakhtin, M. (1986). *Speech genres and other late essays* (V. W. McGee, trans.). Austin: University of Texas Press.

Barnlund, D. (1979). Communication: The context of change. In D. Mortensen (Ed.), *Basic readings in communication theory.* New York: Harper and Row.

Basso, K. (1970). "To give up on words": Silence in Western Apache culture. *Southwest Journal of Anthropology, 26* (3), 213–230. [Reprinted in Carbaugh, 1990b.]

———. (1979). *Portraits of "the whiteman": Linguistic play and cultural symbols among the Western Apache.* Cambridge, England: Cambridge University Press.

———. (1988). "Speaking with names": Language and landscape among the Western Apache. *Cultural Anthropology, 3,* 99–130.

———. (1990). *Western Apache language and culture.* Tucson: University of Arizona Press.

Basso, K., and Selby, H. (Eds.) (1976). Introduction. *Meaning in Anthropology* (pp. 1–9). Albuquerque: University of New Mexico Press.

Bauman, R. (1986). *Story, performance, and event: Contextual studies of oral narrative.* Cambridge, England: Cambridge University Press.

Baxter, L. (1993). "Talking things through" and "putting it in writing": Two codes of communication in an academic institution. *Journal of Applied Communication Research, 21,* 313–326.

———. (1994). The social side of personal relationships: A dialectical perspective. In S. Duck (Ed.), *Social context and relationships* (pp. 139–165). Newbury Park, CA: Sage.

Baxter, L., and Goldsmith, D. (1990). Cultural terms for communication events among some American high school adolescents. *Western Journal of Speech Communication, 54,* 377–394.

Bellah, R., Madsen, R., Sullivan, W., Swidler, A, and Tipton, S. (1985). *Habits of the heart: Individualism and commitment in American life.* Berkeley and Los Angeles: University of California Press.

Berger, P., Berger, B., and Kellner, H. (1973). *The homeless mind.* New York: Vintage.

Bharati, A. (1985). The self in Hindu thought and action. In A. Marsella, G. Devos, and F. Hsu (eds.), *Culture and self: Asian and Western perspectives* (pp. 185–230). New York: Tavistock.

Billig, M. (1987). *Arguing and thinking: A rhetorical approach to social psychology.* Cambridge, England: Cambridge University Press.

———. (1991). *Ideology and opinions: Studies in rhetorical psychology.* London: Sage.

Bilmes, J. (1986). *Discourse and Behavior.* New York: Plenum.

———. (1988). The concept of preference in conversation analysis. *Language in Society, 17,* 161–181.

Braithwaite, C. (1990). Communicative silence: A cross-cultural study of Basso's hypothesis. In D. Carbaugh (Ed.), *Cultural communication and intercultural contact* (pp. 321–327). Hillsdale, NJ: Lawrence Erlbaum.

Briggs, C. (1986). *Learning how to ask: A sociolinguistic appraisal of the role of the interview in social science research.* Cambridge; Cambridge University Press.

Brockmeier, J. (1992).*Anthropomorphic operators of time: Chronology, activity, language and space.* Paper presented at the 8th Triennial conference of the International Society for the Study of Time, Cerisy-la-Salle, France.

Brown, P., and Levinson, S. (1978). Universals of language usage: Politeness phenomena. In E. Goody (Ed.), *Questions and politeness* (pp. 56–289). London and New York: Cambridge University Press.

Brown, R., and Ford, M. (1964). Address in American English. In D. Hymes (Ed.), *Language in culture and society.* New York: Harper and Row.

Brown, R., and Gilman, A. (1960). The pronouns of power and solidarity. In T. A. Sebeok (Ed.), *Style in language* (pp. 253–276). Cambridge: MIT Press.

———. (1987). *Politeness.* London and New York: Cambridge University Press.

Bulmer, M. (1979). Concepts in the analysis of qualitative data. *Sociological Review, 27,* 651–677.

Burke, K. (1937). *Attitudes toward history.* Berkeley: University of California Press.

———. (1965). *Permanence and change.* Indianapolis: Bobbs-Merrill.

———. (1968). *Counter-statement.* Berkeley and Los Angeles: University of California Press.

————. (1969). *A rhetoric of motives*. Berkeley and Los Angeles: University of California Press.

Burns, L., and Stevens, R. (1988). *Most excellent majesty*. Pittsfield, MA: Berkshire Land Trust and Conservation Fund.

Campbell, D. (1975). Degrees of freedom and the case study. *Comparative Political Studies, 8*, 178–193.

Carbaugh, D. (1985). Cultural communication and organizing, *International and Intercultural Communication Annual, 9*, 30–47.

————. (1986). Some thoughts on organizing as cultural communication. In L. Thayer (Ed.), *Organization Communication: Emerging perspectives 1* (pp. 85–101). Norwood, NJ: Ablex.

————. (1988a). Comments on culture in communication inquiry. *Communication Reports, 1*, 38–41.

————. (1988b). *Talking American: Cultural discourses on* Donahue. Norwood, NJ: Ablex.

————. (1988/1989). Deep agony: "Self" vs. "society" in *Donahue* discourse. *Research on Language and Social Interaction, 22*, 179–212.

————. (1989a). Fifty terms for talk: A cross-cultural study. *International and Intercultural Communication Annual, 13*, 93–120.

————. (1989b). *Symbolizing nature: A cultural approach*. Paper presented to the SCA seminar on Environmental Advocacy. San Francisco, November.

————. (1990a). The critical voice in ethnography of communication research. *Research of Language and Social Interaction, 23*, 262–282.

————. (Ed.) (1990b). *Cultural communication and intercultural contact*. Hillsdale, NJ: Lawrence Erlbaum.

————. (1990c). Toward a perspective on cultural communication and intercultural contact. *Semiotica, 80*, 15–35.

————. (1991). Communication and cultural interpretation. *Quarterly Journal of Speech, 77*, 336–342.

————. (1992). "The mountain" and "the project": dueling depictions of a natural environment. In J. Cantrill and C. Oravec (Eds.), *Conference on the discourse of environmental advocacy* (pp. 360–376). Salt Lake City: University of Utah Humanities Center.

————. (1993a). Communal voices: An ethnographic view of social interaction and conversation. *Quarterly Journal of Speech, 79*, 99–113.

————. (1993b). Competence as cultural pragmatics: Reflections on some Soviet and American encounters. *International and Intercultural Communication Annual, 17*, 168–183.

————. (1993c). "Soul" and "self": Soviet and American cultures in conversation. *Quarterly Journal of Speech, 79*, 182–200.

————. (1994). Personhood, positioning, and cultural pragmatics: American dignity in cross-cultural perspective. In S. Deetz (Ed.), *Communication Yearbook 17* (pp. 159–186). Newbury Park, CA: Sage.

———. (in press). The ethnography of communication. In B. Kovacic and D. Cushman (Eds.), *Watershed theories of human communication.* Albany: State University of New York Press.

———. (forthcoming). Naturalizing communication and culture. In J. Cantrill and C. Oravec (Eds.), *Environmental discourse.* Lexington: University of Kentucky Press.

Carbaugh, D., and Hastings, S. O. (1992). A role for communication theory in ethnography and cultural analysis.*Communication Theory, 2,* 156–165.

Carrithers, M., Collins S., and Lukes, S. (Eds.). (1985). *The category of the person.* Cambridge: Cambridge University Press.

Caughey, J. (1984). *Imaginary social worlds.* Lincoln: University of Nebraska Press.

Cheney, G. (1991). *Rhetoric in an organizational society: Managing multiple identities.* Columbia: University of South Carolina Press.

Chick, J. K. (1990). The interactional accomplishment of discrimination in South Africa. In Carbaugh (1990b).

Cohen, A. (1985). *The symbolic construction of community.* London: Tavistock.

Collier, M. J., and Thomas, M. (1988). Cultural identity: An interpretive perspective. *International and Intercultural Communication Annual, 12,* 99–120.

Cooley, C. (1964). *Human nature and the social order.* New York: Schocken.

Corporate Culture. (1980, October 27). *Business Week,* 143–160.

Cronen, V., and Pearce, W. B. (1991/1992). Grammars of identity and their implications for discursive practices in and out of academe: A comparison of Davies and Harré's views to coordinated management of meaning theory. *Research on Language and Social Interaction, 25,* 37–66.

Cushman, D., and Cahn, D. (1985). *Communication in interpersonal relationships.* Albany: State University of New York Press.

Cushman, D., and Craig, R. (1976). Communication systems: Interpersonal implications. In G. Miller (eds.), *Explorations in interpersonal communication.* Beverley Hills, CA: Sage.

Davies, B., and Harré, R. (1990). Positioning: The discursive production of selves. *Journal for the Theory of Social Behaviour, 20,* 43–63.

Dawson, J. (1979). *Validity in qualitative inquiry.* Paper presented at the annual meeting of the American Educational Research Association, San Francisco, April 1979.

Denzin, N. (1993). *Rain Man* in Las Vegas: Where is the action for the postmodern self? *Symbolic Interaction, 16,* 65–77.

———. (in press). Symbolic interactionism. In J. Smith, R. Harré, and L. Van Langenhove (Eds.), *Rethinking psychology, vol. 2: Conceptual foundations.* Newbury Park, CA: Sage.

Dore, J., and McDermott, R. (1982). Linguistic indeterminacy and social context in utterance interpretation. *Language, 58*, 374–398.

Edwards, R., and Potter, J. (1992). *Discursive psychology*. London: Sage.

Eisenberg, E. (1986). Meaning and interpretation in organizations. *Quarterly Journal of Speech, 72*, 90–101.

Eriksen, T. (1991). The cultural contexts of ethnic differences. *Man, 26*, 127–144.

Ervin-Tripp, S. (1972). On sociolinguistic rules: Alternation and co-occurrence. In J. Gumperz and D. Hymes (Eds.), *Directions in sociolinguistics: The ethnography of communication* (pp. 213–250). New York: Holt, Rinehart and Winston.

Everett, J. (1994). Communication and sociocultural evolution in organizations and organizational populations. *Communication Theory, 4*, 93–110.

Fitch, K. (1991). The interplay of linguistic universals and cultural knowledge in personal address: Colombian *Madre* terms, *Communication Monographs, 58*, 254–272.

———. (1994). Culture, ideology, and interpersonal communication research. In S. Deetz (Ed.), *Communication Yearbook 17* (pp. 104–135). Newbury Park, CA: Sage.

Fitzgerald, T. (1993). *Metaphors of identity: A culture-communication dialogue*. Albany: State University of New York Press.

Fitzpatrick, M. A. (1988). *Between husbands and wives: Communication in marriage*. Newbury Park: Sage.

Fortes, M. (1973). On the concept of the person among the Tallensi. In Germaine Dieterlen (Ed.), *La notion de personne en Afrique noire*. Paris: Editions du dentre national de la Recherche Scientifique.

Foss, K. A., and Edson, B. A. (1989). What's in a name? Accounts of married women's name choices. *Western Journal of Speech Communication, 53*, 356–373.

Frentz, T., and Farrell T. (1976). Language action: A paradigm for communication. *Quarterly Journal of Speech, 62*, 333–349.

Gadamer, H.-G. (1977). *Philosophical Hermeneutics* (trans. and ed. by David E. Linge). Berkeley and Los Angeles: University of California Press.

Garrett, M. (1993). Wit, power, and oppositional groups: A case study of "pure talk." *Quarterly Journal of Speech, 79*, 303–318.

Geertz, C. (1973). *The interpretation of cultures*. New York: Bantam.

———. (1976). From the native's point-of-view: on the nature of anthropological understanding. In K. Basso and H. Selby (Eds.), *Meaning in Anthropology* (pp. 221–237). Albuquerque: University of New Mexico Press.

Gergen, K. (1985). The social constructionist movement in modern psychology. *American Psychologist, 40,* 266–275.

———. (1991). *The saturated self: Dilemmas of identity in contemporary life.* New York: Basic.

Giddens, A. (1984). *The constitution of society: Outline of the theory of structuration.* Cambridge: Polity.

Gilligan, C. (1982). *In a different voice.* Cambridge: Harvard University Press.

Gnatek, T. (1992). *Terms for talk in peer-group teaching of literacy.* Unpublished paper. University of Massachusetts, Amherst.

Goffman, E. (1967). *Interaction ritual.* New York: Anchor.

Goodall, H. L., Wilson, G. L., and Waagon, C. L. (1986). The performance appraisal interview: An interpretive reassessment. *Quarterly Journal of Speech, 72,* 74–87.

Goodwin, M. (1990). *He-said, she-said: Talk as social organization among black children.* Bloomington: Indiana University Press.

Gordon, D. (1983). Hospital slang for patients: Crocks, gomers, gorks, and others. *Language in Society, 12,* 173–185.

Gronn, P. C. (1983). Talk as the work: The accomplishment of school administration. *Administrative Science Quarterly, 28,* 1–21.

Gumperz, J. (1982). *Discourse strategies.* Cambridge and New York: Cambridge University Press.

Gumperz, J. J., and Cook-Gumperz, J. (1982). Introduction: Language and the communication of social identity. In J. J. Gumperz (Ed.), *Language and social identity* (pp. 1–21). Cambridge: Cambridge University Press.

Hall, B. J. (1988/1989). Norms, action, and alignment: A discursive perspective. *Research on Language and Social Interaction, 22,* 23–44.

Halloran, M. (1981). Public vs. private: Richard Sennett on public life and authority. *Quarterly Journal of Speech, 67,* 522–535.

Hallowell, A. I. (1955). *Culture and experience.* New York: Schocken.

Harré, R. (1984). *Personal being.* Oxford: Blackwell.

———. (1991a). The discursive production of selves. *Theory and Psychology, 1,* 51–63.

———. (1991b). *Physical being.* Oxford: Blackwell.

———. (Ed.). (forthcoming). *Positioning.* Oxford: Blackwell.

Harré, R., and Gillett, G. (1994). *The discursive mind.* Thousand Oaks, CA: Sage.

Harré, R., and Secord, P. (1972). *The explanation of social behavior.* Oxford: Blackwell.

Harré, R., and Stearns, P. (1995). *Discursive psychology in practice.* Newbury Park, CA: Sage.

Harré, R., and Van Langenhove, L. (1991). Varieties of positioning. *Journal for the Theory of Social Behaviour, 21,* 383–407.

Harris, G. (1989). Concepts of individual, self, and person in description and analysis. *American Anthropologist*, *91*, 599–612.

Hattie, J. (1992). *Self-concept*. Hillsdale, NJ: Lawrence Erlbaum.

Hecht, M. (1993). 2002—A research odyssey: Toward the development of a communication theory of identity. *Communication Monographs*, *60*, 76–82.

Heron, J. (1992). *Feeling and personhood*. Newbury Park, CA: Sage.

Hiemstra, G. (1982). The automated office: Promises to keep. Unpublished manuscript, University of Washington.

Hollway, W. (1984). Gender difference and the production of subjectivity. In J. Henriques, W. Hollway, C. Urwin, L. Venn, and V. Walkerdine (Eds.), *Changing the subject: Psychology, social regulation and subjectivity*. London: Methuen.

Honigman, J. (1970). Sampling in ethnographic fieldwork. In R. Naroll and R. Cohen (Eds.), *A handbook of method in cultural anthropology* (pp. 266–281). Garden City, NY: The Natural History Press.

Hopper, R. (1981). The taken-for-granted. *Human Communication Research*, *7*, 195–211.

Hymes, D. (1961). Linguistic aspects of cross-cultural personality study. In B. Kaplan (Ed.), *Studying personality cross-culturally*. Evanston, IL: Row, Peterson.

———. (1962). The ethnography of speaking. In T. Gladwin and W. Sturtevant (Eds.), *Anthropology and Human Behavior* (pp. 13–53). Washington, D.C.: Anthropological Society of Washington.

———. (1972). Models of the interaction of language and social life. In J. Gumperz and D. Hymes (Eds.), *Directions in sociolinguistics: The ethnography of communication* (pp. 35–71). New York: Holt, Rinehart, and Winston.

———. (1974). Ways of speaking. In R. Bauman and J. Sherzer (Eds.), *Explorations in the ethnography of speaking*. London: Cambridge University Press.

Intons-Peterson, M. J. and Crawford, J. (1985). The meanings of marital surnames. *Sex Roles*, *12*, 1163–1171.

Jackson, J. (1975). Normative power and conflict potential. *Sociological methods and research*, *4*, 237–263.

Jelinek, M., Smircich, L., and Hirsch, P. (Eds.). (1983). Organizational Culture. *Administrative Science Quarterly*, *28*, 331–495.

Johnson, T. (1991, Winter). Caring for the earth: New activism among Hopi traditionals. *The Amicus Journal*, *13*, 22–27.

Katriel, T. (1986). *Talking straight: Dugri speech in Israeli Sabra culture*. Cambridge: Cambridge University Press.

———. (1991). *Communal webs: Communication and culture in contemporary Israel*. Albany: State University of New York Press.

Katriel, T., and Philipsen, G. (1981). "What we need is communication": "Communication" as a cultural category in some American speech. *Communication Monographs, 48,* 301–317.

Ketner, K. L. (1973). The role of hypotheses in folkloristics. *Journal of American Folklore, 86,* 114–130.

Killingsworth, J. R. (1984). Idle talk and modern administration. *Administration and Society, 16,* 346–384.

Kondo, D. (1990). *Crafting selves: Power, gender, and discourses of identity in a Japanese workplace.* Chicago: University of Chicago Press.

La Fontaine, J. (1985). Person and individual: Some anthropological reflections. In M. Carrithers, S. Collins, and S. Lukes (Eds.), *The category of the person* (pp. 123–140). New York: Columbia University Press.

Lange, J. (1990). Refusal to compromise: The case of Earth First! *Western Journal of Speech Communication, 54,* 473–494.

———. (1993). The logic of competing information campaigns: Conflict over old growth and the spotted owl. *Communication Monographs, 60,* 239–257.

Levinson, S. (1989). Putting linguistics on a proper footing: Explorations in Goffman's concepts of participation. In P. Drew and A. Wootton (Eds.), *Goffman* (pp. 161–293). Cambridge: Polity.

Liberman, K. (1990). Intercultural communication in Central Australia. In Carbaugh (1990b).

Lutz, C. (1988). *Unnatural emotions.* Chicago: University of Chicago Press.

MacIntyre, A. (1984). *After virtue.* Notre Dame: University of Notre Dame Press.

Mahoney, J. (1994). *Ritualized communication and identity construction in a Salem, Massachusetts, community.* Unpublished master's thesis. University of Massachusetts, Amherst.

Manning, P. K. (1982). Organizational work: Structuration of environments. *The British Journal of Sociology, 33,* 118–134.

Marcella, A., G. Devos, and F. Hsu (Eds.). (1985). *Culture and self: Asian and western perspectives.* New York: Tavistock.

Marcus, G., and Fischer, M. (1986). *Anthropology as cultural critique.* Chicago: University of Chicago Press.

Marriott, M. (1976). Hindu transactions: Diversity without dualism. In B. Kapferer (Ed.), *Transaction and meaning.* Philadelphia: Institute for the Study of Human Issues.

Mauss, M. (1938). Une categorie de l'espirit humaine: La notion de personne celle de "moi." *Journal of the Royal Anthropological Institute, 68,* 263–282. [Reprinted in M. Carrithers, S. Collins, and S. Lukes (Eds.). (1985). *The category of the person.* Cambridge: Cambridge University Press.]

Maybury-Lewis, D. (1980). Name, person, and ideology in Central Brazil. In E. Tooker and H. Conklin (Eds.), *Naming systems* (pp. 1–10). Washington, D.C.: American Ethnological Society.

Mead, G. (1934). *Mind, self, and society.* Chicago: University of Chicago Press.

Meyrowitz, J. (1984). The adultlike child and the childlike adult: Socialization in an electronic age. *Daedalus, 113,* 19–48.

Mills, C. W. (1940). Situated actions and vocabularies of motive. *American Sociological Review, 5,* 904–913.

Mishler, Elliott. (1979). Meaning in context: Is there any other kind? *Harvard Educational Review, 49,* 1–19.

Mitchell, J. (1991 March). Sour times in Sweet Home. *Audobon,* 86–97.

Moerman, M. (1988). *Talking culture: Ethnography and conversation analysis.* Philadelphia: University of Pennsylvania Press.

Morgan, M. (1989). Television and democracy. In I. Angus and S. Jhally (Eds.), *Cultural politics in contemporary America* (pp.240–253). New York: Routledge.

Murphy, G. (1988). Personal reference in English. *Language in Society* 17, 317–349.

Neumann, M. (1993). Living on tortoise time: Alternative travel as the pursuit of lifestyle. *Symbolic Interaction, 16,* 201–235.

Oldham, G., and Rotchford, N. (1983). Relationships between office characteristics and employee reactions: A study of the physical environment. *Administrative Science Quarterly, 28,* 542–556.

Oravec, C. (1981). John Muir, Yosemite, and the sublime response: A study in the rhetoric of preservationism. *Quarterly Journal of Speech, 67,* 245–258.

———. (1984). Conservationism vs. preservationism: The public interest in the Hetch-Hetchy controversy. *Quarterly Journal of Speech, 70,* 444–458.

Owen, W. F. (1984). Interpretive themes in relational communication. *Quarterly Journal of Speech, 70,* 274–287.

Pacanowsky, M., and O'Donnell-Trujillo, N. (1982). Communication and organizational cultures. *Western Journal of Speech Communication, 46,* 115–130.

———. (1983). Organizational communication as cultural performance. *Communication Monographs, 50,* 124–147.

Pearce, W. B., and Cronen, V. (1980). *Communication, action, and meaning.* New York: Praeger.

Pettigrew, A. M. (1979). On studying organizational cultures. *Administrative Science Quarterly, 24,* 570–581.

Philips, S. (1993). *The invisible culture: Communication in classroom and community on the Warm Springs Indian Reservation.* Prospect Heights, IL: Waveland.

Philipsen, G. (1977). Linearity of research design in ethnographic studies of speaking. *Communication Quarterly, 25,* 42–50.

———. (1987). The prospect for cultural communication. In L. Kincaid (Ed.), *Communication theory: Eastern and Western perspectives* (pp. 245–254). New York: Academic.

———. (1989a). An ethnographic approach to communication studies. In B. Dervin, L. Grossberg, B. J. O'Keefe, and E. Wartella (Eds.), *Rethinking Communication,* vol. 2: *Paradigm exemplars* (pp. 258–268). Newbury Park, CA: Sage.

———. (1989b). Speech and the communal function in four cultures. *International and Intercultural Communication Annual, 13,* 79–92.

———. (1992). *Speaking culturally.* Albany: State University of New York Press.

Pike, K. (1967). *Language in relation to the unified theory of the structure of human behavior* (2nd rev. ed.). The Hague: Mouton.

Platt, J. R. (1964). Strong inference. *Science, 146,* 347–353.

Potter, J., and Wetherell, M. (1987). *Discourse and social psychology.* London: Sage.

Ragan, S. (1983). Alignment and conversational coherence. In R. Craig and K. Tracy (Eds.), *Conversational coherence: Form, structure, strategy* (pp. 157–171). Beverly Hills, CA: Sage.

Rawlins, W. (1983). Openness as problematic in ongoing friendships: Two conversational dilemmas. *Communication Monographs, 50,* 1–13.

———. (1992). *Friendship matters: Communication, dialectics, and the life course.* New York: Aldine de Gruyter.

Ricouer, Paul. (1981). *Hermeneutics and the human sciences* (9th ed., ed. by J. B. Thompson). Cambridge: Cambridge University Press.

Robinson, W. S. (1951). The logical structure of analytic induction. *American Sociological Review, 16,* 812–818.

Rodrick, R., and Beckstrom, M. (1980). The mighty machine: An organizational culture study. Paper presented at the Western Speech Communication Association, Portland, Oregon, 1980.

Rosaldo, M. (1980). *Knowledge and passion: Ilongot notions of self and social life.* Cambridge: Cambridge University Press.

Rosaldo, R. (1980). Ilongot naming: The play of associations. In E. Tooker and H. Conklin (Eds.), *Naming systems* (pp. 11–24). Washington, D.C.: American Ethnological Society.

Sacks, H. and Schegloff, E. (1979). Two preferences in the organization of reference to persons in conversation and their interaction. In G. Psathas (Ed.), *Everyday language: Studies in ethnomethodology* (pp. 15–21). New York: Irvington.

Sacks, H., Schegloff, E., and Jefferson, G. (1974). A simplest systematics for the organization of turn-taking for conversation. *Language, 50,* 696–735.

Sacks, O. (1987). *The man who mistook his wife for a hat*. New York: Harper and Row.

Sapir, E. (1931). Communication. *Encyclopedia of the Social Sciences, 4,* 78–81.

Schall, M. (1983). A communication rules approach to organizational culture. *Administrative Science Quarterly 28,* 557–581.

Schatzman, L., and Strauss, A. (1973). *Field research: Strategies for a natural sociology*. Englewood Cliffs, NJ: Prentice-Hall.

Schneider, D. (1976). Notes toward a theory of culture. In K. Basso and H. Selby (Eds.), *Meaning in Anthropology* (pp. 197–220). Albuquerque: University of New Mexico Press.

Schneider, D., and Smith, R. (1987). Class differences and sex roles in American kinship and family structure. In R. Bellah, R. Madsen, W. Sullivan, A. Swidler, and S. Tipton (Eds.), *Individualism and commitment in American life* (pp. 211–223). New York: Harper and Row.

Schore, A. N. (1994). *Affect regulation and the origin of the self*. Hillsdale, NJ: Lawrence Erlbaum.

Schwartz, H., and Davis, S. (1981, Summer). Matching corporate culture and business strategy. *Organizational Dynamics,* 30–48.

Scollon, R. (1992). *The shifting discourse of American individualism from the authoritarian to the infochild*. Haines, AK: Unpublished manuscript.

Scollon, R., and Scollon, S. (1981). *Narrative, literacy, and face in interethnic communication*. Norwood, NJ: Ablex.

Sebeok, T. (1981). *The play of musement*. Bloomington: Indiana University Press.

Seitel, P. (1974). Haya metaphors for speech. *Language in Society, 3,* 51–67.

Sennett, R. (1977). *The fall of public man: On the social psychology of capitalism*. New York: Vintage.

Sherzer, J. (1983). *Kuna ways of speaking: An ethnographic perspective*. Austin: University of Texas Press.

———. (1987). A discourse-centered approach to language and culture. *American Anthropologist, 89,* 295–309.

Shotter, J. and Gergen, K. (Eds.). (1989). *Texts of identity*. Newbury Park, CA: Sage.

Shoumatoff, A. (1985). *The mountain of names: A history of the human family*. New York: Simon and Schuster.

Shweder, R. (1991). *Thinking through cultures*. Chicago: University of Chicago Press.

Shweder, R., and Bourne, E. (1984). Does the concept of the person vary cross-culturally? In R. Shweder and R. LeVine (Eds.), *Culture theory*. Cambridge: Cambridge University Press. [Also reprinted in Shweder, 1991.]

Shweder, R., and LeVine, R. (Eds.). (1984). *Culture theory: Essays on mind, self, and emotion*. Cambridge: Cambridge University Press.

Silverzweig, S., and Allen, R. (1976, Spring). Changing the corporate culture. *Sloan Management Review*, 33–49.

Singer, M. (1980). Signs of the self: An exploration in semiotic anthropology. *American Anthropologist, 82*, 485–507.

Smircich, L. (1983). Organizations as shared meanings. In L. Pondy, P. Frost, G. Morgan, and T. Dandridge (Eds.), *Organizational symbolism* (pp. 55–65). Greenwich, CT: JAI Press.

Smith, J., Harré, R., and Van Langenhove, L. (Eds.). (1995). *Rethinking psychology*. Newbury Park, CA: Sage.

Smith, L. (1978). An evolving logic of participant observation: Educational ethnography and other case studies. In L. Shulman (Ed.), *Review of research in education* (pp. 11–22). Chicago: Peacock.

Snow, D., and Anderson, L. (1987). Identity work among the homeless: The verbal construction and avowal of personal identities. *American Journal of Sociology, 92*, 1336–1371.

Stewart, J. (1981). Philosophy of qualitative inquiry: Hermeneutic phenomenology and communication research. *Quarterly Journal of Speech, 67*, 109–121.

Stokes, R., and Hewitt, J. (1976). Aligning actions. *American Sociological Review, 41*, 838–849.

Suls, J. (Ed.). (1993). *Psychological perspectives on the self, vol. 4: The self in social perspective*. Hillsdale, NJ: Lawrence Erlbaum.

Tannen, D. (1990). *You just don't understand*. New York: Morrow.

Thomas, J. (1993). *Doing critical ethnography*. Newbury Park, CA: Sage.

Tompkins, P. K. (1993). *Organizational communication imperatives: Lessons of the space program*. Los Angeles: Roxbury.

Turner, J. H. (1988). *A theory of social interaction*. Stanford: Stanford University Press.

Turner, V. (1974). *Dramas, fields, and metaphors*. Ithaca: Cornell University Press.

———. (1980). Social dramas and stories about them. *Critical Inquiry, 7*, 141–168.

Tway, P. (1975). Workplace isoglosses: Lexical variation and change in a factory setting. *Language in Society, 4*, 171–183.

Urban, G. (1991). *A discourse-centered approach to culture: Native South American myths and rituals*. Austin: University of Texas Press.

Varenne, H. (1977). *Americans together*. New York: Teachers College Press.

———. (1990). Review of D. Carbaugh, *Talking American, Language in Society, 19*, 434–436.

Vocate, D. (Ed.) (1994). *Intrapersonal communication: Different voices, different minds*. Hillsdale, NJ: Lawrence Erlbaum.

Walzer, M. (1992). *What it means to be an American*. New York: Marsilio.

Weick, K. (1979). *The social psychology of organizing* (2nd ed.). New York: Random House.

West, C., and Zimmerman, D. (1991). Doing gender. In J. Lorber and S. Farrell (Eds.), *The social construction of gender*. London: Sage.

White, G., and Kirkpatrick, J. (Eds.). (1985). *Person, self, and experience: Exploring Pacific ethnopsychologies*. Berkeley and Los Angeles: University of California Press.

Whorton, J. and Worthley, J. (1981). A perspective on the challenge of public management: Environmental paradox and organizational culture. *Academy of Management Review, 6*, 357–361.

Wieder, L., and Pratt, S. (1990). On being a recognizable Indian among Indians. In Carbaugh (1990b).

Wierzbicka, A. (1989). Soul and mind: Linguistic evidence for ethnopsychology and cultural history. *American Anthropologist, 91*, 41–58.

Wittgenstein, Ludwig. (1958). *Philosophical investigations* (ed. by G. E. M. Anscombe). New York: Macmillian.

Zeitlyn, D. (1993). Reconstructing kinship or the pragmatics of kin talk. *Man, 28*, 199–224.

INDEX

Agent, 3, 10
    Agentive action, 144–145
    Cultural agent, 28–29, 141–153
    See Identity, Voice
Agonistic form, 84
Allen, R., 210
Analytic induction, 212
Anderson, L., 6
Apel, K. -O., 210
Atkinson, D. L., 90

Bakhtin, M., 12, 26, 143
Barnlund, D., 138
Barry, D., 55, 210
Basketball, as Communication Event, 39–60
Basso, K., xi, 12, 26, 56, 137, 187, 209, 214
Bateson, G., 136
Bauman, R., xi
Baxter, L., 9, 31, 152, 213, 214
Beckstrom, M., 210
Bellah, R., 215
Berger, B., 39, 134, 209
Berger, P., 39, 134, 209
Bharati, A., 29
Billig, M., 11
Bilmes, J., 64, 119, 217
Bourne, E., 138
Braithwaite, C., 210, 214
Briggs, C., 15
Brockmeier, J., 153
Brown, P., 31, 138–139, 214
Brown, R., 31, 113–117, 213
Bryant, W. C., 174–175
Bulmer, M., 212, 216
Burke, K., 9, 11, 16, 33, 81–82, 172, 213

Burns, L., 160, 163, 175

Cahn, D., 8
Campbell, D., 212
Carrithers, M., 8
Caughey, J., 138
Cheney, G., 9, 81, 214
Chick, J. K., 10, 137, 138
Code, 206–207
    Defining features of, 108, 134–136
    of Dignity, 134–139
    of Honor, 135–136
    Ecologic, 173–176
    Economic, 167–173
    of Marital names, 108–111
    of Natural space, 167–176
    Political code, 129–130
Cohen, A., 197
Coherence, 13
Collier, M. J., 9
Collins, S., 8
Communal Function of Communication, 57–58, 77–81, 116, 126–134, 198–202
Communication explanation, 151
Communication practice, 142–143
    defined, 14–15
Community, 13, 157–190, 195–202
Consciousness, 148–149
Cook-Gumperz, J., xi, xiii
Cooley, C. H., 4, 5
Craig, R., 8
Cronen, V., 8, 12, 209
Crawford, J., 90
Cultural,
    Communication, xi, 198–202, 209
    Landscape, 16, 26, 27, 32, 34
    Pragmatics, xi, 11–17, 149–153

233